OPTIONS
FOR THE
STOCK INVESTOR

How to Use Options to Enhance
and Protect Returns

James B. Bittman

Second Edition

McGraw-Hill
New York   Chicago   San Francisco   Lisbon   Madrid
Mexico City   Milan   New Delhi   San Juan
Seoul   Singapore   Sydney   Toronto

6 7 8 9 0 IBT/IBT 1 9 8 7 6 5 4 3 2 1 0

P/N 0-07-144305-3
Part of ISBN 0-07-144304-5

This publication is designed to provide accurate and authoritative information in regard to the subject matter covered. It is sold with the understanding that neither the author nor the publisher is engaged in rendering legal, accounting, or other professional service. If legal advice or other expert assistance is required, the services of a competent professional person should be sought.

—From a Declaration of Principles jointly adopted by a Committee of the American Bar Association and a Committee of Publishers.

McGraw-Hill books are available at special quantity discounts to use as premiums and sales promotions, or for use in corporate training programs. For more information, please write to the Director of Special Sales, McGraw-Hill Inc., Two Penn Plaza, New York, NY 10121-2298. Or contact your local bookstore.

 This book is printed on recycled, acid-free paper containing a minimum of 50% recycled de-inked fiber.

Library of Congress Cataloging-in-Publication Data

Bittman, James B.
    Options for the stock investor : how to use options to enhance and protect returns / by James B. Bittman.— 2nd ed.
        p.   cm.
    Includes index.
    ISBN 0-07-144304-5 (hardcover : alk. paper)
    1. Stock options. I. Title.
    HG6042.B57 2005
    332.63'2283—dc22
                                                                        2004021722

The first edition was dedicated to Lyman and Elizabeth Bittman, who taught me the patience required to study the market, and who gave me the optimism needed to hang in there until that patience paid off.

This second edition is dedicated to Grace Elizabeth Bittman. May the options you choose bring you every happiness.

Disclosures and Disclaimers

THROUGHOUT THIS BOOK, HYPOTHETICAL EXAMPLES ARE USED. These examples do not represent and are not intended to represent real people, real situations, or actual advice on particular stocks. Although they are meant to be realistic, the examples used are for illustrative purposes only.

In order to simplify computations, commissions and other transaction costs have *not* been included in the examples used in this book. Commissions will affect the outcome of stock and option strategies and should be considered in real-world situations.

Options involve risk and are not suitable for everyone. Prior to buying or selling an option, a person must receive a copy of *Characteristics and Risks of Standardized Options*. Copies may be obtained from your broker or from Op-Eval, 2406 N. Clark St., Box 154, Chicago, IL 60614. The investor considering options should consult a tax advisor as to how taxes may affect the outcome of contemplated options transactions. A prospectus, which discusses the role of the Options Clearing Corporation, is also available without charge upon request addressed to the Options Clearing Corporation, 440 S. LaSalle, Suite 908, Chicago, Illinois 60605.

Contents

Foreword

LOOKING BACK OVER THE LAST THREE DECADES, THERE HAVE BEEN MASSIVE CHANGES IN THE FINANCIAL INDUSTRY AND THE GLOBAL MARKETPLACE. Few people understood what the grain traders in Chicago were up to when they created the Chicago Board Options Exchange over 30 years ago and launched the trading of listed options on April 26, 1973. On opening day in 1973, when 900 options traded on 16 stocks at the CBOE, who would ever have projected that average daily volume at the CBOE alone would now exceed one million contracts? Today, over three decades later, listed options are a massive global industry, with 55 exchanges across several continents trading in excess of 5 billion contracts annually.

Indeed, there is no end in sight to the growth of the options industry. Last year alone, options volume increased by 16 percent in the United States and 33 percent globally. Worldwide options volume on individual stocks rose 15 percent, and index options volume increased 44 percent. This explosive growth in options volume is a testimony to the utility and versatility of the product.

Options are better understood and more widely accepted today as valuable risk-management tools. Reasons for this include the growing awareness of the need for portfolio protection, and the increased availability of education regarding how investment risk can be managed effectively.

Part of the accelerating investor interest in options is cultural, and can be attributed to the general public's increased awareness that geopolitics, catastrophic events, and unsteady economic growth and recessions can have a severe impact on their investment portfolios. Although this was always true, acute security concerns at home, an unsettled U.S. economy, and the widespread availability of all kinds of information facilitated by the Internet have helped drive the point home. Additionally, widespread corporate abuse scandals in recent years have shaken public trust in institutions and also heightened awareness that self-reliance—or at least self-education—when it comes to finances is critical. The days of incrementally tucking away savings and remaining complacent, secure in the belief that an investment portfolio would take care of itself, are long gone.

Especially as so many of us in the baby boom generation approach retirement and our projected life expectancy increases, we all must take a more active role regarding our investments. Medical costs continue to rise, the social security system as we know it seems increasingly endangered, and we may need to pay for additional education for our children as the employment marketplace continues to grow increasingly competitive.

Fortunately, investors now have every opportunity to learn. Technology allows them "point-and-click" access to virtually every major market and to voluminous amounts of information and research. Today we see a new generation of options users who are independent, Internet-savvy, and continually educating themselves. Stock investors, faced with the challenges of both selecting and protecting their investments, want and need all the practical education they can get to help them manage risk.

There are many helpful educational products out there. I believe one of the most useful is *Options for the Stock Investor*, by James Bittman. Bittman, an acknowledged options expert and international instructor who focuses on the practical applications of trading strategies, has helped to demystify options as risk-management tools for stock investors.

As the baby boomer population rapidly approaches retirement years, more individuals and families will find options a critical tool in safeguarding the investments they accumulated during decades of work and saving. And young professionals, as they begin to compile a portfolio of investments intended to last a lifetime, will find the guidance provided in this book invaluable. *Options for the Stock Investor*, now in its second edition, can assist in educating these motivated populations.

Over 5,000 copies of *Options for the Stock Investor* were sold in its first printing in 1996, and 35,000 copies have been sold in total. Although seasoned investors will find *Options for the Stock Investor* useful, the book is primarily intended for the novice. Mr. Bittman patiently and painstakingly guides the reader through a clear explanation of options vocabulary, the fundamentals of options investing, and the prudent selection of strategies.

As the industry has evolved, innovative variations on the basic option on equity product have been developed. One of these, Long-term Equity Antici-Pation Securities (LEAPS), introduced by the CBOE in 1990, is particularly useful. LEAPS are stock options with an expiration date of up to three years in the future. Mr. Bittman has added a new chapter to his early text explaining the prudent use of LEAPS.

There is also a new full chapter discussing the use of index options. These options gained added visibility in recent years as a hedge against volatility during the bear market. In addition, index options offer a myriad of uses. With index options available on all major stock indexes, holders of portfolios of stocks, as well as those who are long mutual funds, index funds, and exchange-traded funds, can hedge or otherwise manage such positions.

Options for the Stock Investor provides a very practical learning experience by including special option-pricing software, Op-Eval4, that helps potential option investors develop realistic expectations regarding option price behavior. The software also enables the analysis of spreads and multipart strategies.

Accumulating assets may be foremost in the minds of most new investors, but experienced investors know that wise asset allocation and risk management are just as critical to growing portfolio value. Familiarity with and educated use of options can serve the stock investor well. This book provides invaluable guidance.

William J. Brodsky
Chairman and Chief Executive Officer
Chicago Board Options Exchange

ACKNOWLEDGMENTS

I HAVE MANY PEOPLE TO THANK. Anton Karadakov wrote the Op-Eval4 computer program that accompanies this text. It is innovative and easy to use. Advanced traders as well as beginners will find its many features for option analysis both practical and valuable. If anyone needs assistance with software development, Anton has an amazing ability to turn ideas into computer program reality. He can be reached at karadakov@yahoo.com.

The staff of the Options Institute was very supportive of my efforts during the writing process. Marty Kearney, Frank Tirado, Greg Stevens, and Kyle Graham all made contributions to the list of topics, examples, and stories that fill these pages. Debra Peters, vice president of the CBOE and director of the Options Institute, does an excellent job of leading us on our mission to teach options, how they work, and why they are valuable investing and trading tools. She motivates us to produce high-quality courses, and she makes the process fun.

Barry Szurgot and Dave Carlson of CBOE Compliance have both edited and improved my writing for many years. They read everything carefully and made valuable suggestions. They do more than add disclaimers.

Stephen Isaacs, my editor at McGraw-Hill, once again kept his composure and maintained his enthusiasm while tolerating my delays in submitting the manuscript. I'm late only because I insist on turning out a quality product.

Last, but not least, my wife, Laura, has been a saint, tending to our daughter alone on too many weekends while I was holed up in my office working on too many commitments and trying to make the words for this book come out at the same time. I promise not to take on so many tasks at the same time with the same deadline ever again.

The following people also made contributions in a variety of ways, from feedback to moral support:

William Brodsky

Ed Joyce

Ed Provost

Richard Dufour

Martha McGregor

Linda Boland

Marc Allaire

Brian Overby

Felecia Tatum

Michelle Kaufman

Laura Johnson

Floyd Fulkerson

Lisa Harms

James Karls

John Rusin

Shelly Natenberg

Gary Trennepohl

Amit Bansal

Britton Smith

INTRODUCTION

SETTING GOALS

THIS BOOK IS FOR THE STOCK INVESTOR WHO WANTS TO LEARN HOW OPTIONS CAN BE USED TO PURSUE INVESTMENT GOALS. Investors, unlike short-term speculators, have several specific goals
for improving long-term invest-
ment performance. Options can help an investor pursue these objectives:

How do speculators and investors differ?

Buy "good stocks" at "good prices"

Sell stocks at "good prices"

Lower the cost basis of stocks purchased

Enhance income

Insure stocks against a market decline

Insure cash (or liquid investments) against missing a market rally

Reduce the breakeven point on a losing position without increasing risk

This list is enticing to many investors, but it is important not to get too excited too soon. Every successful investor needs
to develop realistic expectations about what can
be accomplished with options, what the costs are,
and, equally important, what is impossible. In
addition, setting and achieving investment goals involves many subjective elements, and the use of options makes the job no less subjective. The chapters in this book are designed to help investors understand, first, how options can be used to pursue stated goals and, second, what the pros and cons of using options are. With this understanding, investors should be able to incorporate options into their investment decision-making process.

What kind of expectations should investors have?

One attribute of options that is typically touted as an advantage is not on the list of investor objectives. "Leverage" is not on this list

Why is leverage not on the list of objectives?

because it is not a goal of most investors. While leverage may be useful for some short-term speculators under certain circumstances, the presence of leverage increases risk, which is not a positive for conservative, long-term investors who are seeking primarily to reduce risk.

To understand what options offer, investors must understand how markets function. One prominent theory about the way markets work is the *efficient market theory*. This theory asserts that many competing market participants have taken all available information (company earnings, industry trends, macroeconomic developments, and so on) and have incorporated this information into the current market price of a company's shares. The market has, effectively, determined the "efficient price" of every security.

Many investment advisors challenge the efficient market theory by claiming that their research (and, therefore, their advice) uncovers "hidden" or "undiscovered" opportunities that are not reflected in current market prices. However, there is not necessarily a contradiction between the general premise of the efficient market theory and the process of researching, selecting, and investing in individual stocks. These competing market participants who attempt to gain advantage by researching investment opportunities and making subjective decisions can be viewed as a necessary component of properly functioning markets.

Assuming that markets present investors with what are essentially "fair" prices, as the efficient market theory asserts, then the key to investing is to research the available information and to make subjective predictions in selecting investments. What adds value in the process is something that

> *What do options give investors?*

increases investing alternatives. This is what options do—they give investors more investment alternatives.

Alternatives are not necessarily better; rather, alternatives offer different trade-offs—a different set of positives and negatives. "Growth versus income" is the classic investment trade-off. Given an investor's specific circumstances and market opinion, an option alternative may be deemed better by that investor; but the option strategy will not be "better" in an absolute sense.

Each option strategy should be understood in terms of the trade-off offered. For an investor making a subjective decision, the option trade-off will sometimes be preferable, and so the option strategy will be selected. On other occasions, the trade-off of buying or selling stock at the current market price will be preferable—and that strategy will be selected.

This book does not assert that options solve all investment problems all of the time. Rather, it is the contention of this book that options help some of the time, that they offer good alternatives to consider, and that they add an interesting diversity to an investor's portfolio. To use options wisely and

> *Do options solve all investment problems?*

efficiently, however, an investor must understand the trade-offs that they offer and when and how those trade-offs fit into the subjective investing process.

THE OUTLINE OF THIS BOOK

This second edition of this book is divided into five sections: "The Fundamentals of Options," "Basic Investing Strategies," "Trading Strategies," "Advanced Topics," and "Investing and Trading Psychology."

Part 1, "The Fundamentals of Options," is updated from the first edition, but is largely unchanged. It thoroughly develops the vocabulary of options, the mechanics of options, and the important concept of why options have value. This section is essential for newcomers to options. Chapter 1, "The Vocabulary of Options," is important because option-related words are sometimes used in a way that differs from everyday usage. Chapter 2, "How Options Work," is perhaps the most important chapter for beginners. It shows in great detail how profit-and-loss diagrams are created. Profit-and-loss diagrams illuminate the potential profit and risk of various strategies. Potential profit and risk become especially important in later sections, when market opinion and investment objectives are matched with the trade-offs of various strategies. Chapter 3, "Why Options Have Value," presents the conceptual reason for an option's value and the important components of value. Chapter 4, "Option Price Behavior," has been revised substantially. It explains important concepts about how option prices change prior to the expiration date. To say the least, the behavior of option prices seems counterintuitive to many newcomers to options. But this is part of the fun of learning to take advantage of new investment tools, and Chapter 4, therefore, is an essential introduction to the trading strategies section presented later.

The theme of Part 2, "Basic Investing Strategies," is that, contrary to the belief of many people, options are *not* primarily speculative instruments. Rather, many option strategies have an investment orientation, and these basic strategies are the subject of Chapters 5 through 10, which cover the following strategies in depth: buying calls with a view to buying the underlying stock (Chapter 5); covered writing, which is perhaps the most popular option strategy (Chapter 6); adjusted covered writes (Chapter 7); married puts, protective puts, and collars (Chapter 8); writing puts with a view to increasing income or acquiring stock (Chapter 9); and, finally, a new chapter on LEAPS, or long-term options (Chapter 10). The important attribute of these strategies is that all of them are investment-oriented and can be used successfully by traditional stock investors. However, a new way of thinking has to be learned.

Part 3, "Trading Strategies," departs from the realm of investment-oriented strategies and examines short-term strategies, where understanding option price behavior prior to expiration is of the utmost importance. Chapter 11 introduces the computer program Op-Eval4, which accompanies this book. This software, now in its fourth complete redevelopment, not only calculates option prices, but also calculates implied volatility and prices of multiple-part strategies, and graphs them and creates tables of theoretical values so that strategy profit and loss over a range of market outcomes can be quickly scanned. Chapter 12 works through, in step-by-step detail, some short-term trading situations, examining the important decisions to be made and illustrating how Op-Eval4 can be used to assist in the process. Computer programs, of course, do not make decisions for traders, and they do not guarantee success. The purpose of computer programs is to get more information and consistent information that can help in the development of realistic expectations and improve the decision-making process. Chapter 13, a new chapter, explains vertical spreads and in what situations traders might choose this strategy over buying or selling an individual option. Chapter 14, another new chapter, extends the discussion of trading strategies and demystifies the use of straddles and strangles.

Part 4, "Advanced Topics," demonstrates that the term *advanced* does not necessarily imply excessive risk. Rather, the strategies presented vary from conservative, stock-oriented strategies to strategies involving various degrees of leverage. Most important, how an investor can monitor the risk level of a particular strategy is explained and illustrated in all cases. Chapter 15, "Ratio Spreads for Investors and Traders," a new chapter, shows ways in which both conservative investors and aggressive traders might benefit from this little-known strategy. Chapter 16, "Covered Combos—Long and Short," another new chapter, demonstrates how a strategy with a reputation for high risk can be used safely with low risk by conservative investors. All that has to be changed is the thinking process and the way capital is managed. Chapter 17, "Cash-Settled Index Options and ETF Options," starts with much of the material on index options from the first edition and then goes on to explain what is perhaps the greatest innovation of the 1990s: the exchange-traded fund.

Part 5, "Investing and Trading Psychology," concludes the book. Chapter 18, "The Difference between Investing and Trading with Options," discusses exactly what its title implies. Chapter 19, "Getting Started," is pretty much the same as in the first edition. It offers some practical advice to beginning option users on what to do first. Studying the stock market, setting goals, and choosing stock-oriented strategies must be done carefully. Chapter 20, "Learning to Trade," another new chapter, offers some practical advice to those who feel the allure of trading.

The Fundamentals of Options

1

THE VOCABULARY
OF OPTIONS

INTRODUCTION

THIS CHAPTER DEFINES ALL OF THE GENERALLY ACCEPTED TERMI-
NOLOGY THAT AN INVESTOR NEEDS TO KNOW. Experienced option
traders may notice, however, that not every term associated with
options is listed. Options are often considered to be far more
complicated than they actually are, a situation that is exacerbated
by industry jargon, which is frequently used incorrectly or with conflicting
meanings. This book will use all essential terms as defined in this chapter:

Call option

Put option

Long call

Short call

Long put

Short put

Long

Short

Strike price (or exercise price)

Expiration date

Exercise

Assignment (and assignment notice)

American-style exercise

European-style exercise

Effective purchase price

Effective selling price

Option buyer

Option writer (or option seller)

Covered

Uncovered (or naked)

In-the-money, at-the-money, out-of-
the-money

Premium	Margin account
Intrinsic value	Marginable transaction
Time value	Initial margin
Cash account	Maintenance margin
Cash transaction	Margin call

If you are familiar with these terms, you may proceed to Chapter 2. If you wish to review their definitions, please keep in mind that these definitions are written on a basic level. The nuances will be explained in later chapters.

This chapter will look first at call options, then at put options. At the end of the chapter, there are questions (with answers following) that are designed to reinforce your understanding.

CALL OPTIONS

A *call option* is a contract between the call owner (or buyer) and the call writer (or seller). A call option gives its owner the right to buy stock from the call writer at a specified price until a specified date. An equity option contract covers 100 shares of stock (one round lot). The *strike price* (or *exercise price*) is the price specified in the option contract at which stock is traded if the call is exercised. The *expiration date* is the date specified in the option contract, after which the right contained in the option ceases to exist.

RIGHTS AND OBLIGATIONS

The buyer of one XYZ September 50 call has the *right* to purchase 100 shares of XYZ stock from the call writer at $50 per share (the strike price) at any time until the September expiration date. The call writer, in contrast, has an *obligation* to deliver 100 shares at $50 per share. If the call owner exercises the right to buy, the call writer must deliver the stock. The call buyer is described as having a *long call* position. The call writer is described as having a *short call* position.

> Call owners have the right to buy.
>
> Call writers have the obligation to sell.

Exercise occurs when the call owner declares the right to buy stock from the call seller and makes the proper notifications. An *assignment notice* is given to a call writer and represents notification that a call owner has exercised the right to buy. The process by which this occurs is as follows: When a call owner decides to exercise, the first step is for the call owner to notify his brokerage firm. The brokerage firm then notifies the Options Clearing

Corporation, which is the central clearinghouse and guarantor of all option transactions. The Options Clearing Corporation then makes a random selection of a brokerage firm with a short call position. That brokerage firm, in turn, selects a customer with a short call position and

> *Option owners*
> *may choose to exercise.*
>
> *Option writers*
> *are assigned and must*
> *fulfill the obligation.*

notifies that customer that the option has been assigned. Brokerage firms typically select customers on either a random or a first-in, first-out basis.

At this point, when an exercise form has been processed and an assignment notice has been sent, a stock transaction has occurred: The call owner is the buyer of stock, and the call writer is the seller of stock. The price of this transaction is the strike price of the option (plus or minus commissions). On the settlement date of the stock transaction, the brokerage firms will transfer the appropriate funds to the seller and shares of stock to the buyer.

A call option ceases to exist after one of two events occurs. First, if the call owner exercises the right to purchase stock, then the call writer must fulfill the terms of the contract. After exercise, the option no longer exists, but stock has been purchased, and the call exerciser pays the amount indicated by the strike price. If a 50 call is exercised, for example, the exerciser must pay $50 per share, or $5,000 for 100 shares. Second, if a call is not exercised prior to expiration, it expires and the right ceases to exist. In this case, the option is said to *expire worthless.*

COVERED AND UNCOVERED (OR NAKED) CALLS

If a call writer owns the stock on which the call is written and can deliver that stock, the short call position is described as *covered*. In contrast, when a call writer *does not* own the stock, the short call position is described as *uncovered* or *naked*. In the case of an uncovered call, receiving an assignment notice means that the investor must acquire the stock to deliver. Since the price at which the stock can be acquired (or even whether it can be acquired) cannot be known, the uncovered, or naked, call writer is taking a risk that is significantly greater than the risk taken by the covered call writer.

INVESTMENT POSITION AFTER EXERCISE
AND ASSIGNMENT OF CALLS

Both the call owner and the call writer will have different investment positions after a call is exercised. Figure 1–1 summarizes the changes. For the call owner with no stock position, the exercised long call becomes a long stock position (100 shares per option). This is described in Figure 1–1a. If the call owner had a short stock position on a share-for-share basis with the long calls,

FIGURE 1–1   Call options—changed positions after exercise and assignment. (a) Long call exercise assuming no stock position; (b) long call exercise if a short stock position existed on a 1-for-1 basis; (c) short call assignment assuming no stock position; (d) short call assignment if a long stock position existed on a 1-for-1 basis

(a)	Exercise of Long Call	*initiates* →	Stock Purchase	*results in* →	Long Stock Position
(b)	Exercise of Long Call	*initiates* →	Stock Purchase	*results in* →	No Position (flat)
(c)	Assignment of Short Call	*causes* →	Stock Sale	*results in* →	Short Stock Position
(d)	Assignment of Short Call	*causes* →	Stock Sale	*results in* →	No Position (flat)

then the call exercise initiates a stock purchase that offsets the short stock position and leaves the investor flat, i.e., with no position (Figure 1–1b). For the call writer, assignment of an uncovered call creates a short stock position (Figure 1–1c). Assignment of a covered call, however, becomes a flat position, because the stock that was owned is sold (Figure 1–1d).

CALLS: EFFECTIVE PURCHASE PRICE
AND EFFECTIVE SELLING PRICE

The price at which the call was bought and sold is significant, because it is an important factor in the ultimate price of the stock transaction. The *effective purchase price* for an exercised call is the price of purchasing stock, taking into account the cost of the call. The *effective selling price* of an assigned call is the price of selling stock, taking into account the proceeds from selling the call. The following example illustrates this point.

If a 50 call that was purchased for $300, or $3 per share, is exercised, the effective purchase price of that stock is $53 per share. This price is calculated by adding the call price to the strike price on a per-share basis. For the assigned call writer, the effective selling price of the stock is also $53: $3 per share is received for selling the call, and $50 is received when assignment occurs. The general

> **For calls:**
> *Effective Purchase Price*
> *equals*
> *Strike Price plus Call Price*
> *equals*
> *Effective Selling Price*

formula—strike price plus call premium—applies equally to the call buyer as the effective purchase price and to the call writer as the effective selling price.

EXERCISE STYLE

American-style exercise means that the right granted by the option may be exercised at any time prior to the expiration date. *European-style exercise* means that the right may be exercised only on the last trading day before the established deadline. In the United States, all equity options and all options on exchange-traded funds (ETFs) are subject to American-style exercise. The pop-

> *American-Style Options*
> *Early Exercise: Yes*
>
> *European-Style Options*
> *Early Exercise: No*

ular OEX index options (options on the S&P 100 Index) are also subject to American-style exercise. Most other index options, however, including SPX index options (options based on the S&P 500 Index) and DJX index options (options based on the Dow Jones Industrial Average), are subject to European-style exercise. All option contract specifications, including exercise style, can be obtained from the exchange on which the options are traded.

CALLS: IN-THE-MONEY, AT-THE-MONEY, OUT-OF-THE-MONEY

The relationship of the stock price to the strike price determines whether an option is in-the-money, at-the-money, or out-of-the-money. An *in-the-money call* has a strike price below the current stock price. If a stock is trading at $55, for example, the 50 call is in-the-money. To be precise, it is $5 in-the-money. This call, however, would not necessarily be trading for $5. In fact, it is very likely to be trading for more than $5. Why options trade for more than the in-the-money amount is discussed in Chapter 3.

An *out-of-the-money call* has a strike price above the current stock price. For example, if the stock is trading at $55, the 60 call option is out-of-the-money. Specifically, this call is out-of-the-money by $5.

At-the-money means that the stock price is equal to the strike price. This term has both a strict definition and a looser, common usage. Theoretically, the 55 call is at-the-money only when the underlying stock is trading exactly at $55. The rest of the time, it is either in-the-money or out-of-the-money. In practice, however, the 55 call is designated as an at-the-money call when the stock price is closer to that strike price than to another strike price. When a stock is trading at $54 or $56, for example, it is common practice to refer to the 55 call as the at-the-money call. Figure 1–2 illustrates the relationship of the stock price to in-, at-, and out-of-the-money calls.

In-the-money, at-the-money, and out-of-the-money are dynamic terms. As stock prices rise, out-of-the-money calls become at-the-money and then

FIGURE 1–2   Call options: in-the-money, at-the-money, and out-of-the-money

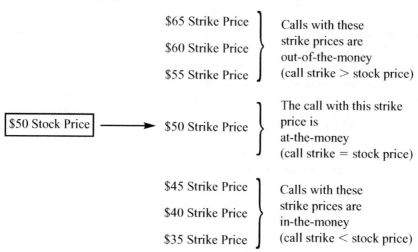

$65 Strike Price	Calls with these strike prices are out-of-the-money (call strike > stock price)
$60 Strike Price	
$55 Strike Price	

$50 Stock Price ──────▶ $50 Strike Price

The call with this strike price is at-the-money (call strike = stock price)

$45 Strike Price	Calls with these strike prices are in-the-money (call strike < stock price)
$40 Strike Price	
$35 Strike Price	

in-the-money. As stock prices fall, the opposite happens: In-the-money calls become at-the-money and subsequently out-of-the-money.

CALLS: PREMIUM, INTRINSIC VALUE, AND TIME VALUE

The term *premium* refers to the price of an option. This premium, or price, consists of two parts: intrinsic value and time value. The *intrinsic value* refers to the in-the-money amount of an option's price, and the *time value* refers to any portion of an option's price that exceeds the intrinsic value. Consider a situation in which the following prices exist:

	(per share)
Stock	$57.00
50 call	8.00
55 call	4.00
60 call	1.50

An analysis of each option's premium (or price) will illustrate the concepts of intrinsic value and time value. First, examine the 50 call. The stock price of $57 is $7 above the strike price. Therefore, the 50 call is $7 in-the-money and has $7 of intrinsic value. The premium (or price) of the 50 call, however, is $8. The $1 difference is the time value.

The $4 premium of the 55 call consists of $2 of intrinsic value and $2 of time value. The premium of the out-of-the-money 60 call, $1.50, consists

FIGURE 1–3   Call options: intrinsic value and time value

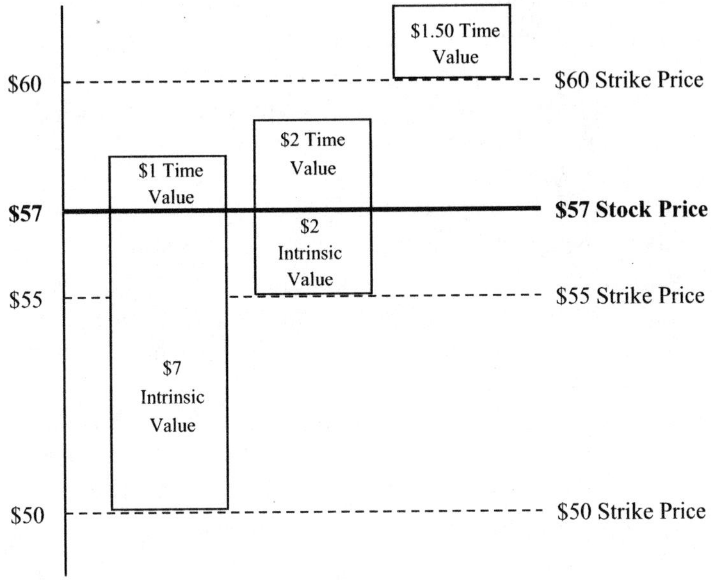

50 Call Premium $8   55 Call Premium $4   60 Call Premium $1.50
Intrinsic Value $7   Intrinsic Value $2   Intrinsic Value $0
Time Value $1   Time Value $2   Time Value $1.50

entirely of time value. Figure 1–3 illustrates intrinsic value and time value for in-, at-, and out-of-the-money calls.

Competition in the market makes it extremely unlikely that in-the-money options will trade for less than their intrinsic value. Assume, for example, a stock price of $56. If the 50 call were trading for $5, investors could buy the call, exercise it immediately, and sell the stock for $56. Since the effective purchase price of the stock is $55, the result would be an immediate profit of $1 per share (not counting transaction costs). A profit opportunity of this nature would attract many professional traders. Competition between professional traders would force the call price up and/or the stock price down, reducing the $1 profit per share to an amount only slightly greater than the transaction costs. For professional traders, transaction costs are very small, and, for this reason, options in U.S. markets rarely trade below their intrinsic value. When they do, they are very near their expiration date and the amount below intrinsic value is only 5 or 10 cents.

MARGIN ACCOUNTS AND RELATED TERMS

Many conservative investors believe that a margin account involves excessive risk. This is not necessarily true. The level of risk depends on the amount of margin debt, if any, and the volatility or "riskiness" of the securities involved. As later chapters explain, the level of risk of a particular strategy depends on the amount of equity capital supporting that strategy. Paying for stock in cash has the lowest level of risk, because the maximum potential loss is known and is fully paid for up front. If the stock price were to suffer a total collapse to zero, the investor would not be called upon for additional funds. In contrast, buying stock "on margin" involves the use of borrowed money, which must be repaid in full. If a stock price declines to below the loan amount, the investor will be called upon to make up the difference. This potential liability is why margin accounts have a reputation for risk.

Investors and traders who use options need to be aware of margin account procedures, because some option strategies are required to be established in margin accounts. The following overview of margin accounts and related terms is presented for newcomers to these topics.

CASH ACCOUNTS, MARGIN ACCOUNTS, AND MARGINABLE TRANSACTIONS

A *cash account* is an account at a brokerage firm in which all purchases are fully paid for in cash or in which sufficient cash is on deposit to meet all potential liabilities. In a *margin account*, a brokerage firm may allow certain types of positions, which are called *marginable transactions*, when there is not sufficient cash to meet all potential liabilities. Different types of marginable transactions, according to regulations, require different amounts of equity capital from the customer. This equity capital is called a *margin deposit*, or simply *margin*.

One common margin transaction is the purchase of stock "on margin." When stock is purchased on margin, there is insufficient cash in the account to purchase the stock. It is also possible that the equity balance of the account will be less than the value of the stock. If the brokerage firm approves the purchase of stock on margin, then the firm will lend the balance of the purchase price. This is known as a *margin loan*. The investor, of course, pays interest on the loan. The use of a margin loan means that market fluctuations will change the equity balance of the account at a greater percentage rate than the same fluctuation would create in the equity balance of a cash account. This is called *leverage*.

Another common marginable transaction is selling stock short. In this transaction, the brokerage firm borrows stock on behalf of the customer, who sells it at the current market price with the hope of buying it back later at a lower price. In a short stock transaction, the customer actually pays nothing when initiating the position (except commissions), but a margin deposit is required to guarantee that the customer will be able to cover any losses.

Certain option transactions are marginable transactions, and certain ones are not. Also, certain option transactions are required to be conducted in a margin account, and others may be conducted in either a cash account or a margin account. Before engaging in option transactions, an investor should be thoroughly familiar with the type of account required for the transactions that are planned. A simple formula to remember is: account equity + margin debt = account value. Account value is the total market value of owned securities. Margin debt is the loan to the investor from the brokerage firm, and account equity is the investor's share after the securities are sold and the margin loan is repaid.

INITIAL MARGIN, MAINTENANCE MARGIN, AND MARGIN CALLS

Initial margin is the minimum account equity required to establish a marginable transaction. Initial margin requirements are frequently expressed as a percentage of the market value of a position or its underlying security. Purchasing stock, for example, is a marginable transaction that currently has an initial margin of 50 percent: The purchase of 100 shares of a $50 stock requires an initial margin of 50 percent of the purchase price plus commissions, or $2,500 plus commissions, and the loan made to the buyer would equal $2,500.

If a margined position loses money, the account equity will decrease, both absolutely and as a percentage of the total account value. *Minimum margin* is the level, expressed as a percentage of account value, above which account equity must be maintained. If account equity falls below the minimum margin level, the brokerage firm will notify the investor through a *margin call* that the account equity must be raised to the maintenance level. Upon receiving a margin call, a customer may either deposit additional funds or securities or close the position. In the previous example, a stock price decline from $50 to $35 would cause a decline in equity to $1,000, because the margin loan of $2,500 remains constant. This $1,000 equity would represent only 28 percent of the account value ($1,000 ÷ $3,500 = 0.28). If the minimum margin were 35 percent, the account equity would be under the requirement, and the customer would receive a margin call.

Although many option strategies are marginable, the real point here is that the amount of equity supporting a position is a key element in capital management, and how an investor manages capital is a decisive factor in determining the risk level of a strategy—that is, whether a particular strategy is speculative or conservative in nature. The importance of this concept will be developed throughout the coming chapters.

PUT OPTIONS

A *put option* gives the put buyer (or owner) the right to sell stock to the put writer (or seller). In the case of American-style options, this right may be exercised at any time prior to the expiration date. In the case of European-style options, the right to sell may be exercised only on the last day of trading prior to an established deadline. The put buyer is described as having a *long put* position, and the put seller is described as having a *short put* position. After exercising, the put buyer must deliver stock. A short put position is an obligation to buy stock if an assignment notice is received. The process by which exercise and assignment occurs for puts is identical to that for calls, described earlier.

> *Put owners have*
> *the right to sell.*
> *Put writers have*
> *the obligation to buy.*

COVERED AND UNCOVERED PUTS

The terms *covered* and *uncovered* do not have as precise meanings when applied to puts as they do when applied to calls. If an investor with a short call position actually owns the stock, the short call is covered. By analogy, if there is sufficient cash to purchase the stock, one would think that this cash-secured short put is covered. In a practical sense, this is true. However, it is not so easy for brokerage firms to monitor cash availability as it is to monitor stock holdings. Many brokerage accounts are used like checking accounts and have widely fluctuating cash balances, and these transactions generate little or no fees to pay for monitoring. Stock transactions, in contrast, are relatively frequent and produce revenue that pays, in part, for the expense of monitoring covered calls. Most brokerage firms, therefore, require that all short put positions be established in a margin account.

INVESTMENT POSITION AFTER EXERCISE
AND ASSIGNMENT OF PUTS

As with calls, the investment positions of put owners and put writers change after a put is exercised. Figure 1–4 summarizes the changes. For the put owner with no stock position (Figure 1–4a), the exercised long put becomes a short stock position. If, however, the put owner holds long stock on a share-for-share basis with the puts, then the put exercise sells that stock and leaves the investor flat, i.e., with no position (Figure 1–4b).

FIGURE 1–4   **Put options—changed positions after exercise and assignment. (a) Long put exercise assuming no stock position; (b) long put exercise if a long stock position existed on a 1-for-1 basis; (c) short put assignment assuming no stock position; (d) short put assignment if a short stock position existed on a 1-for-1 basis**

(a)	Exercise of Long Put	*initiates* ⟶	Stock Sale	*results in* ⟶ Short Stock Position
(b)	Exercise of Long Put	*initiates* ⟶	Stock Sale	*results in* ⟶ No Position (flat)
(c)	Assignment of Short Put	*causes* ⟶	Stock Purchase	*results in* ⟶ Long Stock Position
(d)	Assignment of Short Put	*causes* ⟶	Stock Purchase	*results in* ⟶ No Position (flat)

For the put writer, assignment of a short put requires the writer to purchase stock. If no stock position existed initially, assignment of a short put creates a long stock position (Figure 1–4c). If, however, the put writer has a short stock position on a share-for-share basis with the short puts, then the put assignment leaves the investor flat (Figure 1–4d).

PUTS: EFFECTIVE PURCHASE PRICE AND EFFECTIVE SELLING PRICE

The price at which a put is transacted is significant, because its price is an important factor in the ultimate price of the stock transaction. Consider a 50 put that is purchased for $200, or $2 per share. For the put owner who exercises this put and, consequently, sells stock, the effective selling price is $48 per share. The stock is sold at $50, the strike price of the put, but $2 was paid for the put. This $2 cost reduces the net amount received to $48. Similarly, for

> **For Puts:**
> *Effective Purchase Price*
> *equals*
> *Strike Price minus Put Price*
> *equals*
> *Effective Selling Price*

the writer of the assigned put, the $2 per share received lowers the effective price paid from $50 to $48. The general formula—strike price minus put premium—applies to the put writer as the effective purchase price and to the put buyer as the effective selling price.

PUTS: IN-THE-MONEY, AT-THE-MONEY, AND OUT-OF-THE-MONEY

The relationship to the strike price of in-the-money and out-of-the-money puts is opposite that for calls. An *in-the-money put* has a strike price above the current stock price. An *out-of-the-money put* has a strike price below the current stock price. Consider a situation in which a stock is trading at $55. The 60 put is in-the-money. Specifically, it is $5 in-the-money. The 50 put is out-of-the-money by $5. The 55 put is at-the-money. The term *at-the-money* applies to puts in a similar way as it applies to calls. If the stock price is at or very close to the strike price of the option, that option is referred to as an *at-the-money put*. Figure 1–5 illustrates the relationship of the stock price to in-, at-, and out-of-the-money puts.

PUTS: PREMIUM, INTRINSIC VALUE, AND TIME VALUE

As with calls, *premium* refers to the price of a put, and it consists of two parts: *intrinsic value* and *time value*. Consider a situation in which the following prices exist:

	(per share)
Stock	$57
60 put	5
55 put	3
50 put	1

FIGURE 1–5 Put options: in-the-money, at-the-money, and out-of-the-money

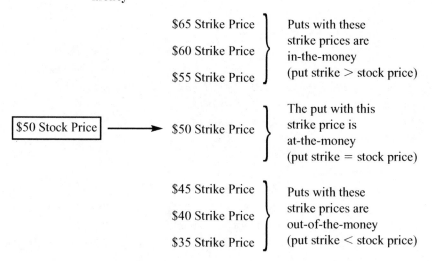

FIGURE 1–6   Put options: intrinsic value and time value

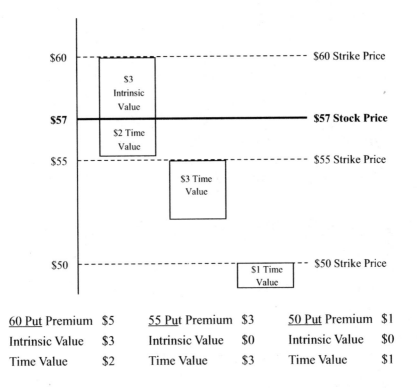

60 Put Premium	$5	55 Put Premium	$3	50 Put Premium	$1
Intrinsic Value	$3	Intrinsic Value	$0	Intrinsic Value	$0
Time Value	$2	Time Value	$3	Time Value	$1

The 60 put is $3 in-the-money. It therefore has $3 of intrinsic value and $2 of time value. The 55 put premium of $3 consists entirely of time value. The $1 price of the out-of-the-money 50 put also consists entirely of time value. Figure 1–6 illustrates intrinsic value and time value for in-, at-, and out-of-the-money puts.

LONG AND SHORT

Many newcomers are confused by the words *long* and *short*, because these words are used in two different contexts. *Long* can mean that a trader owns something or that a trader has a bullish market position. Similarly, *short* can mean that a trader has an obligation or that a trader has a bearish market position.

If a trader owns call options, for example, that person is described as being "long calls." Similarly, a trader can be "long stock" or "long puts." If a trader is "short calls," then that trader has an obligation to deliver the underlying security if an assignment notice is received. A trader who is "short puts" is obligated to buy the underlying security if an assignment notice is received, and a trader who is "short stock" is obligated to repay a stock loan.

If a trader is described as being "long the market," however, it means that this person has a bullish position. This trader could be long calls, short puts, or long stock, because these are bullish positions that tend to profit as the market rises. And, in a like manner, if a trader is described as being "short the market," then that trader has a bearish position, either short calls, long puts, or short stock, for these positions tend to profit as the market declines.

Newcomers to trading should listen carefully to how words are used so that misunderstandings can be avoided.

SUMMARY OF DEFINITIONS—A QUIZ

This chapter concludes with the following quiz. Match the terms below with their correct definitions (some definitions may be used twice). The answers appear immediately after the definitions.

TERMS

Long call	_____	At-the-money call	_____
Short call	_____	Out-of-the-money call	_____
Long put	_____	In-the-money put	_____
Short put	_____	At-the-money put	_____
Strike price	_____	Out-of-the-money put	_____
Exercise price	_____	Premium	_____
Expiration date	_____	Intrinsic value	_____
Exercise	_____	Time value	_____
Exercise notice	_____	Cash account	_____
Assignment	_____	Margin account	_____
European-style option	_____	Cash transaction	_____
American-style option	_____	Marginable transaction	_____
Covered	_____	Effective purchase price—long call	_____
Uncovered	_____	Effective selling price—short call	_____
Naked	_____	Effective purchase price—short put	_____
In-the-money call	_____	Effective selling price—long put	_____

DEFINITIONS

1. A form presented to the Options Clearing Corporation demanding that the terms of an option contract be fulfilled

2. A short option position behind which an investor owns the underlying stock in the case of a short call, or has cash to purchase the stock in the case of a short put

3. A put option with a strike price above the current stock price

4. The process by which a short option position is selected as the one to make good on its contingent obligation

5. A put option with a strike price equal to the current stock price

6. The total price of an option

7. That portion of an option's total price that is in excess of the intrinsic value

8. Strike price minus premium

9. A transaction where there is not sufficient cash to meet all potential liabilities

10. A call option with a strike price below the current stock price

11. An account in which brokerage firms provide special services, such as lending money, facilitating short stock sales, and handling uncovered option transactions

12. A call option with a strike price equal to the current stock price

13. A call option with a strike price above the current stock price

14. An account in which all transactions are fully paid for in cash

15. Strike price plus premium

16. Same as uncovered

17. A short option position behind which an investor does not own the underlying stock in the case of a short call, or does not have cash to purchase the stock in the case of a short put

18. An option that may be exercised only on the last trading day prior to an established deadline

19. That portion of an option's total price that is equal to the in-the-money amount

20. A put option with a strike price below the current stock price

21. A transaction in which the full cash amount is transferred to or from the customer's cash account

22. The right to buy

23. The price specified in an option contract

24. A demand that the terms of an option contract be fulfilled

25. The contingent obligation to buy

26. An option that may be exercised at any time up to and including the expiration date (prior to an established deadline)

27. A contingent obligation to sell

28. The date after which an option ceases to exist

29. The right to sell

ANSWERS

Long call	22	At-the-money call	12
Short call	27	Out-of-the-money call	13
Long put	29	In-the-money put	3
Short put	25	At-the-money put	5
Strike price	23	Out-of-the-money put	20
Exercise price	23	Premium	6
Expiration date	28	Intrinsic value	19
Exercise	24	Time value	7
Exercise notice	1	Cash account	14
Assignment	4	Margin account	11
European-style option	18	Cash transaction	21
American-style option	26	Marginable transaction	9
Covered	2	Effective purchase price—long call	15
Uncovered	17	Effective selling price—short call	15
Naked	16	Effective purchase price—short put	8
In-the-money call	10	Effective selling price—long put	8

2

HOW OPTIONS WORK

ABASIC REQUIREMENT FOR UNDERSTANDING OPTIONS AND USING THEM SUCCESSFULLY IS THE ABILITY TO DRAW PROFIT-AND-LOSS DIAGRAMS FOR STRATEGIES ON THEIR EXPIRATION DATE. Although many readers will have seen the standard profit-and-loss option graphs that will be presented and explained in this chapter, there is a difference between seeing them and truly understanding them. If you are not sure of your ability to draw these diagrams, you must take the necessary time to study this chapter. An investor who can draw expiration profit-and-loss diagrams for option strategies is 90 percent of the way to understanding options. With a firm grasp of these concepts, you will greatly enhance your ability to match option strategies with investment objectives. The skills developed in this chapter will serve you well throughout your investing and trading career.

Investing and trading with options is different from investing and trading with stocks for several reasons. First, the decision to initiate an option trade involves a consequence on the expiration date that depends on the underlying stock price (assuming that the option position is not closed before expiration). The decision to buy a stock, however, has no such consequence. Second, option strategies involve many risk/reward trade-offs. Buying stocks involves only one. In fact, options open a range of investment alternatives; the positives and negatives of these alternatives will be discussed throughout this book.

Third, the time horizon of using options is dictated by the expiration date, while stocks have no expiration date. Fourth, option strategies have different breakeven points from stock strategies.

PROFIT AND RISK CHARACTERISTICS AND IMPORTANT PRICE POINTS TO IDENTIFY

Strategy analysis begins with the basics. When completed, an expiration profit-and-loss diagram reveals three aspects of a strategy: the breakeven point(s), the maximum risk, and the profit potential. Investors also need to know what stock position is created if the option is in-the-money at expiration. An in-the-money long call at expiration, for example, is assumed

What does a P/L diagram reveal about a strategy?

to be exercised and thus to become a long stock position. These are important things to know, because, looked at as a whole, they illustrate the investment trade-off that a strategy offers. A trade-off involves benefits and risks, and an understanding of trade-offs will lead to strategy comparisons and, in turn, improve the decision-making process by clarifying investment choices.

PROFIT-AND-LOSS DIAGRAMS—BASIC STEPS

A profit-and-loss diagram can be created in six basic steps.

Step 1:   *Describe the opening transaction completely.* Write down in words the transaction you want to diagram. For example, "buy a September 50 call for 2" or "sell a May 75 put at 4.25." Do not just write "buy a call" or "sell a put," since you will not have sufficient information to complete the diagram.

Step 2:   *Start a grid.* A profit-and-loss diagram is drawn on a grid that shows the profit or loss of an option strategy at the expiration date over a range of possible stock prices. The vertical grid line represents profit ($+$) or loss ($-$). The horizontal grid line represents a range of stock prices. When making a grid, start with the strike price of the option in the middle of the horizontal grid line and work out in each direction. Figure 2–1 shows a sample grid.

Step 3:   *Select a stock price and calculate the option's value at expiration.* At expiration, an option will be worth either the intrinsic value (the in-the-money amount) or zero. Intrinsic value is discussed in Chapter 1. For example, if the stock price is $56, the 50 call is worth 6 at expiration. If the stock price is $49, this call is worth zero.

FIGURE 2–1 Sample profit-and-loss grid

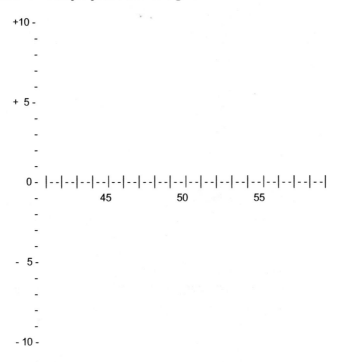

Step 4: *Calculate the profit or loss.* To start your profit-and-loss calculations, choose a stock price within the range of prices on the grid
and determine the value of the option.

For an option that is purchased, calculate the profit or loss by subtracting the purchase price of the option from its value at expiration,
determined in Step 3. A 50 call purchased for 2 with an expiration
value of 6 will show a profit of 4 (the expiration value of 6 minus
the purchase price of 2 equals a profit of 4). The same call with an
expiration value of zero will show a loss of 2 (the expiration value
of -0- minus the purchase price of 2 equals a loss of 2).

For an option that is sold, subtract the value at expiration, determined in Step 3, from the selling price. A 75 put sold at 4.25 with
the stock price above $75 at expiration has a value of zero and yields
a profit of 4.25. The same put with an expiration value of 7, with the
stock price at $68, will show a loss of 2.75.

Profit-and-loss calculations can be easily made and clearly presented if a table such as Table 2–1 is used in conjunction with the

TABLE 2–1   Sample Table for a Two-Component Option Strategy

Stock Price at Expiration	Option Position #1 Profit / (Loss)	Option Position #2 Profit / (Loss)	Total Strategy Profit / (Loss)
$54			
$53			
$52			
$51			
$50			
$49			

profit-and-loss grid. The leftmost column indicates the range of stock prices that appear on the grid. Tables for simple option strategies contain only one column, which indicates the profit or loss of the strategy at each stock price at expiration. Tables for more complicated strategies have columns for the profit or loss of each component of the strategy and a column for the strategy's total profit or loss. Table 2–1 is an example of a table used for a strategy with two components.

Step 5:   *Chart the profit or loss.* Place a dot on the grid above (if a profit) or below (if a loss) the selected stock price at a point even with the profit or loss calculated in Step 4. Figure 2–2 shows the placement of the $4 profit taken from Table 2–2. The 50 call was purchased for 2 and had an expiration value of 6, resulting in a profit of 4.

Step 6:   *Repeat Steps 3, 4, and 5 until the diagram is complete.* Steps 3, 4, and 5 should be repeated over the range of stock prices on the grid. As dots are placed on the grid, a complete profit-and-loss diagram will emerge. The dots can be connected and will always form straight lines, although sometimes the lines will have different slopes.

LONG AND SHORT STOCK POSITIONS

Diagrams of simple stock positions without any options are included here for two reasons. First, it is always good to start on familiar ground. Second, later in this chapter, stock positions will be combined with option positions to pro-

FIGURE 2–2   Illustration of charting a profit or loss. 50 call was purchased for $2. Stock price at expiration is $56. Profit is $4

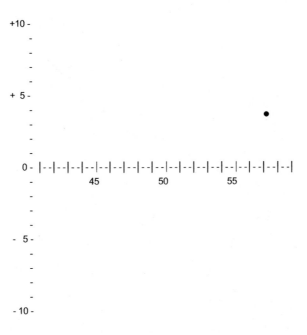

TABLE 2–2   Illustration of Profit Entered in Table

Stock Price at Expiration	Long 50 Call at 2 Profit / (Loss)
$58	
$57	
$56	+4
$55	
$54	
$53	

duce more complicated strategies.

Figure 2–3 illustrates the strategy of buying stock at $50. Table 2–3 contains the profit-and-loss results for such a strategy on a per-share basis. The potential results are straightforward: Buying stock will result in a profit if the

FIGURE 2–3   Long stock at $50

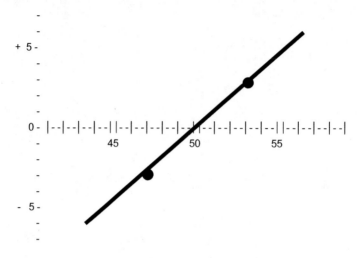

TABLE 2–3   Long Stock at $50 Profit-and-Loss Calculations

Stock Price at Expiration	Long Stock at $50 Profit / (Loss)
$55	+5
$54	+4
$53	+3
$52	+2
$51	+1
$50	-0-
$49	−1
$48	−2
$47	−3
$46	−4
$45	−5

price rises and a loss if the price falls. The two dots on the line in Figure 2–3 correspond to two rows in Table 2–3, $53 and $46. A $3 profit results if the stock is sold at $53. A $3 loss is realized if the stock is sold at $47. The slope of the line in Figure 2–3 is 1 × 1—the profit or loss changes by $1 per share for every $1 change in the stock price.

Figure 2–4 illustrates the strategy of selling stock short[1] at $50. Selling short will result in a profit if the stock price falls and a loss if the price rises. The line in Figure 2–4 has a -1 × 1 slope—the profit or loss changes by $1 per share in the opposite direction for every $1 change in the stock price. Table 2–4

FIGURE 2–4   Short stock at $50

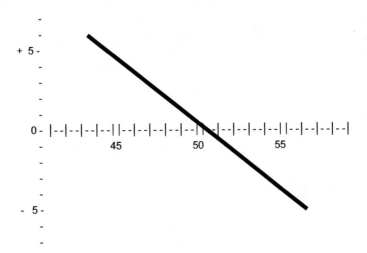

TABLE 2–4   Short Stock at $50 Profit-and-Loss Calculations

Stock Price at Expiration	Short Stock at $50 Profit / (Loss)
$55	−5
$54	−4
$53	−3
$52	−2
$51	−1
$50	-0-
$49	+1
$48	+2
$47	+3
$46	+4
$45	+5

contains the profit-and-loss results on a per-share basis based on stock prices within the range charted.

BASIC OPTION STRATEGIES DIAGRAMMED

We are now ready to tackle option strategies. Profit-and-loss diagrams for four basic option strategies will be presented in detail. After each diagram is explained, the important price points and strategy characteristics will be discussed. The stock price is always assumed to be $50 when an option position is established.

> Strategy: Long call
> Example: Buy 50 call at $3

1.   *Describe the opening transaction completely.* Buy a 50 call at $3.
2.   *Start a grid.* Use the grid shown in Figure 2–1.
3.   *Select a stock price and calculate the option's value at expiration.* If the stock is at $50 at expiration, the 50 call is worth zero.
4.   *Calculate the profit or loss.* Loss of $3 ($-0- value minus purchase price of $3 equals loss of $3).
5.   *Chart the profit or loss.* Figure 2–5a shows a dot indicating a loss of $3 at a stock price of $50.
6.   *Repeat Steps 3, 4, and 5 until the profit-and-loss diagram is completed.* Profit-and-loss results over a range of stock prices from $44 to $55 are presented in Table 2–5. Figure 2–5b shows a second dot indicating a profit of $2 at a stock price of $55, and Figure 2–5c shows additional dots after profit-or-loss outcomes are calculated at stock prices of $53, $49, and $48. Figure 2–5d shows the completed profit-and-loss diagram.

OBSERVATIONS ABOUT THE LONG CALL

> *Breakeven point:* $53. This is calculated by adding the premium paid for the call to the strike price. In this case $50 + $3 = $53.
> *Maximum risk:* This is limited to $3 (per share). No matter how much the stock price declines, purchasing the 50 call can result in losing only the premium paid for the call.
> *Profit potential:* This is theoretically unlimited. If the stock price rises dramatically, the option value will rise as well.

FIGURE 2–5   Long 50 call at $3

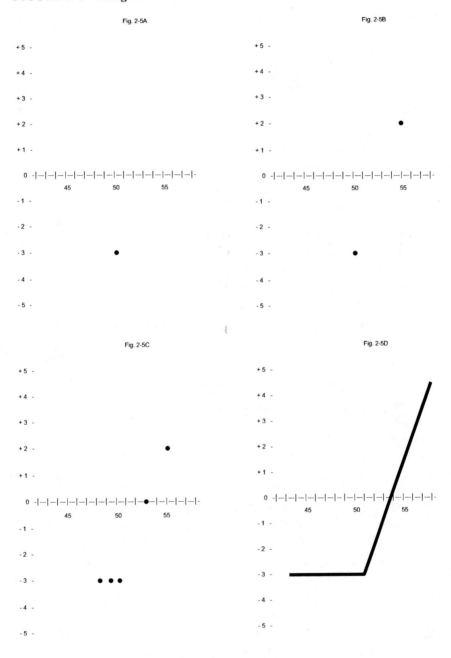

Fig. 2-5A

Fig. 2-5B

Fig. 2-5C

Fig. 2-5D

TABLE 2–5   Long 50 Call at 3—Profit-and-Loss Calculations

Stock Price at Expiration	Long 50 Call at 3 Profit / (Loss)	Stock Price at Expiration	Long 50 Call at 3 Profit / (Loss)
$55	+2	$49	−3
$54	+1	$48	−3
$53	-0-	$47	−3
$52	−1	$46	−3
$51	−2	$45	−3
$50	−3	$44	−3

Position created if option is in-the-money: The long call becomes long stock if the stock price is above the strike price at expiration. (In expiration profit-and-loss diagrams, it is assumed that all in-the-money long options are exercised.)

Investment trade-off: The positive aspect is that risk is limited to $3 per share. This is positive relative to owning stock, which has a theoretical risk of the stock price falling to $-0- and the entire $50 investment being lost. There are two negative aspects: a breakeven point of $53 compared to $50 for buying stock, and a limited time period for the call versus a long stock position, which will not expire.

Desired price action: Bullish. A profit at expiration occurs only if the stock price rises above $53.

Strategy: Short call
Example: Sell 50 call at $3

1.   *Describe the opening transaction completely.* Sell a 50 call at $3.
2.   *Start a grid.* Use the grid shown in Figure 2–1.
3.   *Select a stock price and calculate the option's value at expiration.* With the stock at $50 at expiration, the 50 call is worth zero.
4.   *Calculate the profit or loss.* Profit of $3 (sale price of $3 minus value of $-0- equals profit of $3).
5.   *Chart the profit or loss.* Figure 2–6a shows a dot indicating a profit of $3 at a stock price of $50.
6.   *Repeat Steps 3, 4, and 5 until the profit-and-loss diagram is completed.* Profit-and-loss results over a range of stock prices from $44 to $55 are presented in Table 2–6. Figure 2–6b shows a second dot

FIGURE 2–6   Short 50 call at $3

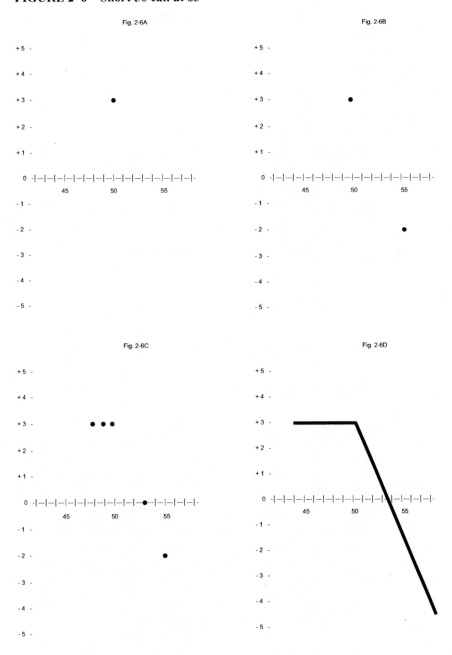

TABLE 2–6   Short 50 Call at 3—Profit-and-Loss Calculations

Stock Price at Expiration	Short 50 Call at 3 Profit / (Loss)	Stock Price at Expiration	Long 50 Call at 3 Profit / (Loss)
$55	−2	$49	+3
$54	−1	$48	+3
$53	-0-	$47	+3
$52	+1	$46	+3
$51	+2	$45	+3
$50	+3	$44	+3

indicating a loss of $2 at a stock price of $55, and Figure 2–6c shows additional dots after profit-or-loss outcomes are calculated at stock prices of $53, $49, and $48. Figure 2–6d shows the completed profit-and-loss diagram.

OBSERVATIONS ABOUT THE SHORT CALL

Breakeven point: $53. This is calculated by adding the premium (per share) received for selling the call to the strike price. In this case, $50 + $3 = $53.

Maximum risk: Theoretically, the risk is unlimited. As the stock price rises, the value of the 50 call will rise, and the loss from the short call position will increase correspondingly.

Profit potential: This is limited to $3 per share. Regardless of how much the stock price falls, the option value at expiration can drop only to zero, thereby earning a profit of $3 per share or $300 per option.

Position created if option is in-the-money: The short call becomes short stock if the stock price is above the strike price at expiration. (In expiration profit-and-loss diagrams, it is assumed that all in-the-money short options are assigned.)

Investment trade-off: There are two positive aspects. First, the breakeven point of $53 is higher than the breakeven point of $50 for a short stock position. Second, the option has a limited life and will expire, but a short stock position could, in theory, exist forever and cause a loss at any time. The negative aspect is that profit potential is limited to $3 per share. This is negative relative to selling stock short, which has the theoretical profit potential of the stock price falling to $-0-.

Desired price action: Neutral to bearish. Profit potential in a neutral market is significant, because this aspect of some option strategies cannot be achieved by stocks alone.

Strategy: Long put

Example: Buy 50 put at $2

1.   *Describe the opening transaction completely.* Buy a 50 put at $2.
2.   *Start a grid.* Use the grid shown in Figure 2–1.
3.   *Select a stock price and calculate the option's value at expiration.* With the stock at $50 at expiration, the 50 put is worth zero.
4.   *Calculate the profit or loss.* Loss of $2 (value of $-0- minus purchase price of $2 equals a loss of $2).
5.   *Chart the profit or loss.* Figure 2–7a shows a dot indicating a loss of $2 at a stock price of $50.
6.   *Repeat Steps 3, 4, and 5 until the profit-and-loss diagram is completed.* Profit-and-loss results over a range of stock prices from $44 to $55 are presented in Table 2–7. Figure 2–7b shows a second dot indicating a profit of $2 at a stock price of $46, and Figure 2–7c shows additional dots after profit-or-loss outcomes are calculated at stock prices of $53, $49, and $48. Figure 2–7d shows the completed profit-and-loss diagram.

OBSERVATIONS ABOUT THE LONG PUT

Breakeven point: $48. This is calculated by subtracting the premium paid for the put from the strike price. In this case, $50 − $2 = $48.

Maximum risk: This is limited to $2 (per share). No matter how high the stock price rises, purchasing the 50 put can only result in losing the premium paid.

Profit potential: Theoretically, this is limited to $48, because the stock price cannot fall below zero.

Position created if option is in-the-money: The long put becomes short stock if the stock price is below the strike price at expiration. (In expiration profit-and-loss diagrams, it is assumed that all long options are exercised.)

FIGURE 2–7   Long 50 put at $2

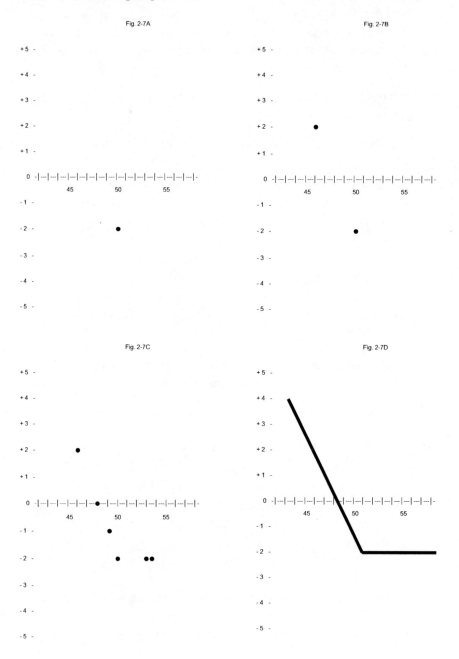

Fig. 2-7A

Fig. 2-7B

Fig. 2-7C

Fig. 2-7D

TABLE 2–7   Long 50 Put at 2—Profit-and-Loss Calculations

Stock Price at Expiration	Long 50 Put at 2 Profit / (Loss)	Stock Price at Expiration	Long 50 Put at 2 Profit / (Loss)
$55	−2	$49	−1
$54	−2	$48	-0-
$53	−2	$47	+1
$52	−2	$46	+2
$51	−2	$45	+3
$50	−2	$44	+4

Investment trade-off: The positive aspect is that risk is limited to $2 per share. This is positive relative to shorting stock, which has unlimited risk. There are two negative aspects: a breakeven point of $48 compared to $50 for short stock, and a limited time period for the put versus the short stock position, which will not expire.

Desired price action: Bearish. A profit occurs at expiration only if the stock declines below $48 at expiration.

Strategy: Short put
Example: Sell 50 put at $2

1. *Describe the opening transaction completely.* Sell a 50 put at $2.
2. *Start a grid.* Use the grid shown in Figure 2–1.
3. *Select a stock price and calculate the option's value at expiration.* With the stock at $50 at expiration, the 50 put is worth zero.
4. *Calculate the profit or loss.* Profit of $2 (sale price of $2 minus value of $-0- equals profit of $2).
5. *Chart the profit or loss.* Figure 2–8a shows a dot indicating a profit of $2 at a stock price of $50.
6. *Repeat Steps 3, 4, and 5 until the profit-and-loss diagram is completed.* Profit-and-loss results over a range of stock prices from $44 to $55 are presented in Table 2–8. Figure 2–8b shows a second dot indicating a loss of $2 at a stock price of $46, and Figure 2–8c shows additional dots after profit-or-loss outcomes are calculated at stock prices of $53, $49, and $48. Figure 2–8d shows the completed profit-and-loss diagram.

FIGURE 2–8 Short 50 put at $2

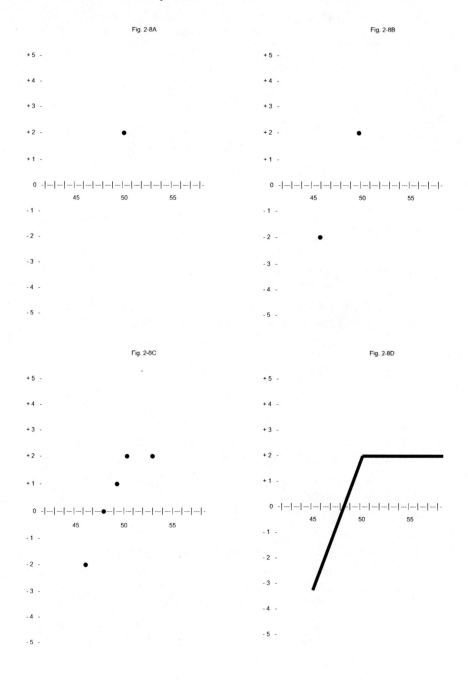

TABLE 2–8   Short 50 Put at 2—Profit-and-Loss Calculations

Stock Price at Expiration	Short 50 Put at 2 Profit / (Loss)	Stock Price at Expiration	Long 50 Put at 2 Profit / (Loss)
$55	+2	$49	+1
$54	+2	$48	-0-
$53	+2	$47	−1
$52	+2	$46	−2
$51	+2	$45	−3
$50	+2	$44	−4

OBSERVATIONS ABOUT THE SHORT PUT

Breakeven point: $48. This is calculated by subtracting the premium for selling the put from the strike price. In this case, $50 − $2 = $48.

Maximum risk: Theoretically, the risk is limited to $48, because the stock price cannot fall below zero.

Profit potential: This is limited to $2 per share. Regardless of how much the stock price rises, the option value at expiration can drop only to zero, thereby earning a profit of $2 per share.

Position created if option is in-the-money: The short put becomes long stock if the stock price is below the strike price at expiration. (In expiration profit-and-loss diagrams, it is assumed that all short in-the-money options are assigned.)

Investment trade-off: There are two positives: a lower breakeven point of $48, and a limited life of the option. The negative aspect is that profit is limited. This is negative only relative to buying stock, which will have an unlimited profit potential.

Desired price action: Neutral to bullish. This is the second example of an option strategy that can make money in neutral markets. (The short call was the first example.)

INTRODUCTION TO MULTIPLE-PART STRATEGIES

The ability to draw profit-and-loss diagrams of the six basic strategies just covered—long and short stock, long and short calls, and long and short puts—is essential for moving forward. The next step is to combine two basic strategies to create more advanced strategies, thus increasing the number of alternatives and expanding the range of investment objectives that can be achieved.

One strategy involving calls and puts will be presented first: the long straddle. Then two strategies involving stock and options will be presented: long stock plus long put, which is also known as the married put strategy, and long stock plus short call, which is also known as covered writing. These three strategies will be diagrammed and analyzed in the same manner as the basic strategies just presented.

Strategy: Long straddle
Example: Buy 1 50 call at $3 *and* buy 1 50 put at $2

1. *Describe the opening transaction completely.* Buy one 50 call at $3 and buy one 50 put at $2.

2. *Start a grid.* Preparation of a grid for a multiple-part strategy is no different from preparation of a grid for a single-option strategy. Use the grid shown in Figure 2–1.

3. *Select a stock price and calculate each option's value at expiration.* With the stock price at $50 at expiration, both the 50 call and the 50 put are worth zero.

4. *Calculate the profit or loss on each option and add the results together.* Total loss of $5
    the call: value of $-0- minus purchase price of $3 equals $3 loss
    the put: value of $-0- minus purchase price of $2 equals $2 loss
    total: $3 loss on call plus $2 loss on put equals $5 loss

5. *Chart the profit or loss.* Figure 2–9a shows a dot indicating a loss of $5 at a stock price of $50.

6. *Repeat Steps 3, 4, and 5 until the profit-and-loss diagram is completed.* Profit-and-loss results over a range of stock prices from $44 to $55 are presented in Table 2–9. Figure 2–9b shows a second dot indicating a loss of $2 at a stock price of $47, and Figure 2–9c shows additional dots after profit-or-loss outcomes are calculated at stock prices of $53, $49, and $48. Figure 2–9d shows the completed profit-and-loss diagram.

OBSERVATIONS ABOUT THE LONG STRADDLE

Breakeven points: $45 *and* $55. This is the first example in which there are two breakeven points. In this case, the upper breakeven point is

FIGURE 2–9   Long 50 straddle at $5

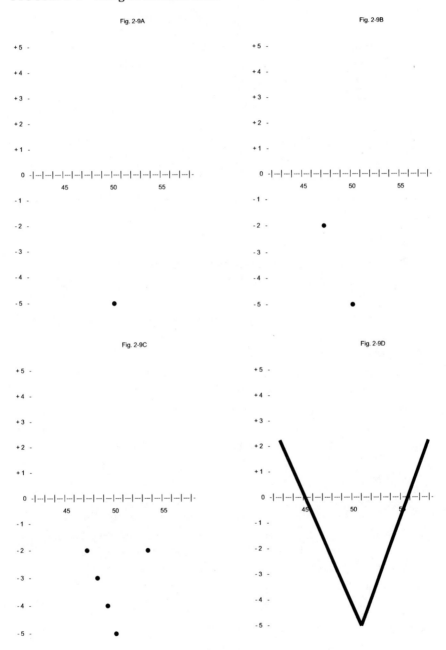

TABLE 2–9   Long 50 Straddle at 5—Profit-and-Loss Calculations

Stock Price at Exp	Long 50 Call Profit/ (Loss)	Long 50 Put Profit/ (Loss)	Total Profit/ (Loss)	Stock Price at Exp	Long 50 Call Profit/ (Loss)	Long 50 Put Profit/ (Loss)	Total Profit/ (Loss)
$55	+2	−2	-0-	$49	−3	−1	−4
$54	+1	−2	−1	$48	−3	-0-	−3
$53	-0-	−2	−2	$47	−3	+1	−2
$52	−1	−2	−3	$46	−3	+2	−1
$51	−2	−2	−4	$45	−3	+3	-0-
$50	−3	−2	−5	$44	−3	+4	+1

equal to the strike price plus the total premiums paid, and the lower breakeven point is equal to the strike price minus the total premiums paid.

Maximum risk: Risk is limited to $5, the total premium paid. If the stock price equals the strike price at expiration, then both options will expire worthless.

Profit potential: This is unlimited. Profit is realized at expiration if the stock price is above $55 or below $45.

Position created if the option is in-the-money: Either long stock or short stock, depending on the stock price at expiration. If the stock price is above the strike price, the long call is exercised, and the position becomes long stock. If the stock price is below the strike price, the long put is exercised, and the position becomes short stock.

Investment trade-off: The positive aspect is that profit can be realized with a stock price move in either direction; this is positive relative to purchasing only a call or a put. There are two negative aspects: The cost is two premiums, and the breakeven points are further from the strike price than with a single-option strategy.

Desired price action: Large movement *either up or down*. This is called a "high-volatility" strategy, because a large move is desired, but its direction is not important.

Strategy: Long stock plus long put (the married put)
Example: Buy stock at $50 *and* buy 50 put at $2

1. *Describe the opening transaction completely.* Buy stock at $50 and buy one 50 put at $2.

2. *Start a grid.* Use the grid shown in Figure 2–1.

3. *Select a stock price and calculate each security's value at expiration.* With the stock price at $50 at expiration, the stock is worth $50 and the 50 put is worth zero.

4. *Calculate the profit or loss on each security and add the results together.*
    Total loss of $2
        the stock: value of $50 minus purchase price of $50 equals $-0-
        the put: value of $-0- minus purchase price of $2 equals $2 loss
        total: $-0- result on stock plus loss of $2 on put equals $2 loss

5. *Chart the profit or loss.* Figure 2–10a shows a dot indicating a loss of $2 at a stock price of $50.

6. *Repeat Steps 3, 4, and 5 until the profit-and-loss diagram is completed.* Profit-and-loss results over a range of stock prices from $44 to $55 are presented in Table 2–10. Figure 2–10b shows a second dot indicating a profit of $1 at a stock price of $53, and Figure 2–10c shows additional dots after profit-or-loss outcomes are calculated at stock prices of $54, $49, and $48. Figure 2–10d shows the completed profit-and-loss diagram.

OBSERVATIONS ABOUT THE MARRIED PUT

Breakeven point: $52. This is calculated by adding the premium paid for the put to the purchase price of the stock. In this case, $50 + $2 = $52.

Maximum risk: $2 per share. The most that can be lost in this example is the premium paid for the put. If the stock price is at or below the strike price, $50 in this example, the put is exercised, and the stock is sold. The result is breaking even on the stock and a loss of $2 on the put.

Profit potential: This is unlimited. Profit is realized if the stock price is above $52 at expiration.

Position created if option is in-the-money: No position. If the stock price is below the strike price at expiration, the put is exercised and the stock is sold.

Investment trade-off: The positive aspect is that risk is limited to $2 per share. This is positive relative to owning stock outright, which has

FIGURE 2–10   Long stock at $50 and long 50 put at $2 (the married put)

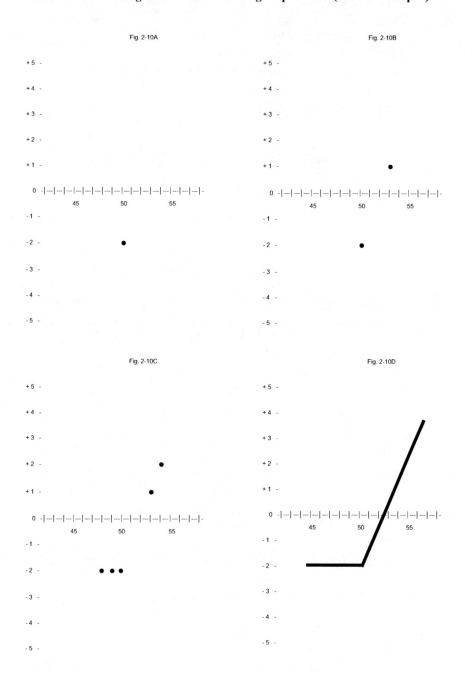

TABLE 2–10   Long Stock at 50 and Long 50 Put at 2—Profit-and-Loss Calculations

Stock Price at Exp	Long Stock Profit/ (Loss)	Long 50 Put Profit/ (Loss)	Total Profit/ (Loss)	Stock Price at Exp	Long Stock Profit/ (Loss)	Long 50 Put Profit/ (Loss)	Total Profit/ (Loss)
$55	+5	−2	+3	$49	−1	−1	−2
$54	+4	−2	+2	$48	−2	-0-	−2
$53	+3	−2	+1	$47	−3	+1	−2
$52	+2	−2	−0	$46	−4	+2	−2
$51	+1	−2	−1	$45	−5	+3	−2
$50	-0-	−2	−2	$44	−6	+4	−2

the theoretical risk of the stock price falling to zero. There are two negative aspects: a breakeven point of $52 compared to $50 for the long stock, and a limited time period for the protection provided by the put.

Desired price action: Bullish. This strategy produces profits if the stock price rises above $52 at expiration. This is equal to the stock purchase price plus the put premium paid.

Strategy: Long stock plus short call (the covered write)

Example: Buy stock at $50 *and* sell 50 call at $3

1. *Describe the opening transaction completely.* Buy stock at $50 and sell one 50 call at $3.

2. *Start a grid.* Use the grid shown in Figure 2–1.

3. *Select a stock price and calculate each security's value at expiration.* With the stock at $50 at expiration, the stock is worth $50 and the 50 call is worth zero.

4. *Calculate the profit or loss on each security and add the results together.* Total profit of $3
    the stock: value of $50 minus purchase price of $50 equals $-0-
    the call: sales price of $3 minus value of $-0- equals $3 profit
    total: $-0- result on stock plus profit of $3 on call equals $3 profit

5. *Chart the profit or loss.* Figure 2–11a shows a dot indicating a profit of $3 at a stock price of $50.

FIGURE 2–11   Long stock at $50 and short 50 call at $3 (the covered write)

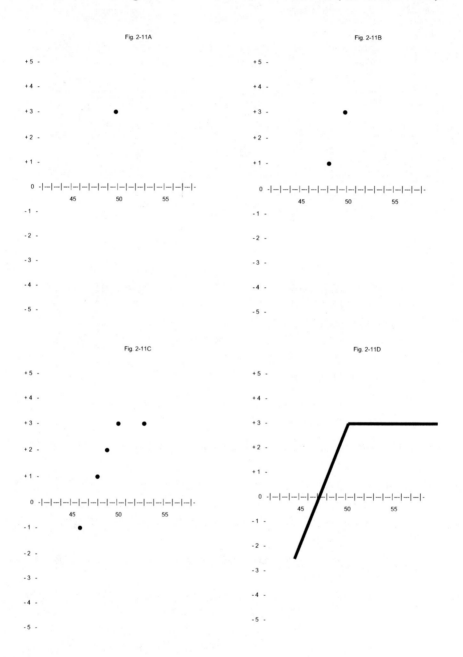

TABLE 2–11   Long Stock at 50 and Short 50 Call at 3—Profit-and-Loss Calculations

Stock Price at Exp	Long Stock Profit/ (Loss)	Short 50 Call Profit/ (Loss)	Total Profit/ (Loss)	Stock Price at Exp	Long Stock Profit/ (Loss)	Short 50 Call Profit/ (Loss)	Total Profit/ (Loss)
$55	+5	−2	+3	$49	−1	+3	+2
$54	+4	−1	+3	$48	−2	+3	+1
$53	+3	-0-	+3	$47	−3	+3	-0-
$52	+2	+1	+3	$46	−4	+3	−1
$51	+1	+2	+3	$45	−5	+3	−2
$50	-0-	+3	+3	$44	−6	+3	−3

6.   *Repeat Steps 3, 4, and 5 until the profit-and-loss diagram is completed.* Profit-and-loss results over a range of stock prices from $44 to $55 are presented in Table 2–11. Figure 2–11b shows a second dot indicating a profit of $1 at a stock price of $48, and Figure 2–11c shows additional dots after profit-or-loss outcomes are calculated at stock prices of $53, $49, and $46. Figure 2–11d shows the completed profit-and-loss diagram.

OBSERVATIONS ABOUT THE COVERED WRITE

Breakeven point: $47. This is calculated by subtracting the premium received for selling the call from the purchase price of the stock. In this case, $50 − $3 = $47.

Maximum risk: The risk is limited to $47, because the stock price cannot fall below zero.

Profit potential: This is limited to $3. If the stock price is above the strike price at expiration, the short call will be assigned, and the stock will be sold. The maximum profit potential of covered writing is equal to the difference between the purchase price of the stock and the strike price of the call plus the call premium.

Position created if option is in-the-money: No position. If the stock price is above the strike price at expiration, the short call will be assigned and the stock will be sold.

Investment trade-off: There are two positive aspects: a lower breakeven price of $47 relative to long stock at $50, and a limited time period for the short call. The negative aspect is that profit potential is limited to $3 per share compared to owning stock outright, which has an unlimited profit potential.

Desired price action: Neutral to bullish. This strategy produces profits if the stock price remains above $47.

SUMMARY

The ability to draw expiration profit-and-loss diagrams is an important skill that enables the investor to understand the potential profits and risks of investing and trading with options. These diagrams are created by following a six-step process: describing the opening transaction completely, starting a grid, selecting a stock price and calculating the value of each option at expiration, calculating the profit or loss, placing a dot on the grid above or below the selected stock price at a point which corresponds to the profit or loss, and, finally, repeating Steps 3, 4, and 5 over a range of stock prices until the profit-and-loss diagram is completed. The six basic strategies are long and short stock, long and short calls, and long and short puts. These basic strategies can be combined to form more complicated strategies.

Once a profit-and-loss diagram has been completed, an investor should make the following observations about the strategy: the breakeven point at expiration; the maximum risk of the strategy, which may be limited or unlimited; the profit potential, which also may be limited or unlimited; the stock position created if the option is in-the-money at the expiration date; and, finally, the investment trade-off that the strategy provides. The concept of a trade-off is that for each strategy, there is some relatively positive aspect and some other relatively negative aspect. Understanding the trade-offs of each individual strategy will lead to strategy comparisons that will aid in the investment decision-making process.

---

[1]Selling short is accomplished by borrowing shares and selling them; the "short position" is closed by purchasing shares and giving them to the lender. The mechanics of selling short are provided by brokerage firms.

3

WHY OPTIONS
HAVE VALUE

INTRODUCTION

OPTIONS HAVE A CLEARLY DEMONSTRABLE VALUE. They also have much in common with another financial product that nearly everyone purchases. This chapter will present an overview of option valuation and the elements that contribute to that value. The next chapter will go into detail about how and why option prices change.

A CONCEPTUAL APPROACH

That options have positive worth is easily illustrated with a simplified stock market example. Consider a scenario in which a stock, currently trading at $100, has a 50 percent chance of rising to $105 and a 50 percent chance of falling to $95. Also, assume that interest rates are zero, so that time becomes unimportant. Given these assumptions, the question is: What is the "expected value" of the 100 call option? This situation is depicted in Figure 3–1.

The expected option value is the average value of the two possible outcomes, and the result may be surprising to some readers. As presented in Figure 3–2, the result is calculated in two steps. First, the probability of each outcome is multiplied by the value of each outcome to arrive at an expected

FIGURE 3–1   Simplified range of outcomes

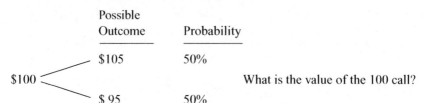

	Possible Outcome	Probability
$105	50%
$95	50%

$100

What is the value of the 100 call?

FIGURE 3–2   Expected value of 100 call

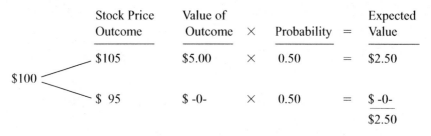

Stock Price Outcome	Value of Outcome	×	Probability	=	Expected Value
$105	$5.00	×	0.50	=	$2.50
$95	$ -0-	×	0.50	=	$ -0-
					$2.50

$100

value of each outcome. Second, the individual expected outcome values are added together to get the total expected value, or, in this case, the expected option value.

If the stock price rises to $105, the 100 call will have a value of $5. If the stock falls to $95, the 100 call will have a value of $-0- and will expire worthless. Therefore, the 100 call has a 50 per-cent chance of being worth $5 and a 50 percent chance of being worth $-0-. Consequently, as shown in Figure 3–2, the expected value of the 100 call is $2.50 [(0.50 × $5.00) + (0.50 × $-0-)].

> *Options are like insurance policies.*

The process just explained is similar to what insurance actuaries go through to determine the premium on an insurance policy. In its simplest form, if there were a 1 percent chance that any house might burn down, the insurance company would charge all homeowners an annual insurance premium of 1 percent of the home's value, plus a mark-up to cover expenses and a profit margin. In fact, options on stocks are just like insurance policies! Consider the components that go into an insurance policy: asset value, deductible, time, interest rates, and risk.

The value of the insured asset directly affects the price of an insurance policy. All things being equal, the more expensive the asset being insured, the higher the premium. The amount of the deductible, however, inversely affects the policy premium—the larger the deductible, the lower the premium. Time affects insurance premiums directly: the longer the time, the greater the cost. Interest rates are a factor, because insurance companies invest the premiums received. In theory, premiums will decrease if interest rates rise, because the increased income will be returned to policyholders in the form of lower insurance rates. Interest rates, therefore, affect insurance premiums inversely. The last factor affecting insurance premiums is risk. Risk has a direct impact on insurance premiums: the higher the risk, the higher the premium.

The components of an option's value correspond directly to the factors that determine insurance premiums. Table 3–1 summarizes the analogy between insurance premiums and option prices.

STOCK PRICE (ASSET VALUE)
Stock price corresponds to asset value. All things being equal, the more expensive an asset is, the more expensive it is to insure. Similarly, the higher a stock's price, the higher the price of an option on that stock.

STRIKE PRICE (DEDUCTIBLE)
The distance from the stock price to the option's strike price corresponds to the deductible of an insurance policy. Policies with small or no deductibles are more expensive than policies with larger deductibles. An at-the-money option is like an insurance policy with no deductible (stock price – strike price = zero). An option with an out-of-the-money strike price is like an insurance policy with a deductible: The first portion of the loss is borne by the insured party (in this case, the stock owner). When a loss exceeds the deductible, the insurance policy kicks in. In the case of options, the "coverage" or "protection"

TABLE 3–1   Components of Option Prices Compared to Insurance Policies

Insurance Policy	Option
Asset Value	Stock Price
Deductible	Strike Price
Time	Time
Interest Rates	Interest Rates and Dividends
Risk	Volatility
= Premium	= Premium

is the option's intrinsic value, which increases as the stock price moves beyond the option's strike price.

TIME (TIME)

Time has a direct impact on option prices, just as it has on insurance policies: the longer the period to expiration, the higher the option value.

INTEREST RATES AND DIVIDENDS (INTEREST RATES)

Interest rates and dividends are factors in option prices because of the time value of money. If call options, for example, could be purchased below the value of interest on the cost of the underlying stock, it would be advantageous for stock investors to buy T-bills and call options rather than the underlying stock. Consequently, the options market adjusts option prices as interest rates and dividends change.

Dividends also have an impact on option prices, but the effect is frequently difficult for option beginners to grasp. Dividends are, in essence, like an interest payment paid by the stock. Owning a stock that pays a dividend is more attractive than owning a stock that does not, all other things being equal. Therefore, call options on dividend-paying stocks are less valuable than calls on non-dividend-paying stocks, all other things being equal. The relationship is that as dividends rise, call values fall and put values rise. This concept will be easier to visualize when the computer program Op-Eval4 is explained in Chapter 11.

VOLATILITY (RISK)

"Risk" in the stock market is called *volatility*. In the normal course of trading, stock prices fluctuate. The larger the price fluctuations, the riskier the stock, and, therefore, the more expensive the options on that particular stock.

Volatility is an important concept that deserves additional explanation. The fluctuation of stock prices can be measured in two ways: direction of price change and size of price change. *Volatility* is a measure of the size of price change without concern about its direction. In other words, volatility is concerned with how much prices move, not with whether they move up or down. In mathematical formulas that calculate option prices, volatility is expressed as a percentage, e.g., 15 percent or 20 percent. In risk management terms, this percentage is the annualized standard deviation of a stock's daily returns. Although this definition can be intimidating to nonmathematicians, volatility can be understood intuitively. The goal for most investors with regard to volatility is to develop a subjective understanding of it and to incorporate that understanding into their investment decisions.

Changing the Volatility

At this point it is useful to revisit the simple two-outcome scenario presented in Figures 3–1 and 3–2. Now, however, we will change the possible outcomes to $110 and $90 and recalculate the expected value of the 100 call. This is done in Figure 3–3.

As Figure 3–3 shows, the wider range of outcomes increases the value of the 100 call to $5.00 from $2.50 in Figure 3–2. The wider range of possible stock prices is, in its simplest form, an increase in volatility, and this leads to an increase in the option's value.

The securities markets, of course, are more sophisticated than the examples in Figures 3–2 and 3–3. Although the possible range of stock prices is infinite, it can be analyzed with a statistical tool commonly known as the *bell-shaped curve*. Option volatilities are stated in percentage terms: 10 percent, 20 percent, and so on. These numbers describe the shape of a bell-shaped curve. Without delving into a detailed mathematical discussion, the volatility percentage is the annualized standard deviation of daily stock returns. A lower volatility percentage means smaller stock price fluctuations, which, in statistical terms, means that most outcomes are expected to be relatively close to the mean. A higher volatility percentage suggests more outcomes occurring in a relatively wider range around the mean.

Although this is not a perfect analogy, the volatility component of an option's price is sometimes compared to the price/earnings ratio (P/E) of a stock. Why do some stocks trade at high P/Es and others at low P/Es? The typical answer is: "The market thinks high-P/E stocks have higher growth potential." Why, then, do P/Es change? "Because the market changes its mind." In the options market, the volatility component of an option's price is the "market's opinion" about the likelihood of a big stock price change—either up or down. When an option price has a low volatility component, this is said to reflect the market's opinion that a big change in stock price is relatively

FIGURE 3–3   Expanded range of outcomes

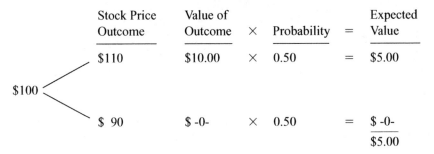

Stock Price Outcome	Value of Outcome	×	Probability	=	Expected Value
$110	$10.00	×	0.50	=	$5.00
$100					
$ 90	$ -0-	×	0.50	=	$ -0-
					$5.00

unlikely. When the volatility component is high, a big change, in the market's opinion, is more likely.

Does the market's opinion, as reflected in the volatility component of an option's price, guarantee a small stock price change or a big one? Absolutely not! Not only can the market "change its opinion," but the market can also be wrong! Referring to the P/E analogy, the market-determined P/E of a stock does not necessarily accurately reflect a company's earnings growth. Similarly, the volatility component of an option price does not indicate, definitively, whether the underlying stock price will or will not make a large change.

Volatility is a subject that takes time to understand and feel comfortable with. Newcomers to options should be patient, and they should remind themselves not to be intimidated by more experienced options traders who understand it. By identifying what is not understood and by asking questions, anyone can grasp the concept of volatility.

INSURANCE ANALOGY CONCLUDED

This chapter has compared the components of an option's value to the factors that determine insurance premiums. The complex concept of volatility corresponds to the risk involved in an insurance policy. To conclude

> *Puts insure stock holdings.*

this insurance analogy, one might reasonably ask, "If options are insurance policies, what do they insure?" For put options, the answer is obvious: Puts insure stock. There is an obvious analogy between buying a put option on a stock you own and buying an insurance policy on the house you own.

What, then, do calls insure? The answer is cash. Call options insure cash deposits against missing a market rally. When investment assets are in Treasury bills (or other cashlike investments), there is no risk of loss of capital. Rather, there is an opportunity risk—the risk of missing a market rally. The investor who buys calls with a small portion of total capital and

> *Calls insure cash.*

invests the rest in Treasury bills will participate in a price rise beyond the breakeven point. The potential loss is the amount invested in calls, which is a limited amount of the total principal compared to having the total principal invested in the market.

When options are seen in this context—as insurance-like instruments—investors begin to think differently about them. Suddenly there are new horizons to explore. In the housing market, of course, individuals can only buy insurance. In the stock market, however, individuals can sell insurance (sell

TABLE 3–2   How Changes in Components Affect Option Prices

Component	Effect on Call Price	Effect on Put Price
Stock Price	Direct	Inverse
Strike Price	Inverse	Direct
Time	Direct	Direct
Interest Rates	Direct	Inverse
Dividends	Inverse	Direct
Volatility	Direct	Direct

Direct effect means   as the component increases, and other factors remain unchanged, the option price will also increase.

Inverse effect means   as the component increases, and other factors remain unchanged, the option price will decrease.

options) just as easily as they can buy it (buy options). For individual stock investors, there are valid reasons for buying insurance and for selling insurance. Which strategy is chosen depends on the investor's market opinion, investment objectives, and risk tolerance. These issues will be discussed throughout the chapters that explain investment and trading strategies.

OPTION PRICE COMPONENTS SUMMARIZED

Table 3–2 lists the components of an option's price and summarizes how changes in the individual components affect that price. Although this subject will be covered in greater depth in Chapter 4, "Option Price Behavior," and in Chapter 11, which explains the computer program, at this point it is sufficient to know the conceptual relationships.

SUMMARY

Option values can best be understood by comparing them to insurance: When there is a statistical possibility of an event's occurring, the theoretical value of an insurance policy is the expected value of that event occurring. The components of option values directly correspond to the components of insurance premiums. For options, the stock price corresponds to the asset value in insurance. The option strike price corresponds to the deductible component in insurance—an at-the-money option is like a no-deductible policy, and an out-of-the-money option is like a policy with a deductible. Time is a component of price for both options and insurance. Interest rates are a component of insurance premiums, and interest rates adjusted for dividends are a component of option prices. Finally, the factor called risk in insurance is called volatility in options.

Volatility is a measure of movement without regard to direction. While it is a statistical concept that is not easily grasped by nonmathematicians, volatility can be understood intuitively and incorporated subjectively into investment decisions.

When seen as insurance-like products, options open a new range of alternatives to investors. As will be explained in coming chapters, there are valid investment reasons for buying and selling insurance (options) on stocks.

C H A P T E R

OPTION PRICE BEHAVIOR

THE WAY IN WHICH OPTION PRICES CHANGE PRIOR TO EXPIRATION IS OF GREATEST CONCERN TO SHORT-TERM TRADERS. Therefore, investors, as opposed to traders, do not need to dwell on the information discussed in this chapter. Investment-oriented strategies, as will be explained in Part 2, generally focus on strategy results at the expiration date, not on price fluctuations during an option's life. Developing realistic expectations about short-term option price behavior, however, is important for options trading.

The value of an option, as explained in Chapter 3, depends on six factors: stock price, strike price, time to expiration, interest rates, dividends, and volatility. In Chapter 3, these factors were explained conceptually, in a static environment. In reality, however, these factors operate in a dynamic environment. This chapter will first discuss the impact of a change in each component, assuming that the other components remain constant. Special emphasis will be placed on volatility, because it is such an important topic in any discussion of option prices. Subsequently, the discussion will cover option price changes when more than one component changes.

The following discussion gets fairly technical, and, again, it is not necessary for investors to comprehend every detail of this chapter. Short-term traders, however, do need to master this material. Newcomers to options may

TABLE 4–1   Example of Inputs to Option Pricing Formula and Outputs

	Inputs
Stock Price	50
Strike Price	50
Dividend Yield	0%
Volatility	30%
Interest Rates	4%
Days to Expiration	90
	Outputs
50 Call Value	3.19
50 Put Value	2.74

prefer to skim this chapter and come back to it when they are more familiar with the investing strategies presented in Part 2.

Table 4–1 shows an example of the use of the six components discussed earlier to calculate theoretical call and put values. The theoretical values were calculated using a mathematical formula known as the *binomial option-pricing model*. This formula involves advanced mathematics, and an explanation of it is beyond the scope of this book. Option values are presented in decimals rounded to the second place for the sake of clarity in explaining several concepts. Listed options in the United States trade in increments of 5 cents if the option price is under $3 per share and in increments of 10 cents if the price is over $3. In this example, the stock price is $50, the strike price is $50, there are no dividends, the volatility is 30 percent, the interest rate is 4 percent, and it is 90 days to expiration. The theoretical values are 3.19 for the 50 call and 2.74 for the 50 put.

An important observation to be made from Table 4–1 is that when the stock price is exactly at the option strike price, the call value is higher than the put value, 3.19 versus 2.74 in this example. This difference occurs because there is an interest component in the call that is not in the put. How option values change as individual inputs change is discussed next.

THE IMPACT OF STOCK PRICE CHANGES

Table 4–2 illustrates how call and put values change when the price of the underlying stock increases. A rise in the stock price from $50 to $51 has a

TABLE 4–2   Impact of Increase in Stock Price

	Initial Inputs	Changed Inputs	
Stock Price	50	51	←Increase in Stock Price Only
Strike Price	50	50	
Dividend Yield	0%	0%	
Volatility	30%	30%	
Interest Rates	4%	4%	
Days to Expiration	90	90	
	Initial Outputs	Changed Outputs	
50 Call Value	3.19	3.80	← Call Value Up
50 Put Value	2.74	2.34	← Put Value Down

direct effect on the value of the 50 call, which increases to 3.80. The effect on the 50 put is inverse; its value decreases to 2.34. Two important observations can be made about these changes.

First, neither the value of the 50 call nor the value of the 50 put changed by as much as the stock price did. The concept is that, if factors other than the price of the underlying security remain constant, then option values change by less than the change in the price of the underlying security. In Table 4–2, the stock price increased by one point (+1.00), the 50 call increased by 0.61, and the 50 put decreased by 0.40. The relationship of an option's price change to the price change of the underlying security is known as *delta*; it will be discussed later in this chapter.

Second, after the one-point change in the stock price, the relationship of the call's time value to the put's time value remained constant. With the stock at $50, the time value of the 50 call, 3.19, is 0.45 greater than the time value of the 50 put, 2.74. With the stock at $51 and other factors unchanged, the time value of the 50 call, 2.80

> *Option prices change less than the change in the underlying stock price.*

(total price of 3.80 minus the intrinsic value of 1.00) is still nearly 0.45 greater than the time value of the 50 put of 2.34. Note that the actual difference is 0.46. The difference of 0.01 can be attributed to rounding error.

Table 4–3 expands upon Table 4–2; it contains the theoretical values of a 50 call at various stock prices and various numbers of days prior to expiration.

**TABLE 4–3   Theoretical Values of 50 Call At Various Stock Prices and
Days to Expiration (Interest Rates, 4%; Volatility, 30%; No
Dividends)**

	Col. 1	Col. 2	Col. 3	Col. 4	Col. 5	Col. 6	Col. 7
Stock Price	90 Days	75 Days	60 Days	45 Days	30 Days	15 Days	0 Days
Row 1	$55	6.59	6.33	6.04	5.75	5.44	5.16	5.00
Row 2	$54	5.83	5.53	5.25	4.93	4.58	4.23	4.00
Row 3	$53	5.11	4.82	4.50	4.15	3.78	3.35	3.00
Row 4	$52	4.41	4.11	3.80	3.45	3.04	2.55	2.00
Row 5	$51	3.80	3.50	3.17	2.80	2.37	1.84	1.00
Row 6	$50	3.19	2.90	2.58	2.21	1.79	1.25	0.00
Row 7	$49	2.69	2.40	2.08	1.72	1.31	0.80	0.00
Row 8	$48	2.19	1.92	1.62	1.30	0.92	0.47	0.00
Row 9	$47	1.80	1.53	1.25	0.94	0.62	0.25	0.00
Row 10	$46	1.40	1.18	0.94	0.67	0.39	0.12	0.00
Row 11	$45	1.11	0.90	0.67	0.46	0.23	0.05	0.00

Table 4–3 contains eleven rows and seven columns. The rows indicate different stock prices, and the columns indicate different numbers of days prior to expiration. By looking up and down the columns and across the rows, one can observe how changes in stock price, time to expiration, or both cause changes in the option's theoretical value. For example, with a stock price of $48 and 75 days to expiration (column 2, row 8), the theoretical value of the 50 call is 1.92. If the stock price is raised by $1, the call value rises to 2.40. If the stock price is decreased by $1, the call value decreases to 1.53. In both cases, the call price moves less than the stock price. Looking anywhere on the table, this is always true. An option's theoretical value always changes less than one-for-one with a change in the stock price. Furthermore, the ratio of the option price change to the stock price change varies. For example, when the stock price rises by $1, from $47 to $48, at 45 days, the call rises from 0.94 to 1.30, or approximately 35 percent of the stock price change. In another situation, when the stock rises from $52 to $53 at 60 days, the call rises from 3.80 to 4.50, or approximately 70 percent of the stock price change.

Figure 4–1 is a graph showing the behavior of the call option price relative to the behavior of the stock price. The option values used to create the line

FIGURE 4–1   Illustration of Delta — the stock price rises $1, and the 50 call rises less than $1

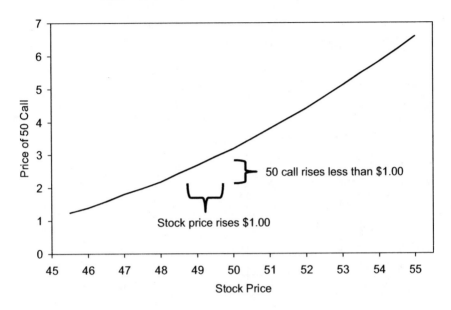

in Figure 4–1 are taken from column 1 in Table 4–3. Figure 4–1 shows graphically that option prices change less than unit-for-unit with price changes in the underlying stock.

DELTA

The ratio of the option price change to the stock price change is an important aspect of option price behavior, and it is referred to as the *delta* of an option. Specifically, the delta is the change in the theoretical value of the option given a one-unit change in the price of the underlying stock. Table 4–4 shows the delta of the 50 call at different stock prices and at different times to expiration. The deltas in Table 4–4 correspond to the option values in Table 4–3. For example, the delta of 0.55 in column 1, row 6 of Table 4–4 (90 days, stock price

> **DELTA**
> *Option Price Change*
> *per unit of*
> *Stock Price Change*

$50) corresponds to the option price of 3.19 in the same cell in Table 4–3. This means that the 50 call has a theoretical value of 3.19 and a delta of 0.55 given the stated inputs (stock price, $50; strike price, $50; days to expiration, 90; interest rates, 4 percent; volatility, 30 percent; no dividends). The term *one unit* is used in the definition of delta rather than $1 because delta is the first

58

OPTIONS FOR THE STOCK INVESTOR

TABLE 4–4 Delta of 50 Call At Various Stock Prices and Days to Expiration (Interest Rates, 4%; Volatility, 30%; No Dividends)

	Col. 1	Col. 2	Col. 3	Col. 4	Col. 5	Col. 6	Col. 7
	Stock Price	90 Days	75 Days	60 Days	45 Days	30 Days	15 Days	0 Days
Row 1	$55	.78	.80	.82	.84	.88	.95	1.00
Row 2	$54	.74	.75	.77	.80	.84	.91	1.00
Row 3	$53	.70	.71	.72	.74	.78	.84	1.00
Row 4	$52	.66	.66	.67	.68	.70	.76	1.00
Row 5	$51	.60	.61	.61	.61	.62	.65	1.00
Row 6	$50	.55	.55	.54	.54	.53	.52	0.00
Row 7	$49	.50	.49	.48	.46	.44	.39	0.00
Row 8	$48	.44	.43	.41	.38	.34	.27	0.00
Row 9	$47	.39	.37	.34	.31	.26	.25	0.00
Row 10	$46	.32	.31	.28	.24	.19	.09	0.00
Row 11	$45	.28	.25	.22	.18	.12	.04	0.00

derivative, or slope, of the curve in Figure 4–1 at a given point. At each point on the curve, the slope changes. Consequently, delta is dynamic: It changes as the stock price changes. For example, with the delta of 0.55, if the underlying stock price rises by $1, the theoretical value of the 50 call will increase from 3.19 to 3.80, which is slightly more than 0.55. The delta is an instantaneous measure of the rate of change in theoretical value, and it changes as the price of the underlying security changes.

Delta is used to gauge the "stock equivalency" of an option. One round lot of stock, 100 shares, is the benchmark. An option with a 0.55 delta will have a change in theoretical value approximately equivalent to 55 shares, all other factors being held constant, for a small price change in the stock. This is what happened in the example just cited. The stock price rose by $1, and the 50 call rose by approximately 0.55 (actually, 0.61). The 100 shares of stock rose $100 in value, and the 50 call rose approximately $55 in value.

Call deltas are positive and range from 0.00 to +1.00. Out-of-the-money call options have deltas between 0.00 and +0.50, at-the-money call options have deltas of approximately +0.50, and in-the-money call options have deltas between +0.50 and +1.00. Put deltas are negative and range from −1.00 to 0.00. This means that the delta of a put approaches −1.00 as the

TABLE 4–5   Theoretical Values of 50 Put At Various Stock Prices and Days to Expiration (Interest Rates, 4%; Volatility, 30%; No Dividends)

	Col. 1	Col. 2	Col. 3	Col. 4	Col. 5	Col. 6	Col. 7
	Stock Price	90 Days	75 Days	60 Days	45 Days	30 Days	15 Days	0 Days
Row 1	$55	1.11	0.93	0.72	0.50	0.28	0.07	0.00
Row 2	$54	1.35	1.13	0.93	0.69	0.42	0.15	0.00
Row 3	$53	1.64	1.43	1.19	0.91	0.62	0.27	0.00
Row 4	$52	1.95	1.72	1.49	1.21	0.88	0.47	0.00
Row 5	$51	2.34	2.12	1.86	1.57	1.22	0.76	0.00
Row 6	$50	2.74	2.52	2.27	1.98	1.63	1.17	0.00
Row 7	$49	3.25	3.03	2.78	2.50	2.16	1.72	1.00
Row 8	$48	3.76	3.56	3.34	3.09	2.78	2.40	2.00
Row 9	$47	4.38	4.19	3.97	3.74	3.49	3.19	3.00
Row 10	$46	5.01	4.85	4.68	4.48	4.27	4.07	4.00
Row 11	$45	5.74	5.59	5.43	5.28	5.13	5.01	5.00

stock price falls. Out-of-the-money puts have deltas between -0.50 and 0.00, at-the-money puts have deltas of approximately -0.50, and in-the-money puts have deltas between -1.00 and -0.50. Tables 4–5 and 4–6 show the theoretical values and deltas, respectively, of a 50 put option at various stock prices and days to expiration.

CALL VALUES RELATIVE TO PUT VALUES

Many investors are confused about the relationship of call and put values. Newcomers to options may believe that calls and puts with the same strike price and expiration should have the same price if the stock price equals the strike price. Actually, this is not true. Assuming no dividends, call prices will be greater than put prices because of an interest component. Evidence of this can be seen from a comparison of Tables 4–3 and 4–5. Row 6 in both tables shows option values with the stock price at $50. At 90 days (column 1), the 50 call has a value of 3.19 and the 50 put has a value of 2.74. The call value is greater than the put value in every square of row 6. The difference is attributed to an interest factor that is part of the call price, but is not part of the put price.

TABLE 4–6   Delta of 50 Put At Various Stock Prices and Days to Expiration (Interest Rates, 4%; Volatility, 30%; No Dividends)

	Col. 1	Col. 2	Col. 3	Col. 4	Col. 5	Col. 6	Col. 7
	Stock Price	90 Days	75 Days	60 Days	45 Days	30 Days	15 Days	0 Days
Row 1	$55	−.22	−.20	−.18	−.16	−.12	−.05	0.00
Row 2	$54	−.26	−.25	−.23	−.20	−.16	−.09	0.00
Row 3	$53	−.30	−.29	−.28	−.26	−.22	−.16	0.00
Row 4	$52	−.34	−.34	−.33	−.32	−.30	−.24	0.00
Row 5	$51	−.40	−.40	−.39	−.39	−.38	−.35	0.00
Row 6	$50	−.45	−.45	−.46	−.46	−.47	−.48	0.00
Row 7	$49	−.50	−.51	−.52	−.54	−.57	−.61	−1.00
Row 8	$48	−.56	−.58	−.59	−.62	−.66	−.74	−1.00
Row 9	$47	−.61	−.64	−.66	−.70	−.74	−.84	−1.00
Row 10	$46	−.68	−.70	−.73	−.77	−.82	−.92	−1.00
Row 11	$45	−.73	−.76	−.80	−.83	−.89	−.97	−1.00

The general concept explaining why call prices are greater than put prices is a relationship known as *put-call parity*. It is beyond the scope of this book to explain this concept in depth, but put-call parity states that stock prices, call prices, and put prices must have a certain relationship with one another or there will be arbitrage opportunities that will permit professional traders to make nearly riskless profits. In fact, one strategy employed by professional floor traders is to look for "market inefficiencies"—situations where prices are out of line with each other—and take advantage of the arbitrage opportunity. Because of the fierce competition between professional traders, such arbitrage opportunities exist for only very short periods of time, and the "inefficiency" typically amounts to only 5 or 10 cents. For readers interested in exploring put-call parity in depth, books by Sheldon Natenberg and the Options Institute discuss this topic thoroughly.

THE RELATIONSHIP OF CALL DELTAS AND PUT DELTAS
Although call deltas are positive numbers and put deltas are negative, one might suspect that, all other things being equal, the absolute value of call and put deltas would be equal. This is not true. A comparison of Tables 4–4 and 4–6 reveals that the absolute values of call and put deltas, when added

together, total 1.00. This phenomenon is another product of the put-call parity relationship. Nonprofessional traders need to know about this difference, because different deltas lead to different price behavior.

THE IMPACT OF TIME

It is well known that options decrease in value with the passage of time (all other factors remaining constant). Table 4–7 shows that, when the number of days to expiration is decreased from 90 to 45, the values of the 50 call and the 50 put decrease to 2.21 and 1.98, respectively. There are two ways of illustrating the impact of time erosion graphically. Figure 4–2 shows option price behavior at three different times prior to expiration and at expiration. The values used to create the four lines in Figure 4–2 are taken from columns 1, 3, 5, and 7 in Table 4–3, which are 90, 60, and 30 days from expiration and at expiration, respectively. Figure 4–2 shows how, as time passes, the graph of call option values approaches the shape of the call option expiration profit-and-loss diagram in Chapter 2 (Figure 2–5).

The values in Table 4–3 are presented differently in Figure 4–3 to illustrate how call prices change as time passes toward expiration, assuming a constant stock price. Consider row 6, a stock price of $50. The 50 call declines in value from 3.19 at 90 days to 2.90 at 75 days to 2.58 at 60 days, and so on. The

TABLE 4–7   Impact of Decrease in Days to Expiration

	Initial Inputs	Changed Inputs	
Stock Price	50	50	
Strike Price	50	50	
Dividend Yield	0%	0%	
Volatility	30%	30%	
Interest Rates	4%	4%	
Days to Expiration	90	45	← Decrease in Days Only
	Initial Outputs	Changed Outputs	
50 Call Value	3.19	2.21	← Call Value Down
50 Put Value	2.74	1.98	← Put Value Down

FIGURE 4–2   Illustration of time erosion for an at-the-money call: 50 call at 90 days, 60 days, 30 days, and expiration

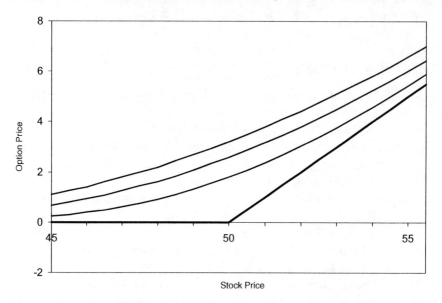

FIGURE 4–3   Illustration of time erosion for an at-the-money call: 50 call with stock price of $50 at various days to expiration

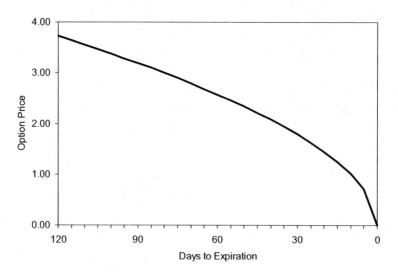

important observation is that time decay affects at-the-money options relatively little initially and relatively more as expiration approaches. Table 4–3 shows that when one-half of the time to expiration has elapsed, from 90 days to 45 days, approximately one-third of the 50 call value has eroded. A similar price/time relationship exists from 60 days to 30 days, when the 50 call declines from 2.58 to 1.79, and from 30 days to 15 days, when the decline is from 1.79 to 1.25. Figure 4–3 illustrates time decay graphically for a 50 call with the stock price held constant at $50. Table 4–5 reveals a similar time-decay rate for put options.

The name for time decay in options is theta. *Theta* is the change in option price given a one-unit change in time. The term *one unit* is not specific; it could refer to one day, one week, or some other time period. In the Op-Eval4 option-pricing program, the unit of time for theta is seven days if the time to expiration is greater than seven days and one day if the time to expiration is seven days or less.

> **THETA**
> *Option Price Change*
> *per unit of Time*

TIME DECAY VARIES

Unfortunately for newcomers to options, the impact of time decay on option values is not as simple as it may appear at first. While time decay for at-the-money options is low initially and increases per unit of time as expiration approaches, time decay for in-the-money and out-of-the-money options is different. Remember, it is only the time-value portion of an option that decays. Consequently, with a stock price of $53, 90 days to expiration, and a 50 call value of 5.11, time decay will affect only 2.11 of the value. Time decay during the first 15-day period is 0.29, and it increases to 0.43 during the 30- to 15-day period. During the last 15 days prior to expiration, however, the option decreases in value by only 0.35. A similar rate of time decay for the 50 call occurs when the stock price is $47. The time decay is 0.27 from 90 to 75 days and 0.27 from 30 days to 15 days. But time decay is only 0.25 between 15 days and expiration. The passage of time has an identical effect on put options; at-the-money puts erode at an increasing rate, and in-the-money and out-of-the-money puts decrease least in the last period immediately prior to expiration.

CHANGE IN INTEREST RATES

A change in interest rates has a direct effect on call prices and an inverse effect on put prices. The 1 percent rise in interest rates illustrated in Table 4–8 caused

TABLE 4–8   Impact of Increase in Interest Rates

	Initial Inputs	Changed Inputs	
Stock Price	50	50	
Strike Price	50	50	
Dividend Yield	0%	0%	
Volatility	30%	30%	
Interest Rates	4%	5%	← Increase in Interest Rates Only
Days to Expiration	90	90	
	Initial Outputs	Changed Outputs	
50 Call Value	3.19	3.25	← Call Value Up
50 Put Value	2.74	2.69	← Put Value Down

a 0.06 rise in the value of the 50 call value and a 0.05 decrease in the value of the 50 put. While it is possible for interest rates to change 1 percent in a short time frame, this is not a common occurrence. Consequently, traders of short-term stock options should be aware of the impact of changes in interest rates, but this need not be a primary concern. The impact of interest rates over longer periods of time can be significant, however, and traders of longer-term options must pay much closer attention to the impact of interest rates.

THE IMPACT OF DIVIDENDS

The impact of dividends on option prices is opposite to that of interest rates. With no dividends, the call price is greater than the put price by the cost of money (the interest rate). With positive dividends, however, the cost of money is effectively reduced—the dividend proceeds can be used to pay part or all of the interest. Also, an underlying security that pays a dividend is more attractive on a relative basis than a security that does not. Consequently, owning calls on an underlying stock that pays a dividend is relatively less attractive, while owning puts is relatively more attractive. Table 4–9 illustrates that, as dividends rise, the call price decreases and the put price increases. The call and put prices are equal when the dividend yield equals the interest rate.

TABLE 4–9   Impact of Increase in Dividend Yield

	Initial Inputs	Changed Inputs	
Stock Price	50	50	
Strike Price	50	50	
Dividend Yield	0%	1%	← Increase in Dividend Yield Only
Volatility	30%	30%	
Interest Rates	4%	4%	
Days to Expiration	90	90	
	Initial Outputs	Changed Outputs	
50 Call Value	3.19	3.13	← Call Value Down
50 Put Value	2.74	2.77	← Put Value Up

THE IMPACT OF VOLATILITY

The volatility component in options is analogous to the risk component in insurance. Higher risk means higher insurance premiums, and higher volatility means higher option prices. Table 4–10 confirms this. When volatility increases from 30 percent to 31 percent, both the 50 call and the 50 put increase in value. Changes in volatility have a direct effect on option values.

Note also that when call and put values change as a result of a change in volatility, the relationship of their time values does not change. In Table 4–10, the new time value of the 50 call is 0.45 greater than the new time value of the 50 put, just as it was before the change in volatility.

As described in Chapter 3, volatility is a measure of movement without regard to direction. The greater the volatility, the higher the option price. Volatility is stated in percentage terms. For example, the past price action of a particular underlying security is said to "trade at 25 percent volatility," or an option's theoretical value is said to be calculated "using a 30 percent volatility."

Because volatility is such an important topic in any discussion of options, the following observations are warranted. Although the explanation will get involved, do not lose track of the main goal. Traders must learn to understand volatility conceptually, as part of the subjective decision-making process. With practice and experience, any option user can master the topic of volatility.

TABLE 4–10   Impact of Increase in Volatility

	Initial Inputs	Changed Inputs	
Stock Price	50	50	
Strike Price	50	50	
Dividend Yield	0%	0%	
Volatility	30%	31%	← Increase in Volatility Only
Interest Rates	4%	4%	
Days to Expiration	90	90	
	Initial Outputs	Changed Outputs	
50 Call Value	3.19	3.29	← Call Value Up
50 Put Value	2.74	2.84	← Put Value Up

The direct relationship between volatility and option values illustrated in Table 4–10 is only one of several important observations. Three more observations about volatility are: (1) Volatility is a completely different concept from beta, (2) each stock has its own volatility characteristics, and (3) the volatility characteristics of individual stocks can and, in fact, do change frequently.

VOLATILITY VERSUS BETA

Volatility is a measure of the size of price movements without regard to direction. Volatility answers this question: Can the price of a stock be expected to fluctuate a great deal or only a little over the next time period as a percentage of the base price, regardless of direction or correlation with the overall market? *Beta*, in contrast, is a measure of correlation with the overall market. Beta answers this question: If the market is up by 1 percent, will this stock be up by 1 percent, more than 1 percent, or less than 1 percent?

> **BETA**
> *A stock's correlation with market movement.*

Any combination of beta and volatility is possible: high, high; high, low; low, high; or low, low. An example of low beta and high volatility might be a stock that is the subject of takeover rumors. As each new piece of information

hits the market, this stock may move up or
down sharply (high volatility); all the while,
the overall market is moving steadily in one
direction. Consequently, this stock would have
a low correlation with the market's overall
trend (low beta).

> **VOLATILITY**
> *A statistical measure
> of a stock's movement
> without regard to direction.*

An example of a high-beta and high-volatility stock might be a technology stock at a time when technology stocks, as a group, are leading the overall market. A low-beta, low-volatility stock might be an interest-sensitive issue, such as a utility, that fails to rise during a broad market rally because interest rates are holding steady or inching up slightly.

EACH STOCK HAS ITS OWN VOLATILITY CHARACTERISTICS

It seems intuitive that each stock would have its own volatility characteristics, and yet there seems to be a belief that stocks in the same industry tend to have similar price action. Obviously, these notions are in conflict, so which is correct?

Within industry groups, there can be a wide range of volatility characteristics. Using options, therefore, requires careful judgment about volatility, when making comparisons between stocks and their options. For example, Sandy, a San Francisco doctor, had extensively researched a medical technology company and became accustomed to a 90-day 50 call trading at $4 when the underlying stock was trading at $50. Sandy then discovered a 90-day 50 call on a new medical technology firm (also trading at $50) that was trading for $2, and he automatically assumed that this option was "cheap." By not doing any research on the new firm and its options, Sandy could be making an erroneous (and possibly expensive) assumption if the volatility characteristics of the two stocks are in fact very different.

VOLATILITY CHARACTERISTICS CAN CHANGE

An important point that is too frequently overlooked is the changing nature of the volatility characteristics of individual stocks. These characteristics change frequently, and they can change by a large amount. The classic example is that of an old, stodgy company that becomes the subject of a takeover battle. Prior to the battle, the stock may have been priced at $40 and fluctuated $0.50 per day (a 1.25 percent daily price fluctuation). After the announcement of the original offer, which is followed by new offers and rebuffs, the stock could fluctuate $2 per day around a price of $60 (a 3.50 percent daily price fluctuation). Although this is a dramatic example, much less dramatic events can change the volatility characteristics of a stock. Any number of news events, such as unexpected earnings, reorganizations, new product introductions, or news about a competitor, can affect a stock's price action. Just as the entire market goes through more volatile and less volatile periods, so too can individual stocks go through similar changes. Knowledge of past changes in a stock's volatility characteristics can be helpful when investing and trading with options. This information is available from options newsletters and data vendors.

FOUR MEANINGS OF THE WORD *VOLATILITY*

Volatility is perhaps the most talked about and least understood topic in the options business. This is understandable, because volatility is a complicated statistical concept. The nondirectional aspect of the concept is especially confusing to many investors, as they spend most of their time trying to predict the direction of the market. Adding to the confusion is the fact that the term *volatility* is used in four different ways: historical volatility, future volatility, expected volatility, and implied volatility.

The actual volatility of a stock's price fluctuation is calculated by statistical methods. Time periods studied vary from the most recent 10 days to 200 days, but a common period is 90 days. *Historical volatility* is a measure of actual stock price changes during a period of time in the past. There are two important observations to be made about historical volatility. First, the results of historical volatility calculations depend on the time period chosen; different time periods yield different volatility calculations. Second, there is no guarantee that stock price volatility in the future will be the same as the calculated historical volatility. Although historical information is a good place to start when making a prediction, there are many factors that can cause stock price volatility to change over time. Ultimately, predicting volatility is an art, not a science.

Future volatility is (1) unknown and (2) the determinant of an option's true theoretical value. This is what causes the most confusion for new options users. If an option's theoretical value depends upon something that is unknown, which it does, then how can the theoretical value be calculated? Obviously, it cannot be. However, the future volatility can be estimated, and a theoretical-value calculation can be made using that estimate. Therefore, any number presented as the theoretical value of an option is actually only an estimate of the theoretical value.

Expected volatility is an individual's estimate of future volatility; it is used by that individual in theoretical-value calculations. Frequently, traders use historical volatility as the expected volatility in calculating the theoretical values of options. This is fine as long as the trader is aware of more information on the historical volatility, such as the high and low for the year and recent changes. Such awareness aids traders in interpreting theoretical values and making strategy-selection decisions. Too often, however, traders are presented with "theoretical values" and advised not to pay more or sell for less. Such advice is often short-sighted and not properly set in a broader decision-making framework.

Implied volatility is the volatility number that justifies the market price of an option. In other words, it is the volatility number required for an option-pricing formula to calculate the current market price of an option as the theoretical value. In Chapter 11, the process of determining implied volatility using the computer program Op-Eval4 will be explained.

Summarizing the Differences

Distinguishing among these four uses of the word *volatility* may best be accomplished with an example. Consider a company whose stock has traded for the last 90 days at a volatility of 24 percent, as calculated by the statisticians. Recent reports about the company have been both good and bad: There have been successful new product introductions, on the one hand, but rumors abound of a pending "one-time" write-off because of a plant closing. Also, an earnings report is due in three weeks. One well-known option strategist is advising clients to base option theoretical-value calculations on a volatility estimate of 30 percent, but the market is currently trading the options as if 35 percent volatility is expected.

In this example, each use of the word *volatility* can be matched with its proper adjective. The historical volatility of the stock price is 24 percent. Because of recent events and an imminent earnings report, however, the future volatility (which is unknown) is likely to be different. The expected volatility as seen by one advisor is 30 percent, but the implied volatility in the market is 35 percent. Which is the "right" volatility number? Unfortunately, there is no answer to this question—just the information. An option user must combine an interpretation of this information with a specific market forecast and choose a strategy that has, in the person's opinion, a good chance of succeeding.

The preceding example is not intended to confuse newcomers to options. Rather, it is presented as a reminder that certain words in the options business often do not mean the same thing as in everyday usage. Many options-related terms have very specific meanings, because the field is technical for full-time, professional traders. However, individual investors with longer-term investment objectives need not be scared off by all the technical talk, which can be intimidating. As will be explained in Part 2, "Basic Investing Strategies," investors should concern themselves with whether an option and its price meet their objectives. It is not necessary for longer-term investors to get involved with computers and detailed talk about volatility.

DYNAMIC MARKETS

The discussion up to this point has assumed that one component of value changes while the rest stay constant. In the real world, of course, more than one component changes at a time. Market forecasts do not call for a stock to move up or down on a single day while volatility remains unchanged. Rather, stock prices and volatility commonly change over a period of time. All of these factors—stock price, time, and volatility—will affect the option price. An investor's forecast must, therefore, take all three into account. Referring back to Table 4–3, if a prediction called for the stock price to rise from $47 at 90 days to $51 at 75 days, the call price might be expected to rise from 1.80 to 3.50, assuming that interest rates and volatility do not change. If either or both of these change, the result will be a different option price.

Traders, therefore, must take into account the dynamic nature of markets. Tables of theoretical values, such as those presented in this chapter, help traders to develop realistic expectations about the price behavior of options. The computer program that accompanies this book was used to create these tables. Using the program will be explained in Chapter 11. The benefit of the program is that with it, given a realistic expectation for option prices, traders can more easily select a strategy that matches the market forecast. With practice, any trader can master this.

SUMMARY

The short-term behavior of option prices is the realm of the trader rather than the investor, who, as is explained in Part 2, focuses on the results of the strategy at expiration. Prior to expiration, option prices always move less than one-for-one with stock price changes. Delta is the name for the expected option price change given a one-unit stock price change. The passage of time causes option prices to decrease, all other things being equal. At-the-money options decrease with the passage of time in a nonlinear manner: less initially and more as expiration nears. The time decay of in-the-money and out-of-the-money options is different, with increasing time decay for a while and then less time decay very close to expiration. Changes in interest rates have a direct effect on call prices and an inverse effect on put prices. Changes in dividends are the opposite of changes in interest rates: When dividends are up, call prices are down and put prices are up.

Volatility has a direct impact on option prices: The higher the volatility, the higher both put and call prices will be. Volatility is a measure of movement without regard to direction. While it is a statistical concept that is not easily grasped by nonmathematicians, volatility can be understood intuitively and incorporated subjectively into trading decisions.

The term *volatility* is used in four ways: historical, future, expected, and implied. Historical volatility is the measure of actual price movements over a period of time. The selection of a time period is arbitrary, but the most commonly used period is six months. Future volatility is the actual stock price movements that occur between the present and an approaching option expiration. Future volatility is unknown, and it is what option users are trying to predict. Expected volatility is a trader's estimate of future volatility; it is used in mathematical formulas to calculate theoretical option values. Implied volatility is the volatility number that justifies the current market price of an option.

Volatility means movement, and the challenge for options traders is to develop a subjective understanding of numbers such as 30 percent, 40 percent, and so on, that describe option volatility in mathematical terminology. The goal for traders is to gain perspective on such questions as: What is a "normal" volatility level for this stock? What is its recent volatility? What is its current volatility? And, what volatility is forecast?

Markets are dynamic, not static. While the impact of the factors listed earlier on option prices may be confusing at first, having both an understanding of option price behavior and realistic expectations are necessary for the successful use of options as either investing or trading instruments.

Basic Investing Strategies

5

BUYING CALLS—AN INVESTOR'S APPROACH

INTRODUCTION

ALLS CAN BE PURCHASED FOR A VARIETY OF REASONS. Short-term trading, or speculating, is perhaps the most commonly known reason, and that strategy will be discussed in Chapter 12, but this chapter will explain investment-oriented reasons for purchasing calls. In the introduction to this book, an investor, as opposed to a speculator, was defined as someone who was interested in the benefits of long-term stock ownership, and one investment use of options was described as facilitating the buying or selling of "good stocks" at "good prices." Call options, of course, involve the right to buy stock, and this chapter will explain the use of purchased calls in an effort to enhance the stock-purchasing process.

In Chapter 3, options were compared to insurance policies. Essentially, because there is a probability that an event will occur, insurance policies have a value equal to the financial consequences of that event times the probability of its occurring. Call options are insurance policies that insure investment capital held in short-term liquid investments against missing a stock price rise. An investor who owns a call will participate in a stock price rise above a certain price level. Below a certain price level, the call will expire, but the investment capital will not decrease in value. A call owner, of course, does not have the right to vote on corporate affairs and will not receive dividends, if any, paid by the underlying stock.

The question is: Under what circumstances would an investor choose to own an insurance policy against a stock's rising rather than own the stock itself? The answer, like the reasoning that goes into selecting any investment, is largely subjective, but this chapter will describe and present some historical examples. Although some of the examples will seem obvious, given 20/20 hindsight, they will be helpful in exploring the psychology of purchasing calls for investment purposes and will enable readers to examine their personal investing activities and identify similar situations.

DIFFERENT STRATEGIES OFFER DIFFERENT TRADE-OFFS

When an investor is facing the need to select an investment strategy, it would be nice to know "which one is best." Focusing on this question, however, misses an important point about options. If knowledgeable participants are competing in the marketplace described by the efficient market theory (mentioned briefly in the introduction), then all strategies, in a theoretical sense, should be equal. The difference between strategies is not that one is "better" than another, but that they offer different trade-offs. The concept of a trade-off is that each strategy has a relative advantage and a relative disadvantage compared to another strategy. Figure 5–1 compares the purchase of stock at $50 to the purchase of a 50 call for $3. Purchasing stock at $50 breaks even at $50 (the positive), but risks $50 (the negative). The 50 call, however, has a limited life and breaks even at $53 (the negatives), but risks only $3 (the positive).

DIFFERENT CALLS, DIFFERENT TRADE-OFFS

As defined in Chapter 1, calls are categorized as in-the-money, at-the-money, or out-of-the-money. Figure 5–2 illustrates the trade-offs each type of call offers. The assumptions are a stock price of $50 and three call options, the 45, 50, and 55 calls, priced at $6, $3, and $1, respectively. The calls differ in premium and in effective purchase price. The premium, it will be recalled, is the total price of the option; and the effective purchase price is the price paid for the underlying stock, taking into consideration the option premium. The 45 call, for example, has a premium of $6 and an effective purchase price of $51. If the 45 call is exercised, the stock is effectively purchased at $51 per share (not including transaction costs). The effective purchase price is calculated by adding the call premium to the strike price. If a call is exercised, the exerciser

FIGURE 5–1   Long stock vs. long call

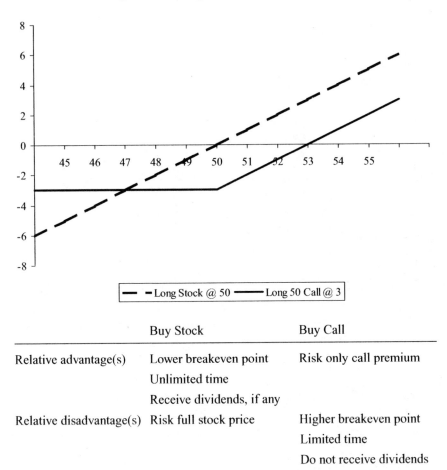

	Buy Stock	Buy Call
Relative advantage(s)	Lower breakeven point	Risk only call premium
	Unlimited time	
	Receive dividends, if any	
Relative disadvantage(s)	Risk full stock price	Higher breakeven point
		Limited time
		Do not receive dividends

must pay the amount of the strike price in return for receiving the stock, but the total price (or effective price) includes the price paid for the call.

The 45 call, in comparison to the 50 and 55 calls, has a breakeven point of $51 (the positive) but risks $6 per share (the negative).

The 50 and 55 calls offer different trade-offs relative to the stock and the 45 call. The 50 call has a premium and risk of $3 per share and an effective purchase price of $53. Relative to the 45 call, the premium of the 50 call is lower, but the effective purchase price is higher. The 55 call has the lowest premium and lowest risk, $1 per share, but the highest effective purchase price, $56.

FIGURE 5–2   Comparison of three long calls

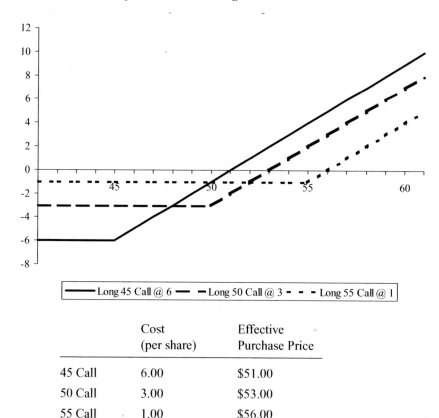

	Cost (per share)	Effective Purchase Price
45 Call	6.00	$51.00
50 Call	3.00	$53.00
55 Call	1.00	$56.00

Consequently, none of the four strategies—buying stock or buying one of the three calls—is "better" in an absolute sense; each just offers a different set of trade-offs. The strategy with the lowest effective purchase price has the highest risk, and the lowest-risk strategy has the highest effective purchase price.

CALLS AS INSURANCE

Susan, a marketing research analyst in Chicago, has been watching the stock of a soft drink bottler in Seattle (call it "SoftDrink") for some time and wants to buy the stock as a long-term investment. She is nervous, however, about a pending earnings report and rumors of a new product introduction. Susan believes that this is the time to take the plunge and buy the stock, especially if the new product is successful, but she is concerned enough to want to limit her risk. Buying stock has a risk/reward profile that every experienced investor knows: There is substantial profit potential and substantial risk. If Susan believes the stock could move up or down $10 as a result of pending developments, then the purchase of SoftDrink stock involves a $10 risk/reward profile. How do call options change the situation? Read on.

For simplicity, assume that Susan has $5,300 to invest in SoftDrink stock and that the 50 call is trading at $300 ($3 per share). Again, if Susan believes that the stock could move up or down $10 during the option's life, the 50 call offers a different risk/reward profile from purchasing the stock outright. The risk of buying the call is $3 per share. The profit potential, Susan believes, is $7 per share if the stock price rises $10. In addition to the different risk/reward ratio, the 50 call also offers a significantly different method of adding Soft-Drink stock to Susan's investment portfolio.

THE CALL OPTION ALTERNATIVE—BUY CALL PLUS T-BILL

The strategy involving the 50 call involves two steps. The first step is to purchase the call for $300, or $3 per share, and simultaneously deposit $5,000 in an interest-bearing account. The second step has two possibilities. The first possibility is that SoftDrink is above $50 on the option's expiration date. With this outcome, Susan can purchase the stock by exercising the call and using the funds on deposit to pay for the shares. SoftDrink will have been purchased, effectively, for $53 and will be in Susan's investment portfolio. If SoftDrink is $60, she will have a $7 profit per share in the stock. Susan can then proceed to monitor this stock investment in the same manner as her other holdings. There is no reason, necessarily, for her to use options on this particular holding again.

The second possibility is that SoftDrink is below $50, a likely outcome if the earnings report is below expectations or if the reaction to the new product is abysmal. If the stock price is below $50 at option expiration, Susan can let the call expire unexercised. Her maximum risk is the $3 per share that she paid for the call. At this point, she can reexamine her decision to purchase the stock. If new information compels her to forget SoftDrink, Susan can feel relieved that she risked only $3 per share. Alternatively, if she judges SoftDrink to be a better buy than ever, she can purchase the stock at the current market price.

In the SoftDrink example, the call option helped a long-term investor purchase a good stock and limit her risk during the crucial initial holding period. The trade-off was a higher effective purchase price (the negative) versus limited risk (the positive).

Another alternative for Susan would be to wait until after SoftDrink's pending development before purchasing any stock. In this case, there would be a $10 potential benefit versus a $10 opportunity loss. If she made no investment and the stock declined $10, Susan would be better off by $10 per share, as she could buy the stock at $40 versus $50. If the stock rose to $60, however, Susan would have missed the buying opportunity at $50 and would be $10 worse off, as she would have to pay $60 per share if she still wanted to buy the stock. Regardless of whether the stock is purchased prior to or after the pending development, given the assumptions in this example, Susan faces a $10 potential benefit versus a $10 risk.

> *What is the risk/reward profile of buying stock?*
>
> *What is the risk/reward profile of buying a call?*

Compared to the stock purchaser, who faces a $10 risk/$10 reward ratio, the call buyer faces a $3 risk/$7 reward ratio. While this, in itself, is significant, it is not the only advantage of using the call.

In the real world, of course, there are more possible outcomes than the stock price moving up or down $10. First, if the news event is negative, it could cause a larger drop in the stock price than $10. Second, a negative report could change the investor's fundamental view of the stock, leading her not to want to invest in this stock at all. In either of these cases, purchasing the call, while resulting in a loss, would be less costly than buying the stock.

Another possibility is that a rising stock price could cause a stock purchaser to believe that he had missed the opportunity and lead to his not investing at all. Only time would tell how this scenario would play out, but many investors have "stocks that got away." In this situation, the call might have changed the short-term risk/reward ratio in the investor's favor.

> *Stop-Loss Order:*
> *Dependent on price*
>
> *Call Option:*
> *Dependent on time and price*

Still another possibility is the frustrating "stop-loss scenario," in which a stock purchaser places a stop-loss sell order below the purchase price. The intent of this action is to limit risk. But in the worst-case scenario, the stock price dips to the stop-loss price that triggers the sell order, then rises dramatically—a frustrating series of events that many investors have experienced. The call option, while having a limited life and limited loss, does not have a limiting price. If the stock price dips and rallies during the option's life, the call purchaser still participates in the price rise above the option's breakeven price. While this is a tremendous advantage in favor of options, this benefit is not free. The call had a cost and a higher effective purchase price relative to purchasing the stock.

Remember, options offer trade-offs, not alternatives that are "better" in an absolute sense. The higher effective purchase price is the cost of getting the benefit of limited risk. A stock purchaser will profit more than a call purchaser if the price rises. A stock purchaser, however, has a higher risk potential than a call purchaser. Seen in this light, the call alternative demands somewhat different thinking from that typically required of stock investors.

REAL-WORLD EXAMPLES

Let's move from the hypothetical to the actual by reviewing some historical situations in which options actually did help the long-term investor. In the two scenarios presented, the market view will be correct one time and wrong the other.

The first situation is January 2004, when H&R Block (HRB), the firm known for its tax preparation service, approached $60 per share, a new all-time high. There was some controversy about whether HRB represented a good investment opportunity at this price. Some investment advisors were touting HRB for its diversification into mortgage origination, and its steadily growing dividend was another attraction. Nevertheless, HRB had significant competition in what analysts believed was a saturated industry. An investor considering HRB should have been aware of these conflicting opinions. If the stock's current price was viewed as "risky, but an excellent opportunity," then call options offered a way to take advantage of this opportunity and limit risk at the same time.

On January 22, 2004, HRB closed at $59.42, and the June 2004 60 call closed at $5.40. An investor with approximately $6,000 to purchase 100 shares of HRB stock had the alternative of buying one June 60 call for $540 and leaving $5,460 in an interest-bearing account until the third Friday in June. The call offered the advantage of limiting the investor's risk to $540 minus any interest earned. The accompanying disadvantage was an effective purchase price of $65.40 per share, approximately $6 above the then-current market price of $59.42.

Those who were following HRB in 2004 knew that the stock price fared poorly during the first half of the year. By June 18, 2004, when the June options expired, the price of HRB had dropped to $47.66 per share, a loss of nearly $12 per share for stock purchased at $59.42. The investor who purchased the June 60 call was equally wrong in her outlook for HRB's share price, but lost only $5.40 per share.

The option expiration date, however, is not the end of the story. The investor who purchased the call and watched it expire worthless still has $5,460 in a money market account. The question for this investor is, What to do with this money? The alternatives are numerous, but they include buying HRB at the current price, buying another HRB call, and looking elsewhere to invest the funds. The stock buyer, in contrast, has to decide whether to hold or to sell. Whichever decision is made, the stock owner, in this example, has only $4,700 of equity in the stock, about $700 less than the call purchaser.

The second situation begins in December 2003, when eBay rose to a new all-time high of $60. Its stock price had more than doubled in the preceding 13 months, and the company had recently split its shares 2 for 1. Boosters of eBay claimed that this company was "the leader of an industry of tomorrow." They argued that the share price had to rise as more and more institutions accumulated the stock. The negative view was that eBay was overvalued at 90 times earnings, and that any stumble could cause the price to come crashing down. With eBay's closing price of $61.37 on December 19, 2003, the June 2004 60 call was offered at $8.80.

An investor who was considering the purchase of eBay stock at this time had to decide whether to take the plunge into the stock and potentially risk a substantial portion of the $61.37 purchase price or to purchase a six-month call with risk limited to $8.80.

After December 19, 2003, eBay's stock price continued to trade straight up, nearly without interruption, and reached $86.50 on June 18, 2004, the expiration day for June options. In hindsight, a buyer of the stock at $61.37 would have made more than a buyer of the 60 call. From the first day, however, the call buyer knew the maximum risk. And this is a situation that many investors can live with more easily than the anxieties of watching an investment fluctuate dramatically, not knowing when, where, or if the losses will stop. Investing is sometimes an anxiety-provoking endeavor, and one use of call options is to reduce that anxiety when initiating new investment positions.

USING IN-THE-MONEY CALLS

The previous examples illustrate how at-the-money calls can act as insurance policies that limit risk and insure against missing a price rise. In-the-money calls offer a different set of trade-offs. In-the-money calls, it will be remembered, cost more than at-the-money or out-of-the-money calls (the negative). However, in-the-money calls offer a lower effective purchase price than other options (the positive). When, then, would an investor want this choice? There are a number of situations.

Follow Tom, the owner of a car dealership in Houston, as he works through several investment strategies.

First, purchasing an in-the-money call can be used as a short-term risk management technique that is an alternative to buying stock and placing a stop-loss sell order. Tom has been watching a chemical manufacturing stock, Chemco, that shows promise. Potential environmental concerns, however, could cause a dramatic change in the company's fortunes. Chemco stock is trading at $50, and the 90-day 45 call is available for $6. Tom could purchase Chemco for $50 and place a stop-loss sell order at $45, to act as a loss-limiting mechanism. Tom needs to realize, however, that a stop-loss order does not guarantee that the loss will not be larger, because the market can trade through and below a stop-loss price for a number of reasons. One possibility is that a large volume of sell orders appear at the same time (perhaps as the result of a rumor or a news item during market hours), and the stock trades down through and below $45 before buyers and sellers can find a new equilibrium between supply and demand. Another possibility is a "gap opening" below $45. Such a situation could occur when news released after the previous day's close causes an imbalance of sell orders on the next morning's opening. In situations like this, it is possible for a stock to open significantly lower than the previous day's closing price.

If Tom purchased a 90-day 45 call for $6, instead of purchasing stock and using a stop-loss order, he could accomplish two things that he could not accomplish with the stop-loss order. First, if he does not exercise the call, his maximum loss is limited to $6 per share—the price of the call. Second, the call is not price-dependent like the stop-loss order, which is triggered by a trade or offer at $45 and immediately becomes a market sell order when that occurs. Thus, Chemco could trade down to $45, trigger the stop-loss sell order, and then reverse direction and trade higher. This is not an uncommon occurrence, as many experienced investors are undoubtedly aware. Although the limited life of Tom's call is a negative, Chemco could trade at or below $45 during the call's life, but the call would still be intact to participate in any price rise above $45 until its expiration date. Many investors find this time-dependent aspect of call options irresistible.

PLANNING FOR FUTURE CASH FLOWS

A second situation in which an investor might choose an in-the-money call is when the cash needed to purchase the stock is not immediately available, but its receipt is anticipated. Assume that Tom wants to purchase Chemco, but he needs his dealership's third-quarter dividend in order to have the full purchase price. The dividend will be declared and paid prior to the option's expiration. Investors regularly experience these situations, such as when a bond is about to mature, a year-end bonus is anticipated, or an investor is a regular saver and can anticipate when the needed amount will be available.

In Tom's situation, he wants the lowest possible price, and that leads to the in-the-money call. If Chemco is trading at $50 and a 90-day 45 call is available for $6, then purchasing the call costs an extra $1 in terms of effective purchase price. During the period of the call ownership, of course, Tom will not receive dividends, if any, paid by the stock. He will, however, participate in any price rise in the stock above $51. Also, his risk is limited to $6 per share before the call is exercised. If his own fortunes decline and his dealership fails to pay the expected dividend, he will have shown great wisdom in limiting his risk by using the option strategy.

Some investors to whom this strategy is new may have the initial reaction that paying $51 for a stock that is trading at $50 is the waste of a dollar per share. In this case, of course, it was assumed that Tom did not have sufficient funds on hand immediately to purchase the stock at $50. Waiting until the money is available has its risks, too. The stock may rally during the waiting period and reach a price greater than $51 per share. Of course, the price could also decline during the waiting period. Once again, the point is not that the call strategy is "better" in an absolute sense. Rather, the call offers the investor a different set of trade-offs: buying now rather than waiting (the positive), but paying, effectively, $1 more per share (the negative).

An alternative to purchasing the in-the-money call is purchasing the stock on margin. When stock is purchased on margin, an investor pays 50 percent or more initially and borrows the balance of the purchase price from the brokerage firm until the anticipated cash is received. Purchasing on margin is a viable alternative to purchasing an in-the-money call. The interest cost can be compared to the higher effective purchase price of the call. Buying on margin, however, assumes the immediate availability of at least 50 percent of the purchase price or other marginable securities which can act as collateral for the margin loans. The in-the-money call strategy in the previous example required less than 15 percent of the stock price immediately.

GETTING THE BEST OF BOTH

A third situation in which in-the-money calls can be used is to facilitate those difficult times when there are two stocks that have caught an investor's fancy, but the investor does not have sufficient capital to purchase both. Again consider Tom, who wants to purchase Chemco stock. However, he also has his eyes on a grocery giant, Foodco, that has been growing rapidly in recent years. In this case, Tom purchases Foodco stock and, at the same time, purchases an in-the-money call on Chemco. This gives him total exposure to Foodco with total risk and high exposure to Chemco with limited risk. Purchasing both stocks on margin would mean total exposure with total risk on both stocks.

With the in-the-money call on Chemco, Tom can participate in both stocks until a later date at or prior to the option expiration date, when he makes a final decision. If Foodco has performed better and is the preferred choice, then the Chemco call is sold (if it is in-the-money) or expires (if it is out-of-the-money), and that stock is forgotten. If Chemco is the choice, then Foodco is sold. The proceeds from Foodco's sale can then be used to purchase Chemco when the call is exercised.

The risks of this third use of in-the-money calls should not be overlooked. If a 45 call is purchased for $6 per share, then the investor who purchases one stock and this call on another stock is, in fact, taking an additional $6 risk (per share). A number of market scenarios could follow. Both stocks could rise in price, and the purchased stock and the call could both show a profit. Both could fall and both show a loss. Or, one could rise and show a profit and the other fall and show a loss. There is no guarantee that the strategy described here will perform better than another strategy. The call option has, however, presented a new alternative that was not previously available.

A final point: This third strategy, attempting to get the best of both worlds, need not be limited to in-the-money calls. However, in-the-money calls offer the lowest effective purchase price (if exercised) and the highest short-term price participation (if the stock price rises) relative to at-the-money or out-of-the-money calls. The trade-off is that in-the-money calls cost more than in-the-money or out-of-the-money calls.

SUMMARY

This chapter introduced the idea that call options can be used like insurance policies to help investors buy stocks with limited risk during the life of the call. Relative to purchasing stock, call options offer a different set of trade-offs, limited risk in return for a higher effective purchase price. Calls are a time-dependent risk management tool; they are not price-dependent like stop-loss orders. Finally, calls offer an alternative to buying stock on margin until the funds are available to pay for the stock in full.

C H A P T E R

COVERED WRITING

INTRODUCTION

COVERED WRITING IS ONE OF THE MOST POPULAR OPTION STRATEGIES. Unfortunately, it is also a frequently misunderstood strategy. Many investors either fail to recognize the many differences between covered writing and buy-and-hold investing or have one of many misconceptions about the strategy.

This chapter has two parts. First, the basics of covered writing will be explained, and this explanation will include examples that review the standard rate-of-return calculations. Second, some common misconceptions and myths about covered writing will be addressed. Throughout this chapter there will also be several comments about the psychological adjustment that covered writing requires and how it differs from traditional buy-and-hold investing.

THE BASICS OF COVERED CALLS

The covered call strategy involves the purchase of stock and sale of calls on a share-for-share basis. The following example will include explanations of how the strategy works, a profit-and-loss diagram, the profit potential and risk, the standard rate-of-return calculations, and an investor's motivation for using the strategy.

Assume that Marc, an engineer in Boston, decides to engage in covered writing. He has been watching the price of Gasco, a major refiner. He likes the stock and would not mind holding it in his portfolio; on the other hand, he would also be happy with a reasonable profit should the stock price rise. He buys 100 shares of Gasco stock at $48.75 per share and sells one 60-day 50 call for $1.60. An expiration profit-and-loss diagram is presented in Figure 6–1, and supporting calculations are given in Table 6–1. For simplicity, transaction costs and the possibility of early assignment have been ignored. Early assignment may mean that a covered writer will not receive a dividend. Also, transaction costs can significantly influence the desirability of covered writing and, therefore, must be included in any analysis.

MAXIMUM PROFIT POTENTIAL
As illustrated in Figure 6–1, Marc's maximum profit potential is $2.85. If the price of Gasco is at or above the strike price at expiration, the call owner will exercise, and Marc, the call writer, will be assigned. If Marc's short call is

FIGURE 6–1   Marc's covered write on Gasco—buy stock and write call

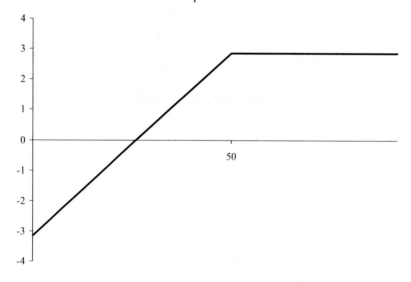

TABLE 6–1   The Covered Write—Buy Stock and Write Call Profit-and-Loss Calculations at Expiration

Stock Price at Expiration	Buy Stock @ $48.75 Profit or Loss	Sell 50 Call @ $1.60 Profit or Loss	Total Profit or Loss
$53	+4.25	− 1.40	+2.85
$52	+3.25	− 0.40	+2.85
$51	+2.25	+ 0.60	+2.85
$50	+1.25	+1.60	+2.85
$49	+0.25	+1.60	+1.85
$48	− 0.75	+1.60	+0.85
$47	− 1.75	+1.60	− 0.15
$46	− 2.75	+1.60	− 1.15
$45	− 3.75	+1.60	− 2.15

assigned, his stock will be sold at $50, and the result for Marc is a profit of $2.85. This profit is calculated by adding the option premium of $1.60 to the stock gain of $1.25. The stock gain is the difference between the strike price of the call and the purchase price of the stock. Regardless of the stock price, if the covered writer is assigned, the stock will be sold at the strike price of the call.

THE BREAKEVEN STOCK PRICE AT EXPIRATION

An advantage of the covered writing strategy over purchasing stock outright is the lower breakeven point. Covered writing breaks even, at expiration, at a stock price equal to the purchase price of the stock minus the amount received for selling the call. In Marc's case, the breakeven stock price of $47.15 is calculated by subtracting the call premium of $1.60 from the purchase price of the stock of $48.75.

SELECTING A COVERED WRITE

Analyzing any investment requires answering this question: Is the potential profit worth the potential risk? When choosing a covered write, stock selection is the most important element. Compare Marc's risk to his profit potential: His profit potential is limited to $2.85 if the call is assigned, but his risk, theoretically, is $47.15 if the stock falls to $-0-. While not many stocks fall to $-0-, some stocks do suffer substantial price declines. Because of this risk, an investor must be thoroughly confident of the stock investment itself before using this strategy.

BENCHMARK MEASURES OF PROFIT

Although there are no absolute measures of profit, there are two benchmark measures for covered writing. With some experience, these measures can be included as part of the analysis in deciding whether a particular covered write is "worth it."

The Static Rate of Return

There are two standard measures of a covered write's attractiveness. The first is the static rate of return or, simply, the static return. The *static return* is the annualized percentage profit on a covered write, assuming that the stock price is unchanged from the purchase price at option expiration and the call expires unexercised.

The static return calculation is made by dividing the income by the net investment and annualizing the result.

The *income* is the net call premium received plus dividends received, if any. Net call premium is the total call premium less transaction costs (assumed here to be zero). For Marc, income is $1.60.

The *net investment* is the total price of the stock minus the net call premium received. The total price of the stock includes transaction costs. Since Marc purchased stock for $48.75 and sold the call for $1.60, his net investment, on a per-share basis, is $47.15 ($48.75 minus $1.60).

Dividing the income of $1.60 into the investment of $47.15 results in a profit of 0.034, or 3.40 percent, for Marc *in 60 days*. To annualize the earnings, this amount is multiplied by the number of days per year and divided by the days to expiration. In this example, 0.034 is multiplied by 365 days per year and divided by 60 days. The result, 0.210 or 21.0 percent, is the static return. The assumption is that the 3.40 percent earned in 60 days can be earned in every 60-day period for the rest of the year. Since there are just a tad more than six 60-day periods in a 365-day year, the result is 6.08 times 3.40 percent, or 21.0 percent. Of course, the assumption about repeating a given performance may not be realistic. Remember that this is a benchmark measure and that achieving an excellent return one time does not guarantee future results. The static return calculation is summarized in Table 6–2.

The If-Called Rate of Return

The second standard benchmark measure is the if-called rate of return or, simply, the if-called return. The *if-called return* is the annualized percentage profit

TABLE 6–2   Marc's Static Rate of Return (Annual Rate)

Assumptions:	Stock price is unchanged from purchase price at option expiration	
	Call expires unexercised	
Marc's example:	Stock Purchase Price	$48.75
	50 Call Price	1.60
	Dividends	0
	Days to Expiration	60

$$\text{Static Return} = \frac{\text{Income}}{\text{Investment}} \times \text{Annualization Factor}$$

$$= \frac{\text{Call Premium} + \text{Dividend}}{\text{Stock Purchase Price} - \text{Call Premium}} \times \frac{\text{Days per Year}}{\text{Days to Expiration}}$$

$$= \frac{1.60 + 0}{48.75 - 1.60} \times \frac{365}{60} = 0.210 = 21.0\%$$

on a covered write, assuming that the stock price rises to the strike price of the short call and the stock is sold at that price on the option expiration date.

The if-called return is calculated in three steps. First, the income is added to the gain. Second, this sum is divided by the net investment. Third, the quotient is annualized.

The *income* is the same as for the static return: the net call premium plus dividends. The *gain* is the difference between the option strike price and the stock purchase price. In this example, the gain is $1.25, the difference between $50, the strike price of the call, and $48.75, the purchase price of the stock.

The *net investment* is the same as for the static return, $47.15, which is the total stock price minus the net call premium.

Adding the income of $1.60 to the gain of $1.25 and dividing that sum of $2.85 into the net investment of $47.15 results in a profit for Marc of 0.061, or 6.10 percent, *in 60 days*. To annualize the earnings, this amount is multiplied by the number of days per year and divided by the days to expiration. In this example, 0.061 is multiplied by 365 days per year, and the product is divided by 60 days. The result is 0.371 or 37.1 percent, the annualized rate. The assumption is that the 60-day profit can be earned in every 60-day period for the rest of the year, which, as stated earlier, may be unrealistic. But this is only a benchmark calculation. The if-called return calculation is summarized in Table 6–3.

TABLE 6–3   Marc's If-Called Rate of Return (Annual Rate)

Assumptions: Stock price rises to or above strike price at option expiration

Call is assigned and stock is sold at the option strike price

Marc's example: Stock Purchase Price $48.75

50 Call Price   1.60

Dividends   0

Days to Expiration   60

$$\text{If-Called Return} = \text{Income} + \frac{\text{Gain}}{\text{Investment}} \times \text{Annualization Factor}$$

$$= \frac{\text{Call Premium} + \text{Dividend} + (\text{Call Strike Price} - \text{Stock Purchase Price})}{\text{Stock Purchase Price} - \text{Call Premium}}$$

$$\times \frac{\text{Days per Year}}{\text{Days to Expiration}}$$

$$= \frac{1.60 + 0 + (50 - 48.75)}{48.75 - 1.60} \times \frac{365}{60} = 0.371 = 37.1\%$$

USING THE STATIC AND IF-CALLED CALCULATIONS

For newcomers to these calculations, the process of annualizing returns may raise some eyebrows. After all, it may be asked, how can one be sure of repeating this performance five more times in a row? This is a reasonable question, but it misses the point. The static and if-called calculations are not absolute measures; they are objective calculations that can assist in the subjective decision-making process of investment analysis and selection. Even though selecting a covered write is as subjective as selecting any investment, these calculations provide a basis for comparison. By comparing several covered writing opportunities, an investor can get a feel for what the market is. The final choice is based on a combination of some objective information and some subjective information. The result is a more informed decision, and therefore a wiser selection.

SELLING IN-THE-MONEY CALLS—A PURE INCOME STRATEGY

When covered writing involves an in-the-money call, the price of the underlying stock is above the strike price of the sold call. As an example, consider Diane, an income-oriented investor who likes the shares of Blue Chip Co., currently trading at $61.50. Her concern is the $0.25 quarterly dividend, which equates to an annual dividend yield of only 1.6 percent. The annual dividend yield is calculated by adding the four quarterly dividends and dividing the total by the stock price. In Diane's case, $(0.25 \times 4) \div 61.5 = 0.016 = 1.6$ percent. The strategy of selling an in-the-money call, however, changes the income situation.

Assume that Diane purchases 100 shares of Blue Chip at $61.50 and sells a 90-day 60 call for $4.25. The static return calculation assumes that the stock price is unchanged at $61.50 at expiration. At this price, Diane's 60 call would be assigned, and her stock would be sold at $60. Since the if-called return assumes that the stock is called away, there is no difference, in Diane's case, between the static return and if-called return calculations.

Diane's income from the covered write has three parts: the option premium received, +$4.25; the dividend received, +$0.25; and the stock loss, -$1.50, the difference between the purchase price of $61.50 and the selling price of $60. Diane's total income, therefore, is $3.00, not including transaction costs. Diane's net investment is the stock purchase price of $61.50 minus the call premium of $4.25, or $57.25. Given 90 days to expiration, the static return, not including transaction costs, is calculated in Table 6–4.

Diane's actual annualized return will be lower than 23 percent because of transaction costs, which include two stock commissions, one for buying stock at $61.50 and one for selling at $60.

If the stock price is above $60 at expiration and her call is assigned, then Diane's objective will have been met. She will have her cash back along with a 23 percent annualized profit (approximately). She can then look for another investment.

While some investors are reluctant to sell in-the-money calls, no one should automatically reject this strategy. As will be discussed next, there are

TABLE 6–4   Diane's In-the-Money Covered Write Strategy Static Return Equals If-Called Return

Return = ((income + gain) ÷ net investment)×(days per year ÷ days to expiration)

= ((4.50 − 1.50) ÷ 57.25) × (365 ÷ 90) = 23%

where: income = call premium received (4.25) plus dividends (0.25) = 4.50

gain   = strike price (60.00) minus stock price (61.25) = − 1.25

net investment = stock price (61.50) minus call premium (4.25) = 57.25

The unchanged stock price is above the strike price, and, therefore, it is assumed that the stock will be called away on the expiration date. The result is a "pure income" strategy. The result is a loss if the stock price is below $57.25.

several considerations that should be included in the selection of a specific covered write.

GUIDELINES FOR USING COVERED WRITING

Covered writing is a stock-oriented strategy. This means that a large part of the investment and risk is in the stock itself. Although the success or failure of all option strategies depends on the price behavior of the underlying stock, so-called stock-oriented option strategies are those in which an investor actually owns or has an interest in owning the underlying stock. This is different from short-term trading strategies with options, where there is no interest in owning the underlying stock.

Guideline 1: Be Comfortable with the Stock

Because of this stock orientation, the first guideline is: *An investor who employs covered writing must be comfortable owning the underlying stock.* In this regard, covered writing involves a stock selection process similar to regular investing.

Guideline 2: Be Comfortable Selling the Stock

The strategy of covered writing, however, involves an aspect that ordinary stock investing lacks: the obligation to sell. While a typical investor purchasing a stock may not focus on a target selling price, the covered writer is obligated to sell at a price that is effectively equal to the call strike price plus the call premium. (The term *effective selling price* is defined in detail in Chapter 1.) Guideline 2, therefore, is: *An investor who employs covered writing must be comfortable with selling the stock at the effective price dictated by the short call (strike plus premium).* This guideline has an important psychological implication for the investor. If an investor is satisfied selling the stock at the effective price of the short call, then receiving an assignment should be anxiety-free. In fact, selling the stock should be viewed as a positive event, because this means that the if-called return—*the maximum possible profit*—has been earned.

Guideline 3: Go for Acceptable Returns

Guideline 2 leads to guideline 3: *An investor who employs covered writing must calculate the static and if-called rates of return (including transaction costs) and enter the covered write only if those rates of return are deemed acceptable.* Although "acceptable" returns are impossible to define, returns on covered writing can be compared with other returns, such as the prevailing short-term risk-free rate on Treasury bills, the average yield on the S&P 500 stock index, and the long-term government bond rate. A desirable covered writing return, of course, should be higher than these, because covered writing involves the risk of owning individual stocks, which is substantially greater than the risk of owning government bonds or a diversified portfolio.

Although some investment professionals have touted rules like "at least two to three times the three-month T-bill rate after commissions," such rules can be misconstrued to place too much emphasis on the return calculations and not enough emphasis on stock selection and market forecasting. Since stock ownership is the largest element of risk in the covered writing strategy, it is important to place the most emphasis on this aspect of the covered writing strategy.

Guideline 4: Interpret Return Calculations Carefully

Guideline 4 relates to the return calculations themselves: *An investor who employs covered writing must interpret the return calculations very carefully.* This is necessary because for very short time periods, the calculations can be misleading. Assume, for example, that a 20 call with one week to expiration is sold for 25 cents, after commissions, when the stock price is $19.80. This covered write may, theoretically, have a high annual rate of return, but how often and with what degree of investment confidence can such transactions be repeated? Such trades are often much more speculative than prudent investments.

Guideline 5: Focus on 60 Days or Longer

Consequently, an expansion of guideline 4 is guideline 5: *An investor who employs covered writing should concentrate on time periods of 60 days or longer.* A 90-day time frame is common, and investors should not be reluctant to look at 120 days or longer. Indeed, Allaire and Kearney, in their excellent book *LEAPS* (McGraw-Hill, 2002), discuss the advantages of covered writing with long-term options.

Guideline 6: Include All Costs

The final guideline places emphasis on the real-world factor of transaction costs: *An investor who employs covered writing must include all transaction costs in the return calculations.* The static return calculation should include all costs related to the initial stock purchase (one commission) and the call sale (a second commission). The if-called return calculation should include all costs of option assignment and sale of stock, which involves a third commission. Table 6–5 is a worksheet for covered writing that includes all costs.

TABLE 6–5   Covered Call Writing—Static Return and If-Called Return Calculations

Stock / Price _____   Stock Cost _____   Total Call Proceeds _____

Call / Price _____   Stock Comm. _____   Call Comm. _____

Days to Exp. _____   If-Called Proceeds (Strike × # shrs) _____

Net Income = Net Call Proceeds + Dividends

Total Call Proceeds	− Commissions	= Net Call Proceeds	+ Dividends	=	Net Income
_____	− _____	= _____	+ _____	=	_____

Net Investment = Total Stock Cost − Net Call Proceeds

Stock Cost	+ Commissions	= Total Stock Cost	− Net Call Proceeds	=	Net Investment
_____	+ _____	= _____	− _____	=	_____

Gain (If-Called) = Net If-Called Proceeds − Net Investment

If-Called Proceeds	− Commissions	= Net If-Called Proceeds	− Net Investment	=	Gain (If-Called)
_____	− _____	= _____	− _____	=	_____

Static Rate of Return (Annual Rate)

$$\frac{\text{Net Income}}{\text{Net Investment}} \times \frac{\text{Days per Year}}{\text{Days to Expiration}} \times \text{Static Rate of Return}$$

$$\underline{\hspace{2cm}} \times \frac{365}{\underline{\hspace{1cm}}} = \underline{\hspace{1cm}}$$

If-Called Rate of Return (Annual Rate)

$$\frac{\text{Net Income + Gain}}{\text{Net Investment}} \times \frac{\text{Days per Year}}{\text{Days to Expiration}} = \text{If-Called Rate of Return}$$

$$\frac{\underline{\hspace{1cm}} + \underline{\hspace{1cm}}}{\underline{\hspace{2cm}}} \times \frac{365}{\underline{\hspace{1cm}}} = \underline{\hspace{1cm}}$$

REAL-WORLD CONSIDERATIONS—TRANSACTION COSTS

An important point about commissions and other transaction costs is the concept of *quantity discounts*. Virtually all brokerage firms have commission schedules that decrease on a per-share basis as the quantity of shares transacted increases. For example, it may cost substantially less on a per-share basis to trade 300 shares than to trade 100 shares. Similarly, the existence of minimum commission charges often means that four or five calls can be sold for the same commission as one call. The implication of these factors for covered writers is economies of scale. In general, to be cost-effective, covered writing transactions must involve more than 100 shares. Transaction costs are likely to lower the static and if-called returns to the point of making a covered write on 100 shares undesirable. Consequently, investors must determine whether they have sufficient capital to engage in covered writing.

MYTHS ABOUT COVERED WRITING

Covered writing is a popular option strategy. Virtually every broker and every investor who has used options either knows about covered writing or has used this strategy. Even so, a number of myths and misconceptions about covered writing have developed that are worth discussing. With a more complete awareness of an investment strategy's strengths and weaknesses, an investor can achieve a certain psychological comfort. And what better way to increase awareness than to discuss the negative things people say?

MYTH 1: "BEING ASSIGNED IS BAD"

When some investors initiate a covered write, they are not sure what they want to have happen. On the one hand, there is the desire to have the stock price rise. On the other hand, there is the desire for it not to rise too far for fear of their being required to sell the stock. These ambiguous feelings may stem from a sense of having given up control—a covered writer is obligated to sell at the whim of the call owner. Consequently, there is a feeling one might "lose" the stock or have it "taken away."

If this same investor were to choose to sell the stock at the effective price of the short call, however, such an action would be viewed as a proactive decision. It might be seen as a "good sale" or "taking profits."

Here is a conundrum: Covered writing is the only strategy in which a profit is sometimes described as a loss! Consider Herman, an academic in Chicago, who regularly invests in stocks and follows the market carefully. In one trade, he buys a pharmaceutical stock at $48 and sells it at $52, only to see it rise to $54 one week later. He is still pleased, saying, "At least I made money" or "You never go broke taking a profit."

But Herman then decides to try his hand at options and starts with a covered write. He buys a high-tech stock for $48 and sells the 50 call for $2. The stock price then rises to $55 at option expiration, and Herman's short call is assigned, which gives him an effective selling price of $52 and a profit of $4. His first reaction is one of dismay. Herman says, "That option cost me $3" and "I had my stock taken away." His $4 profit became a "$3 loss"—the difference between $52 and $55! For some reason, the handsome if-called return is forgotten.

Perhaps Herman's different reactions to the two trades arise from the difference between making a proactive decision to sell and having no control over when a short call is assigned. Whatever the reason, investors like Herman who employ covered writing must make every effort to adapt psychologically to this investment strategy. No matter what one's investment strategy may be, there is always "something better" that could have been done. One almost never buys at the exact bottom or sells at the exact top. "Selling early" is certainly not only caused by covered writing. All experienced investors have had some stocks they wish they had never sold.

Being assigned on a short call is a part of covered writing. On the positive side, it means that the maximum possible return on that covered write has been earned. This is a good event. Adjusting to the reality of this psychologically is an important step in learning to use covered writing successfully.

MYTH 2: "COVERED WRITING IS A GOOD STRATEGY, BECAUSE MOST OPTIONS EXPIRE WORTHLESS"

This misconception is a commonly held belief, but it is illogical, and there are some facts that support the idea that this belief is illogical. If most options expired worthless, then there would be excess returns to be made from selling options. If this were true, then, in a competitive marketplace, opportunity-seeking capital would rush in to realize those excess returns. To earn these supposed returns, many options would be sold, driving down option prices to the point where excess returns were no longer available. At such a point, it would no longer be true that "most options expire worthless."

The fact is, most options do *not* expire worthless. The Chicago Board Options Exchange (CBOE) publishes an annual statistics booklet that discloses the percentage of CBOE equity options in customer and firm accounts that are closed prior to expiration, exercised, and expire worthless. Two years from the last decade were chosen, and the monthly numbers for 1993 and 2004 are presented in Table 6–6. These figures are percentages of the number

**TABLE 6–6   Equity Options—Liquidations, Exercises, and Expirations (%)
1993 compared to 2002**

1993	Closing Sells			Exercises			Long Expirations		
	Total	Call	Put	Total	Call	Put	Total	Call	Put
JAN	56.1	47.8	58.9	9.9	11.3	9.4	34.0	40.9	31.7
FEB	47.2	47.9	46.9	11.2	18.4	8.1	41.6	33.7	44.9
MAR	55.8	48.7	58.8	9.0	11.3	8.1	35.2	40.0	33.2
APR	55.0	53.1	55.8	9.7	12.4	8.4	35.4	34.5	35.8
MAY	56.7	49.6	60.3	10.2	12.6	8.9	33.1	37.8	30.8
JUN	55.4	54.5	55.8	8.8	12.8	7.1	35.8	32.7	37.1
JUL	54.7	51.1	56.3	10.4	15.2	8.3	34.9	33.7	35.4
AUG	56.0	53.3	57.6	10.3	12.5	9.2	33.6	34.2	33.3
SEP	53.2	51.4	54.1	10.8	14.4	9.0	36.0	34.1	36.9
OCT	57.8	47.9	62.0	11.3	11.3	11.3	30.9	40.8	26.8
NOV	57.2	52.9	59.1	11.8	15.1	10.3	31.0	32.0	30.5
DEC	55.9	49.2	58.8	10.0	9.8	10.1	34.0	41.0	31.0
AVG (12 mo)	55.4	50.7	57.4	10.3	12.9	9.2	34.3	36.4	33.4
2002	Total	Call	Put	Total	Call	Put	Total	Call	Put
JAN	39.9	42.6	35.8	21.6	11.4	37.0	38.5	46.1	27.2
FEB	47.0	43.2	52.0	14.8	11.0	20.0	38.2	45.8	28.0
MAR	49.2	51.3	46.9	14.4	17.6	10.7	36.4	31.1	42.4
APR	44.3	43.4	45.6	15.6	13.8	18.0	40.1	42.7	36.4
MAY	17.8	60.6	5.7	33.0	2.7	41.6	49.2	36.8	52.7
JUN	46.2	40.1	54.1	16.5	5.7	30.6	37.3	54.2	15.3
JUL	47.3	42.1	53.8	16.3	3.7	32.2	36.4	54.3	13.9
AUG	53.9	51.5	56.8	13.3	13.0	13.6	32.8	35.5	29.5
SEP	49.8	45.1	55.9	13.8	5.1	25.2	36.5	49.7	18.9
OCT	47.8	44.5	51.4	15.6	12.2	19.2	36.6	43.3	29.4
NOV	NA	NA	NA	NA	NA	NA	NA	NA	NA
DEC	NA	NA	NA	NA	NA	NA	NA	NA	NA
AVG (10 mo)	44.3	46.4	45.8	17.5	9.6	24.8	38.2	43.9	29.4

Source: CBOE

of option contracts that were opened during the contract life. One must be careful not to read too much into these numbers, because they do not include equity options in market makers' accounts or index options, and they give no indication of whether money was made or lost. The CBOE statistics indicate that, in 1993, 35 percent or fewer of total option contracts expired worthless. In 2004, the percentage for the full year was higher, 38.2 percent, and there was one month where the percentage of options expiring worthless approached 50 percent. Nevertheless, statistics going back 30 years indicate that nowhere near 90 percent of options expire worthless.

Simply stated, investors should not write calls on stocks that they believe will appreciate beyond the option's breakeven point. Seen in its proper light, covered writing is a strategy that offers a different set of trade-offs from the outright purchase of stock. The strategy of buying stock has a breakeven price equal to the purchase price, makes nothing if the stock price does not rise, and has unlimited profit potential. The covered write strategy, by comparison, has a lower breakeven price, profits in an unchanged price environment, but has limited profit potential. The two strategies, buying stock outright and covered writing, offer different trade-offs. No one knows in advance which will be better, or even if either will be profitable, but competing forces in the marketplace determine the prices, and investors must select the strategy that, based on their judgment, is most likely to succeed and will best suit their risk preferences and investment objectives.

The options market simply presents investors with more alternatives, each of which is, in some sense, equal in the estimate of the combined market forces that determine prices. There are no excess returns. Coming to grips with this notion will make it easier to move forward with the work of investing— researching investment opportunities and making decisions.

MYTH 3: "COVERED WRITING IS A BAD STRATEGY BECAUSE IT FORCES INVESTORS TO SELL THEIR WINNERS AND KEEP THEIR LOSERS"

It is easy to see how this idea developed. When a stock price is above the strike price of the short call on the expiration date, an assignment notice is received and the stock is sold. Thus the notion arises that "one loses one's winners." Similarly, if a stock falls in price, the call expires unexercised, and the "loser" is kept. But who or what is responsible for selling winners and keeping losers—options or investors? Where is it written that a stock that has been sold, whether it was sold by option assignment or by a conscious decision, cannot be repurchased? And where is it written that a stock that has declined in price cannot be sold outright if it is not called away by an option assignment?

Why are the events just described the fault of options? Every investment must be managed if good results are to be expected. When stock prices start to go down, it is the investor's job to recognize the new trend and take appropriate action. Some investment professionals employ strict rules about stop-loss orders if a stock price declines by a certain percentage. Other experienced investors believe that investing is too subjective to have one rule that fits all situations. Nevertheless, making decisions about selling stocks that are not performing or that have a changed trend is the responsibility of every investor. Stock investments must be managed. Investors do not abdicate their management responsibilities when option strategies are employed.

MYTH 4: "COMMISSIONS MAKE COVERED WRITING IMPOSSIBLE"

Commissions and other transaction costs are definitely important factors to be considered. Although there is a strong argument that transaction costs often make it prohibitive to purchase 100 shares and sell one call, transaction costs, as a general rule, decrease significantly as the number of shares increases. Many firms have a minimum commission, which means that two, three, or sometimes as many as five options can be traded for the same cost as one option. The result is lower costs on a per-share basis. Such a difference can have a significant impact on the static return and if-called return calculations. As stated earlier, investors must determine whether they have sufficient capital to engage in covered writing.

MYTH 5: "COVERED WRITING IS BORING"

Any successful investor will agree that the task of identifying good investment opportunities is time-consuming. Whether an investor does fundamental research independently, relies on investment letters or newspaper columns, or uses one of the many methods of technical analysis, getting good ideas takes time. Furthermore, once an investment idea has been selected and acted on, the role of patience increases; it does not decrease. Buying and holding stocks is a classic example. Once a stock has been purchased, it requires discipline and patience not to take a quick profit (or a quick loss!) if the investment was intended for the long term.

Covered writing is similar. Entering a position for 60 days or longer may take more patience than short-term traders are accustomed to, but covered writing is a different kind of activity from short-term trading. It is prudent to commit a substantial amount of capital to covered writing, and covered write positions do not have to be monitored as frequently as short-term trades. If a covered writer is comfortable with the stock selection (as one must be), the position need not be reviewed any more often than longer-term holdings in a portfolio. At option expiration, either the short call expires or an assignment notice is received (indicating that the stock was sold). At this point, another decision has to be made. If the stock is sold, the decision is among a wide range of alternatives, including, but not limited to, repurchasing the same stock, buying another stock, entering into another covered write, or leaving the funds in an interest-bearing account. If the call expires unexercised, the range of choices is equally wide, starting with whether to hold or sell the stock. *The call's expiration or being assigned does not make a decision for the investor:* The smart investor consciously chooses the best investment given the current market environment.

Covered writing can be much more active than traditional buy-and-hold investing. If an investor has two or three covered write positions at a time, then it is possible to stagger the expiration dates so that new decisions have to be made on a regular basis. This kind of activity is certainly not boring. In fact, it adds variety and interest to the individual investor's management tactics.

MYTH 6: "COVERED WRITING UNDERPERFORMS"
Only a few studies have been conducted on the investment performance of a portfolio of stocks that consistently employed the covered writing strategy. One of the best studies is by Professor Robert Whaley of Duke University. Professor Whaley was commissioned by the Chicago Board Options Exchange to create a passive buy-write strategy calculated for the period beginning June 1, 1988. That is when Standard & Poor's began reporting daily dividends. The result of Professor Whaley's work is the BXM index, formally named the CBOE BuyWrite Monthly Index. The index is based on S&P 500 index options (SPX), which are written against an S&P 500 portfolio. The index call option is sold at the bid price. It has an exercise price just above the prevailing index level (i.e., slightly out-of-the-money), and it is held until expiration and cash-settled. At that time, a new one-month SPX call option is written. The results of Professor Whaley's study from June 1, 1988, through July 30, 2004, are presented in Figure 6–2, in which the BXM index is compared to the S&P 500 Total Return Index (SPTR). Complete details of the BXM index, including current data, are available at www.cboe.com/bxm. The BXM index is designed to represent a hypothetical buy-write strategy. Like many passive indexes, the BXM index does not take into account significant factors such as transaction costs and taxes, and, because of factors such as these, many or most investors should be expected to underperform passive indexes.

For the full 16-year period, the BXM index slightly outperformed the S&P 500 Total Return Index. The BXM index also had a lower variance of

FIGURE 6–2   Stocks and the BXM Index

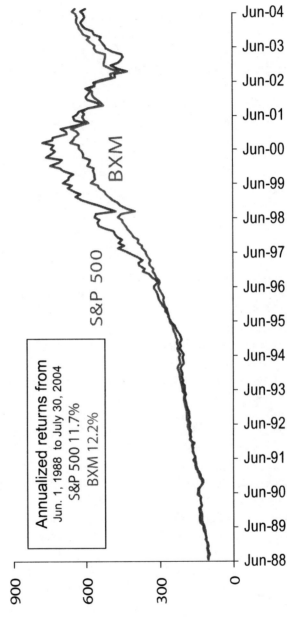

Annualized returns from
Jun. 1, 1988 to July 30, 2004
S&P 500 11.7%
BXM 12.2%

BXM

S&P 500

Month-end prices (scaled so that both = 100
on inception date of June 1, 1988)

returns during the 16 years studied. As one would expect, the BXM did not outperform the SPTR in every month, or even in every year. Investment strategies designed to produce income, as opposed to growth, generally underperform the S&P 500 during big up years, such as the late 1990s. However, even during such periods, some income-oriented investors probably still preferred (or needed) the income and would not have switched to growth strategies. Consequently, the fact that covered writing was not the best performer at one time does not diminish its importance in an investment portfolio. For income-oriented investors, the proper role of covered writing is undoubtedly larger than it is in growth portfolios. If one believes, however, that the current stock market environment is more like the stock market of the early 1990s, then more emphasis might be placed on this strategy in one's overall investing activities.

SUMMARY

Covered writing is a conservative option strategy involving the purchase of stock and the selling of calls on a share-for-share basis. Selling a call when one owns the underlying stock pursues one of three investment objectives. In stable or sideways-trading markets, the call expires worthless, and the premium is kept as income. In rising markets, a selling price for the stock is established above the current stock price at the time the call is sold. In declining markets, the call premium acts as limited downside protection and lowers the breakeven price on the owned stock.

Two traditional measures of covered writing positions are the static return, which assumes that the stock price is unchanged at expiration, and the if-called return, which assumes that the stock price is at or above the strike price at expiration and that the stock is sold at the strike price. These are benchmark measures to be used as part of the subjective decision-making process; they are not absolute measures.

The stock purchase decision is the most important element of selecting a good covered write. Investors who employ the covered writing strategy must be willing to own the stock selected, and they must be willing to sell the stock at the effective price dictated by the sold call. When properly understood, assignment of the short call, which requires the sale of the purchased stock, is not a "bad" event. Rather, assignment means that the maximum possible return from the covered write has been earned. If an investor determines that the if-called return is satisfactory prior to establishing a covered write position, then assignment must be viewed as a "good" event.

There are a number of myths and misconceptions about covered writing that, upon reflection, are either illogical or incorrectly blame options for outcomes that are actually the result of an investor's failure to make conscious decisions. To employ covered writing, an investor must understand that the covered writing strategy is different from the traditional buy-and-hold strategy. When an investor comes to grips with the psychological differences required by covered writing, it is easier to find the proper place for this strategy in the total sphere of an investor's activities.

ADJUSTED COVERED WRITES

INTRODUCTION

THE COVERED WRITING STRATEGY DOES *NOT* "LOCK IN" AN INVESTOR UNTIL THE EXPIRATION DATE. When a market forecast proves inaccurate, when a forecast changes, or when market conditions change, a covered writer may need to take action. Sometimes the appropriate action is to close the position and take a loss. Sometimes the profit potential and breakeven point of a covered write position can be adjusted to match the revised forecast. Adjusting a covered write position is accomplished by a two-part trading action known as rolling.

This chapter will discuss alternative courses of action available to covered writers when, for whatever reason, their market forecast has changed. Changing a market forecast, of course, is subjective, and for the purposes of the following examples, no attempt will be made to explain how the forecast was reached.

ROLLING DEFINED

The typical adjustment to a covered write is to roll the short call. In the context of a covered write position, *rolling* means closing an existing short call position by purchasing it in the market and, at the same time, establishing another short call position by selling a call with a different strike price and/or expiration. The result of this process is to change the breakeven point and the profit potential of the original covered write.

ROLLING UP

Rolling up means repurchasing (or covering) an existing short call (to close the position) and selling a call with the same expiration date but a higher strike price. Rolling up raises both the maximum profit potential and the breakeven point. Assume, for example, that 30 days ago Linda, a master gardener in Chicago, entered a 90-day covered write on a large transportation stock, Railco. She purchased 100 shares of Railco at $64 and sold the 90-day 65 call for $3. The stock pays no dividends, so Linda calculated the static and if-called returns to be 19.9 percent and 26.6 percent, respectively, not including transaction costs. In the last 30 days, Railco has done better than Linda expected. The price rose to $70 and has recently pulled back to $67. The 65 call is now at $4.50, and Linda's market forecast has changed. She originally thought that Railco would trade at around $65; she now thinks it will trade closer to $70. With the 70 call trading at $2, and there being 60 days to expiration, Linda sees an opportunity to improve her profit potential.

Linda can roll up by repurchasing her short 65 call for $4.50 (to close the position) and simultaneously selling the 70 call for $2. The cost, or *net debit*, of this action is $2.50 (plus commissions), the difference between the purchase price of the 65 call and the selling price of the 70 call. Linda's changed profit potential is calculated in three steps. First, the new net purchase price is calculated by adding the net cost of the roll to the original net purchase price. Second, the new selling price is identified; this is simply the strike price of the new call, just as the original selling price was the strike price of the original call. Third, the new maximum profit potential is calculated by subtracting the new net purchase price from the new selling price.

Linda's new selling price is $70, the strike price of the new call. The original selling price was $65, the strike price of the original call. It must be noted that the selling price is not equal to the call strike price plus the call premium. In calculating the net purchase price, the call premium was subtracted from the purchase price of the stock. If the call premium were also added to the call strike price, then it would be counted twice.

Linda's original maximum profit potential was $4, the original strike price of $65 minus the original net purchase price of $61. Her new maximum profit potential is $6.50, the new strike price of $70 minus the new net purchase price of $63.50. Again, for simplicity in explaining the concepts, none of these figures or calculations has included commissions. In real-world examples, however, commissions and other transaction costs are significant and must be included in all calculations. Figure 7–1 compares Linda's original position with her new one.

Which is better? There is no objective answer to this question. Linda's new situation has a higher profit potential, but it also has a higher breakeven stock price. Her decision was a subjective one based on her revised forecast for Railco stock. Using the options market did not give Linda a better situation; it just gave her another alternative with different trade-offs.

FIGURE 7–1   Linda's original and adjusted covered write positions

	Original Covered Write	Adjusted Covered Write
Net Purchase Price	$61.00	$63.50
Selling Price (If-Called)	$65.00	$70.00
Maximum Profit Potential	$ 4.00	$ 6.50

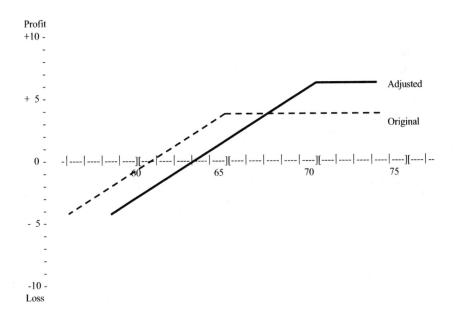

ROLLING DOWN

Rolling down means repurchasing (or covering) an existing short call (to close the position) and selling a call with the same expiration date but a lower strike price. Rolling down lowers both the maximum profit potential and the break-even point. In the following example, Bob, a traveling salesman who spends his spare time looking for good covered writes, uses the rolling down technique to salvage a bad situation. Twenty-five days ago, Bob bought stock in Surgeco, a large electrical equipment manufacturer, at $48 and sold the 75-day 50 call for $1.50. Surgeco pays a $0.50 dividend two weeks before expiration, so Bob calculated the static return at 20.9 percent and the if-called return at 41.9 percent (not including commissions). Surgeco, however, is now trading at $45, and the 50 call is now $0.25. Bob realizes that this was a bad trade and is now forecasting that Surgeco will continue to trade near $45 until expiration in 50 days. Bob could take a net loss of $1.75 per share by selling the stock at $45 (-$3) and buying back the 50 call at $0.25 (+$1.25). Instead, given his new forecast, Bob has identified an opportunity that, in his opinion, is likely to do better. He decides to roll down to the 45 call, which is trading at $2.25.

Bob can roll down by repurchasing his $50 call for $0.25 and selling the $45 call for $2.25. The amount received, or *net credit*, from this action is $2.00 (less commissions), the difference between the selling price of the 45 call and the purchase price of the 50 call. Bob's changed profit potential is calculated in three steps, similar to the calculations made for Linda.

Bob's original net purchase price was $46.50 per share (not including commissions). Subtracting the net credit of $2.00 received for rolling down, the new net purchase price is $44.50.

Bob's original selling price, if assigned, was $50, the strike price of the original call. The new selling price is $45, the strike price of the new call. Consequently, with a net purchase price of $44.50 and a selling price of $45, Bob's new maximum profit potential is $0.50, not including commissions or the $0.50 dividend. Figure 7–2 compares Bob's original position with his new one.

While Bob's original position was much better than his new position, unfortunately, he is not choosing between these two. He is choosing between taking a $1.75 loss at current prices or rolling down and hoping to make $0.50 if the stock price remains at or above $45. Readers must remember that rolling is *not* necessarily preferable to taking the loss. Which strategy will turn out to be better depends on the actual stock price action, and, as every investor knows, forecasting stock prices is an art, not a science. Consequently, only time will tell whether Bob made the "right" choice. But whatever the outcome,

FIGURE 7–2   Bob's original and adjusted covered write positions

	Original Covered Write	Adjusted Covered Write
Net Purchase Price	$46.50	$44.50
Selling Price (If-Called)	$50.00	$45.00
Maximum Profit Potential*	$ 3.50	$ 0.50

*The 0.50 dividend is not included.

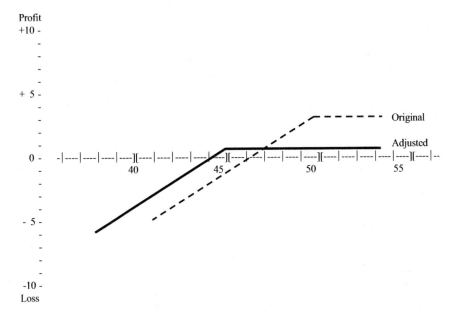

the option market gave Bob a viable alternative that does not exist in the stock market alone.

ROLLING OUT

Rolling out means repurchasing (or covering) an existing short call (to close the position) and selling a call with the same strike price but a later expiration. Rolling out increases the maximum profit potential, lowers the breakeven point, and extends the time period. In this example, Joe, an attorney with the government in southern Illinois who gets good investment advice from a friend in Chicago, has had a very successful covered writing experience. Eighty days ago he entered a covered write on the stock of Grainco, a large animal feed distributor. Joe purchased stock at $96 and sold the December 100 call for $3.10. It was 90 days to December expiration at that time. The stock paid a $0.75 dividend last week, so the static return was 17 percent and the if-called return was 35 percent (before commissions). Grainco has traded in a narrow range since this covered write was initiated and is now trading at $97. December expiration is now 10 days away, and the 100 call is now selling at $0.20. Joe is happy with this covered write and, based on advice from his friend in Chicago, forecasts that the stock will continue to trade between $95 and $100. The March 100 call, 108 days to expiration, is trading at $3.60. Joe sees an opportunity, given his forecast, to extend this attractive income-oriented investment.

Joe can roll out by repurchasing the December 100 call for $0.20 and selling the March 100 call for $3.60. The net credit from this action is $3.40 (less commissions). Joe's adjusted profit potential is calculated in three steps. His original net purchase price was $92.90 per share (not including commissions). His new net purchase price is $89.50, the $92.90 original net purchase price less the $3.40 credit received for rolling out. His original maximum profit potential was $7.10, not including the $0.75 dividend or commissions. His new maximum profit potential is $10.50, not including next quarter's dividend or commissions, *but this is for a longer time period.*

MAKING NEW STATIC AND IF-CALLED CALCULATIONS

Because of the longer time period, the decision to roll out should not be based on the market forecast alone, but should also include new static and if-called return calculations. To make these calculations, Joe must assume that he is making a *fresh start*, buying the stock at $97 and selling the 97-day 100 call for $3.40. Note that the figure used for the price of the March 100 call is the net credit received for making the roll (less commissions, which are not included here for simplicity). In this case, the December 100 call is repurchased (or covered) for $0.20 and the March 100 call is sold for $3.60, for a net credit of $3.40. An additional positive factor in the new static return calculation is the absence of a commission for purchasing the stock, since it is already owned, although an extra commission will be paid for repurchasing the December 100 call. Joe's static return for the covered write extended to March is calculated in Table 7–1. The if-called return will, of course, include a commission for selling the stock. The calculation of Joe's if-called return for the covered write extended to March is shown in Table 7–2.

Now all the pieces of the puzzle are in place, and Joe can make a decision with complete information. His market forecast is that Grainco will trade

TABLE 7–1   Joe's Adjusted Covered Write Position New Static Rate of Return Calculation

Current Stock Price: $97.00

100 Call − Net Received: 3.40 (3.60 − 0.20)

Dividends: 0.75

Days to Expiration: 108

$$\text{New Static Return} = \frac{\text{New Income}}{\text{New Investment}} \times \text{Annualization Factor}$$

$$= \frac{\text{Net Call Premium} + \text{Dividend}}{\text{Current Stock Price} - \text{Net Call Premium}} \times \frac{\text{Days per Year}}{\text{Days to Expiration}}$$

$$= \frac{3 + 0.75}{97 - 3} \times \frac{365}{108} = 0.149 = 14.9\%$$

TABLE 7–2   Joe's Adjusted Covered Write Position New If-Called Rate of Return Calculation

Current Stock Price: $97.00

100 Call − Net Received: 3.35 (3.60 − 0.25)

Dividends: 0.75

Days to Expiration: 108

$$\text{New If - Called Return} = \frac{\text{New Income} + \text{New Gain}}{\text{New Investment}} \times \text{Annualization Factor}$$

$$= \frac{\text{Net Call Premium} + \text{Dividend} + (\text{Call Strike Price} - \text{Current Stock Price})}{\text{Current Stock Price} - \text{Net Call Premium}}$$

$$\times \frac{\text{Days per Year}}{\text{Days to Expiration}} = \frac{3 + 0.75 + (100 - 97)}{97 - 3} \times \frac{365}{108} = 0.257 = 25.7\%$$

between $95 and $100 for the next 97 days. The static return of 15 percent and the if-called return of 26 percent (before commissions) are in line with the returns on the previous covered write, which he finds acceptable. Furthermore, Joe is willing to sell the Grainco stock and realize a profit if the short call is assigned. Being satisfied with the return calculations and courageously believing in his market forecast, Joe instructs his broker to buy the December 100 call and sell the March 100 call.

COMMON MISTAKES IN ROLLING

The only real reason to adjust a covered write position (or to change any investment position, for that matter) is a changed market forecast. Linda felt that her stock would trade closer to $70 than $65 and decided to increase her profit potential. Bob believed that Surgeco would stay above $45, and he adjusted his covered write in an effort to recoup his loss. Joe extended the time horizon of his original forecast and rolled out to the March option because it offered a desirable return, given his perception of the risk.

Rolling involves transaction costs and has implications for returns; therefore, a covered writer must make a conscious decision to adjust a covered write and not roll just for the sake of rolling. Some of the reasons for *not rolling* are the following: Do not roll for fear of "losing the stock" or "paying extra commissions due to assignment." Do not roll for fear of "early exercise." Do not roll "to get my money back." Each of these will be explained in turn.

ROLLING TO AVOID "LOSING THE STOCK"

The previous chapter warned the covered writer to be ready and willing to sell the underlying stock at the price dictated by the short call. If assignment occurs, therefore, an investor is not "losing the stock" but realizing the maximum profit, the if-called return. The covered writer is seeing the logical consequence of a conscious decision. Some investors struggle with this idea when they first engage in covered writing.

ROLLING TO AVOID "PAYING EXTRA COMMISSIONS DUE TO ASSIGNMENT"

The initial analysis of static and if-called returns must include an accurate estimate of commissions, including a commission for selling stock in the if-called scenario. If those returns are deemed satisfactory, then being assigned and selling the stock does not incur extra commissions. Those costs were included in the original return calculations.

ROLLING TO AVOID "EARLY EXERCISE"

Equity options in the United States are American-style, which means that the option owner has the right to exercise the option at any time prior to expiration. If a call option is deep in-the-money and/or expiration is very close, then it may be exercised just prior to a dividend payment. Consequently, covered writers may be required to sell their stock and, as a result, will not be eligible to receive the dividend. While there is no way to avoid this situation, there is a way to anticipate it and to determine whether it is an acceptable event.

All that needs to be done is an additional return calculation. For lack of a better name, this return is dubbed the *called-at-dividend return*, the assumption being that the call is assigned immediately prior to the ex-dividend date and the stock is sold at the strike price of the short call. There are two differences between this return and the if-called return: There is no dividend in the "income," and the number of days is lower. If the called-at-dividend return is deemed acceptable, then being assigned early and not receiving the dividend is acceptable.

An unacceptable called-at-dividend return does not, however, automatically disqualify a covered write. This is just another subjective element of the investment-selection decision. The investor must consciously make a decision about the likelihood of the scenario's occurring. If an out-of-the-money or at-the-money call is being considered, there is less chance of an early assignment than if an in-the-money call is being considered.

ROLLING "TO GET MY MONEY BACK"
A covered write position will lose money if the stock price is below the breakeven price at expiration. If the stock price drops below this point prior to expiration, it is only natural for an investor to feel anxiety. In the example of rolling down presented earlier, Bob faced this situation and decided to roll down to the 45 call. It was clearly stated that Bob's forecast called for the stock to trade at or above $45 until expiration in 50 days. There are no hard and fast rules about what to do in such a situation, but an investor's action should be consistent with the market forecast. Hope will not cause a declining stock price to stop declining. Sometimes it is best to close out a position and take a loss. This is just as true for covered writing as it is for other investment situations.

SUMMARY

Rolling up, rolling down, and rolling out involve the repurchase (to close) of a short call and the simultaneous sale of another call at a different strike price and/or later expiration. Rolling will change the maximum profit potential and breakeven point of the original position. When rolling out to a later expiration, new static and if-called return calculations should be made as if the investor were starting over. In these calculations, the investor should use the net credit received for the roll as the price of the sold call. Any decision to roll should be based on a consciously made market forecast and not out of fear of losing the stock, paying extra commissions, or being assigned early, or in an effort to recover losses.

MARRIED PUTS, PROTECTIVE PUTS, AND COLLARS

INTRODUCTION

THERE ARE TIMES WHEN INVESTORS ARE TORN. They are bullish and want to own stocks, and yet they have a nagging concern that the market is due for a sell-off. If they stay invested in stocks and the market declines, they will suffer. However, if they sell their stocks and the market rallies, they will miss out. While this is a typical investor's dilemma, options offer some alternatives aimed at getting the best of both worlds—staying in the market with only limited risk. As you may have already guessed, insurance strategies are the topic of this chapter.

The three strategies discussed will be presented in the same format: The strategy will be defined, a profit-and-loss diagram will be presented, and the expiration mechanics will be explained. A case study of a situation in which an investor might employ the strategy will then be presented. Special emphasis will be placed on the thinking process that the investor goes through to arrive at the decision to employ the strategy. Also in this chapter, using put options as protection will be compared to another risk-limiting technique, the stop-loss order, and the concept of put-call parity will be introduced. The risk profile of the married put strategy is identical to the risk profile of another option strategy, and the put-call parity concept explains why.

THE MARRIED PUT STRATEGY DEFINED

The married put strategy is, simply, a two-part strategy in which stock and put options are purchased simultaneously. The puts are purchased on a share-for-share basis with the stock, i.e., 100 shares and one put, or 600 shares and six puts. The put option acts like an insurance policy on the stock. If the stock declines in price, then the loss is limited to the strike price of the put plus the

Why not insure your stocks like you insure your house?

cost of the put. If the stock rises, then the put expires, but the investor keeps the profit from the stock, less the cost of the put. Any time an investor wants to invest, but is worried about short-term price action, the married put strategy offers a way to purchase stock and limit risk at the same time.

Diane, the Cautious Investor

Consider Diane, an experienced investor with a keen sense for opportunity and an equally keen desire to limit her risk. Diane has been following Healthco, a medical supply company. The stock hit an all-time high of $75 two years ago, but it fell out of favor after a poor earnings report. Its price declined to $32.50 six months ago, and since then it has traded in a narrow range around its current price of $36. The quarterly reports have discussed cost cutting and new marketing efforts, and the monthly sales figures have been favorable. Diane predicts that the next earnings report, which is due in two weeks, will surpass expectations and cause the stock price to rise. She realizes, of course, that her assessment could be wrong. An unfavorable report could send the stock to new lows.

Diane wants to buy Healthco stock in order to take advantage of her bullish opinion, but she wants to limit her risk in case her forecast is incorrect. In Diane's case, the married put strategy involves purchasing 100 shares of Healthco at $36 per share and simultaneously purchasing one 60-day 35 put for $1. This strategy offers Diane an opportunity to participate if the stock price rises, and at the same time, it limits her risk if the price declines.

Figure 8–1 is a profit-and-loss diagram of Diane's position at expiration. The hyphenated line is the long stock, the dotted-and-dashed line is the long put, and the solid line is the combined position. Table 8–1 shows how the calculations are made. The top line of Table 8–1, for example, illustrates the outcome at $40. The purchased stock has increased in value by $4 per share,

FIGURE 8–1   The married put strategy

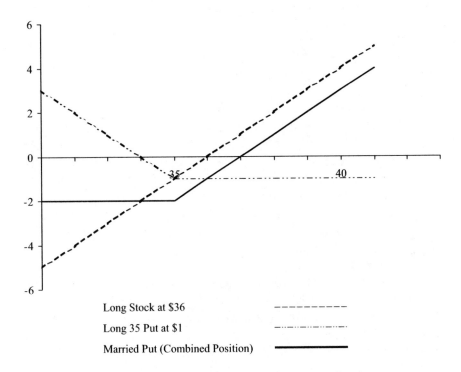

Long Stock at $36	- - - - - - -
Long 35 Put at $1	-..—..—..—..—.
Married Put (Combined Position)	▬▬▬▬▬▬

TABLE 8–1   The Married Put Strategy Calculation of Profit or Loss at Expiration

Stock Price at Expiration	Long Stock @ $36 P/(L)	Long 35 Put @ $1 P/(L)	Combined Position P/(L)
$40	+ 4	(1)	+ 3
$39	+ 3	(1)	+ 2
$38	+ 2	(1)	+ 1
$37	+ 1	(1)	-0-
$36	-0-	(1)	(1)
$35	(1)	(1)	(2)
$34	(2)	-0-	(2)
$33	(3)	+ 1	(2)
$32	(4)	+ 2	(2)

and the purchased put expires worthless, losing $1 per share. The combined position, therefore, earns $3 per share, not including commissions. In another example, at a stock price of $32, the purchased stock loses $4 per share, and the put earns a profit of $2. The result of the combined position with a stock price of $32 is a loss of $2 per share, not including commissions.

Expiration Mechanics

The owned put gives Diane the right to sell her Healthco stock at the strike price, in this case $35 per share, at any time until the expiration date. However, even if the stock is trading below the strike price of the put, $35 in this example, Diane has two alternatives. First, she can exercise the put and, as a result, sell her Healthco stock at $35 per share. She will then be left with no stock position. She will, of course, have cash of $3,500 (less commissions) from selling her 100 shares. She can then look for the next investment opportunity. As indicated in Figure 8–1 and Table 8–1, Diane will have a $2-per-share loss if the stock price is at or below $35 at expiration. The stock will have declined from $36 to $35, and the expiring put will lose $1.

Alternatively, if Diane were favorably disposed toward holding the stock at its current price, she could choose to sell the put in the open market and collect, in cash, the put's market price (less commissions). On the last day prior to option expiration, the put will be trading at, or very near, its intrinsic value. Prior to expiration, there may or may not also be some time value in the market price of the put. If Diane chooses to sell her put, then she will own the 100 shares of Healthco stock she originally purchased plus the cash proceeds from selling the put. Assuming that the stock price is below $35, and assuming that she sells the put very close to expiration, then her total holdings, stock plus cash, will be approximately the same $3,500 as if she chose to exercise the put. As explained earlier, Diane's loss will be $2 per share with a stock price of $35 or lower at expiration.

Which is the better course of action, to exercise the put or to sell it? The answer to this question is a subjective decision that only Diane can make, based on her forecast for Healthco stock.

If the price of Healthco is at or above $35 at expiration, Diane also has two choices. With the stock price above $35 at expiration, the 35 put will expire worthless, but Diane can still review whether or not to keep the stock. If no new information has caused her to change her forecast, then she can continue to hold. She may, in fact, include Healthco among her long-term holdings and never employ an option strategy on the stock again. Alternatively, if for any reason she has changed her opinion about the stock, Diane can sell it in the open market and look for another investment opportunity.

PROTECTIVE PUTS

Protective puts are puts that are purchased on a share-for-share basis with *previously purchased* stock. Protective puts differ from married puts only in their timing. Married puts are purchased simultaneously with the stock purchase, and protective puts are purchased subsequent to the stock purchase.

While the difference may seem small, it is important to the IRS, and therefore it should be important to investors. According to "Taxes and Investing" a pamphlet published by the Options Industry Council,

> In order for a "married put" to be "married," the put must be acquired on the same day as the stock and the stock must be identified as the stock to be delivered upon exercise of the put. Furthermore, the married put criteria may only be met either by delivering the married stock or by allowing the put to expire. If the put expires, the cost of the put is added to the basis of the stock.

Protective puts (i.e., puts purchased on a date after the stock purchase date) are subject to the "offsetting position rules." According to "Taxes and Investing," "In general, any offsetting position that includes stock and provides a substantial diminution of risk of loss is subject to the anti-straddle provisions." Because of these complications, and because of evolving interpretations of the tax code, it is good practice to seek the advice of a tax professional regarding options transactions.

Consider Amit, the very happy owner of VideoTeck stock, which has risen sharply since he purchased it 10 months ago. Amit purchased 300 shares of VideoTeck at $30 per share on February 5. Today is December 17, and the stock is trading at $77. On the one hand, Amit would like to own the stock until at least next February 6. If he sells at a gain after February 5 of next year, then the profit will qualify as a long-term capital gain, which has a lower tax rate than he would incur if he sold now and paid the tax rate applicable to a short-term capital gain. On the other hand, Amit is forecasting a near-term drop in the stock's price, because the price of VideoTeck stock has been showing technical weakness by failing to break resistance in the high 70s. Also, the major market averages have recently sunk below their short-term moving averages on increasing volume. Amit interprets both of these signs as very negative for the outlook for VideoTeck.

What Amit would like to do is purchase three protective puts. There are 90-day, 75 puts on VideoTeck that expire next February 17, and they are trading for $4 per share. Amit's thinking is this: "If the stock price declines, then the worst result is a long-term profit on a selling price of $75 less the cost of the puts. Alternatively, if the stock price rises, then the long-term gain will be higher." Unfortunately, this strategy runs afoul of the tax rules affecting protective puts. According to "Taxes and Investing," "The holding period of any position that is part of a straddle does not begin earlier than the date the investor no longer holds an offsetting position." The logic of this ruling is that investors must own a security with *unhedged risk* for more than one year in order to qualify for long-term capital gains treatment.

This means that if Amit implements his protective put strategy, then when the February 75 put expires or when Amit sells it, his holding period for his VideoTeck stock starts over, and he must hold it for another 12 months unhedged before he can qualify for long-term capital gains treatment.

MOTIVATIONS FOR MARRIED AND PROTECTIVE PUTS

Any time an investor is bullish, but worried, married puts or protective puts can be employed. An investor could have a bullish opinion on a particular stock but a negative opinion on the market in general. An appropriate time for purchasing a married put to limit risk is when the investor is trying to pick the bottom on a particular stock. Some investors like to limit their risk on new positions and use married puts because they cannot follow those positions closely enough to be sure of selling if a particular loss level results. Any time an investor views an investment opportunity as a "good price, but a risky time," the married put strategy is one method of managing risk. Buying stock outright at such a time could prove costly if a sharp price decline occurs. *Not* buying, however, could mean missing a profitable opportunity.

Since the stock is already owned when the purchase of a protective put is being considered, the motivation for a protective put is slightly different from that for a married put. An investor who is not worried about getting long-term tax treatment and who uses a protective put either is considering selling or is worried about a short-term market decline when the longer-term forecast is bullish. For example, it is quite logical to expect a stock to pull back after a steep runup. However, it is impossible to know whether the runup has come to an end or will continue. Some investors take comfort from a protective put; they can profit more if the price rise continues, and most of their profits are locked in if the price declines.

Protective puts offer relatively high-cost insurance, but they do not limit profit potential if the stock price rises. They should be purchased when a stock owner is bullish on a holding, but is nervous about something. That "something" could be an upcoming earnings report or a government announcement.

Remember the old saying, "Cut your losses short and let your profits run"? Protective puts allow investors to stay in the market with limited risk during times that are perceived to be high-risk.

Although investors face difficult choices frequently, the married put and protective put strategies offer an alternative that has its own set of positives and negatives, an alternative that does not exist without options. As Figure 8–1 illustrates, the married put and protective put strategies limit risk, the advantage relative to buying stock outright. The disadvantage is a higher breakeven price, $37 versus $36 for purchasing stock alone. Which alternative is better— simply buying the stock, or buying both the stock and the put? Again, there is no objective answer to such a question. Investors must evaluate their stock price forecast in conjunction with their tolerance for risk.

The Psychology of Insurance

Many investors find the logic of "puts as insurance" difficult to accept. After all, if an investor is bullish, why purchase insurance? Why buy something that you hope will expire worthless? When one stops to think about it, however, this is actually something that people do all the time. Think about home insurance, car insurance, or health insurance. No honest person wants her home to burn in order to collect the insurance proceeds. No one wants to get into a car accident. Everyone wants these insurance policies to expire worthless. But these same people rest easy knowing that they are protected.

The married put and protective put strategies apply the same logic to investments. Investors buy puts so that they can rest easy; they hope that the stock rises in price and that their insurance policies, the puts, expire worthless. One difference, of course, is that no one is forcing an investor to buy insurance, whereas lenders and state laws compel homeowners and car owners to buy insurance. Investors are also subject to "Monday-morning-quarterback"-type thinking. If the stock rallies after the investors have bought both stock and puts, they kick themselves for having bought the puts. If the stock declines, even though the put limits their loss, they kick themselves for having bought the stock. This is a quandary for new investors, but experienced investors realize that making a certain percentage of losing investments is inevitable. Many experienced investors believe that the discipline of limiting an initial loss provided by the married put is well worth the cost.

Married and Protective Puts versus a "Stop-Loss" Order

Some investors may ask, "Why spend money on the put? Why not just use a stop-loss order?"

A stop-loss order is an order to sell at the market price, contingent on a stock's trading at or being offered at a specified price that is below the current market price. For example, an investor who owns 100 shares of a stock trading at $45 might place a stop-loss order at $42. If the stock trades at or is offered at $42, the stop-loss order

> *Stop-loss orders*
> *do not assure*
> *a limited loss.*

becomes an order to sell at the market, and the shares are sold at the best available price. The motivation behind stop-loss orders is a desire to limit risk.

Stop-loss orders do not assure a limited loss, however, because it is impossible to say for certain at what price the stock will be sold. Stock prices do not have to change in an orderly price sequence. They can "gap" between trades, an occurrence that is most common at the start of trading each

> *Puts do*
> *limit losses.*

morning, since there is no guarantee that prices will open today where they closed yesterday. Stock prices can also gap during trading hours when a news item or an announcement from the company is made.

Married and protective puts, however, do limit the loss from holding a stock during the put's life. Regardless of how much lower a gap trade might be, the owner of a put can exercise that put and sell the stock at the option strike price, thus limiting the potential loss.

> *Stop-loss orders*
> *are price-dependent.*

> *Puts are*
> *time-dependent.*

The most significant difference between the married or protective put and the stop-loss order is the nature of the limiting factor. A stop-loss order is price-dependent; a married put is time-dependent. During the life of the put, it is possible for the stock price to trade down to or below the specified stop-loss price level and then rebound higher, much to the dismay of the investor who placed a stop-loss order. The negative scenario for the married put investor is a stock price decline occurring after the put option expires worthless.

For these reasons, it cannot be said that a married put is "better" than a stop-loss order. Married puts just offer a different set of trade-offs: A limit on loss is the positive; limited life and the cost are the negatives. A stop-loss order, in contrast, does not guarantee a maximum risk (the negative), but its positives are an unlimited life and that it costs nothing.

PUT-CALL PARITY INTRODUCED

Figure 8–2 compares the profit-and-loss diagrams for the married put strategy introduced in this chapter and the call plus Treasury bill strategy presented in

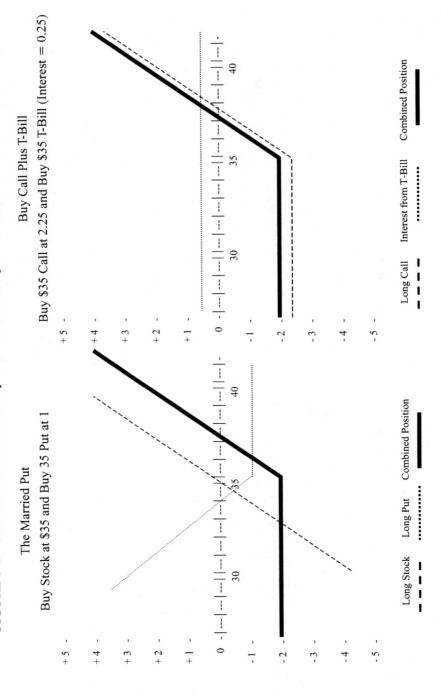

FIGURE 8–2   The Married Put Versus Buy Call Plus T-Bill Expiration Profit and Loss Diagrams

The Married Put

Buy Stock at $35 and Buy 35 Put at 1

Buy Call Plus T-Bill

Buy $35 Call at 2.25 and Buy $35 T-Bill (Interest = 0.25)

Long Stock   Long Put   Combined Position

Long Call   Interest from T-Bill   Combined Position

Chapter 5. The components and the combined positions of both strategies are illustrated. The combined positions appear to be identical, and this confuses many newcomers to options. It is, therefore, important to discuss why strategies with different components have similar risk profiles.

The concept of put-call parity is that the prices of calls, puts, and stock are related by interest rates. If the prices are not in line with one another, then arbitrage opportunities will exist. An in-depth explanation of put-call parity is beyond the scope of this book, but the following comments are warranted because they reinforce an understanding of the mechanics of option strategies at expiration.

Essentially, put-call parity means that calls, puts, and stock can be added together in different combinations to create identical risk profiles, or profit-and-loss diagrams. The married put strategy and the "buy call plus Treasury bill" strategy are two strategies whose results are identical, assuming no commissions, because of the put-call parity concept. Figure 8–2 shows that the two strategies have the same risk profile. Table 8–2 shows how the two strategies result in positions that are identical or of equal market value at expiration.

TABLE 8–2   Position at Expiration Married Put versus Buy Call Plus T-Bill

Buy Call + T-Bill	Stock Price at Expiration	Married Put
LONG STOCK Call exercised and stock is purchased with proceeds from T-Bill	Stock Price Above Strike Price	LONG STOCK Put expires and long stock position is unaffected
NO POSITION Call expires Investor may or may not choose to purchase stock with proceeds from T-Bill	Stock Price At Strike Price	LONG STOCK Put expires and long stock position is unaffected
NO POSITION Call expires Investor may or may not choose to purchase stock with proceeds from T-Bill	Stock Price Below Strike Price	NO POSITION Put exercised, stock sold Investor may or may not choose to repurchase stock

In both strategies, if the stock price is above the strike price at expiration, the resulting position is long stock. In the case of the call plus T-bill, the in-the-money call is exercised, and the purchased stock is paid for with the proceeds from the maturing T-bill. In the case of the married put, the put expires worthless when the stock price is above the strike price, and the investor is left with the stock position originally purchased.

If the stock price is below the strike price at expiration, both strategies result in no stock position, only cash. The call plus T-bill investor is left with cash from the maturing T-bill when the out-of-the-money call expires worthless. The married put investor is left with cash when the in-the-money put is exercised and the stock is sold.

In the third possible outcome, the stock price being exactly at the strike price at expiration, the call plus T-bill investor is left with the amount of the strike price in cash when the call expires and can decide to keep the cash or convert it to stock (by buying stock). The married put investor has stock valued at the amount of the strike price and can decide to keep the stock or convert it to cash (by selling the stock). Consequently, with the stock price exactly at the strike price, both investors have exactly the same market value and can choose either stock or cash.

The conclusion to be drawn from Figure 8–2, Table 8–2, and the preceding discussion is that the call plus T-bill investor has the same risk profile and ends up, at expiration, with the same outcome as the married put investor. This is the result of the put-call parity concept.

The Real-World Choice

Knowing that the positions of call plus T-bill and stock plus put are theoretically equivalent, the question becomes: What are the advantages and disadvantages of each in the real world? Speculative strategies versus investment strategies will be discussed in Chapter 18, but the important criterion is the amount of equity capital available to pay for a position in the underlying stock as introduced in Chapter 1. A clear advantage of the married put strategy is that the stock is purchased, so the capital is obviously available. The married put strategy can, therefore, be easily defined as "investment-oriented."

Buying a call does not, by itself, involve the underlying stock. To make this strategy investment-oriented, it is therefore necessary to set aside sufficient cash to pay for the underlying stock. This requires discipline at the very least and segregation of funds at the most. Consequently, it is not always easy to tell whether calls are purchased speculatively or as a short-term risk-management technique for entering the underlying stock unless cash, or liquid investments, readily available to pay for the stock can be identified.

The disadvantage of the married put strategy is extra up-front transaction costs: one commission to purchase the stock and one to purchase the put. There is also the possibility of a third commission for selling the stock if the put is exercised. Buying a call plus a Treasury bill involves related commissions that are typically less than stock commissions. However, there will be a stock commission if the call is exercised. In the theoretical world, where commissions are ignored and the discipline to maintain cash reserves is assumed, these two strategies are identical. In the real world, an investor must choose between extra commissions and maintaining discipline.

THE COLLAR STRATEGY

Many investors like the risk-reducing aspect of married and protective puts, but they are concerned about the cost. The *collar* is a two-part option strategy that addresses this concern. The first part of a collar is a married or protective put. The second part is a covered call. As described in Chapter 6, covered calls are calls that are sold on a share-for-share basis against owned stock. In return for receiving a premium, the seller of a covered call assumes the obligation of selling the stock at the strike price at any time prior to the expiration date. When a covered call is used as part of a collar, the premium received from selling the covered call is used to reduce the cost of the married or protective put.

Collars: The Trade-Offs

The advantage of a collar relative to a married put is its lower net cost. Part or all of the premium received from the covered call is used to pay for the put. The disadvantage of a collar is the limit it places on the stock's profit potential. The covered call establishes a ceiling on how much can be made from a price rise in the stock. Figure 8–3 shows how, with XYZ trading at $72, selling an 80 call for $2 and purchasing a 70 put for $3 creates a collar that limits the total risk to $3 per share. It also limits profit potential to $7 per share.

How does an investor who is looking to reduce risk decide between a married put and a collar? First, make sure you understand the trade-offs of each strategy, and, second, consider the market forecast that justifies each one.

Married puts offer relatively high-cost insurance, but they do not limit profit potential if the stock price rises. As mentioned earlier in the chapter, married puts should be purchased when an investor is bullish on a stock but nervous about something.

A collar offers relatively low-cost insurance, but it places a limit on the stock's profit potential. The covered call, remember, is an obligation to sell stock at the strike price. If an investor is unwilling to sell the stock, perhaps for tax reasons or because his long-term forecast is bullish, then the presence of

**FIGURE 8–3   The collar long stock at $72, long 70 put at $3, and short 80
call at $2**

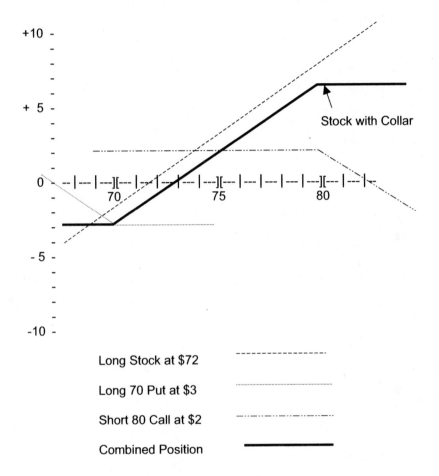

Long Stock at $72

Long 70 Put at $3

Short 80 Call at $2

Combined Position

the short call and the existence of the obligation to sell the stock must be
addressed. Therefore, before a collar is established, a decision must be made
as to when, and at what point, the call will be repurchased to close out the obligation. It is then necessary to have the discipline to follow through on that
decision.

Married puts and collars are insurance strategies with trade-offs. The married put, for a cost, provides protection and leaves the unlimited profit potential of the stock intact. In contrast, the collar offers lower-cost protection but
involves the obligation to sell the stock and therefore limits profit potential.

SUMMARY

The married put strategy offers investors an advantage relative to the outright purchase of stock, because it combines the purchase of stock with limited risk for a limited time. The disadvantage of this strategy relative to the simple purchase of stock is the higher breakeven point at expiration. While implementation of this strategy is subjective, it is appropriate when a stock purchaser is thinking, "This is a good price, but a risky time."

The married put strategy offers a different set of trade-offs from stop-loss orders. A stop-loss order involves no up-front payment, it is price-dependent and has no time limit; but it does not assure a limited loss. The married put, in contrast, has a limited life and requires an up-front payment, including commissions, all of which might be lost if the put expires worthless. The married put, however, places a limited loss on owning the stock during its life.

Because of the put-call parity concept, the married put strategy and the buy call plus T-bill strategy are theoretically equivalent. There are real-world differences, however, involving transaction costs and disciplined cash management.

Collars combine the sale of a covered call with the purchase of a protective or married put. Collars offer a different set of trade-offs. The net cost for a collar is typically lower, but the upside potential in the stock is limited to the strike price of the short call.

Mastering the psychology of insurance and applying it to options is difficult because, in hindsight, the chosen strategy will always be second-best. Nevertheless, using put options as insurance to protect new or existing stock positions gives some investors the ability to rest easy.

C   H   A   P   T   E   R

WRITING PUTS

INTRODUCTION

THIS CHAPTER PRESENTS A FULL AND BALANCED PICTURE OF WRITING PUTS. After briefly reviewing the strategy mechanics, this chapter will explain how put writing can be used in an effort to achieve one's investment objectives. The subject of put-call parity will emerge again, and put writing will be compared to another option strategy. Finally, the focus will shift to risk and an explanation of why selling puts is too often viewed as involving an unacceptable level of risk.

PROFIT-AND-LOSS DIAGRAM AND STRATEGY MECHANICS

The maximum theoretical risk of writing a put is the purchase of 100 shares of stock at a price equal to the strike price minus the premium received. Figure 9–1 illustrates a profit-and-loss diagram at expiration of a short 50 put sold for $200, or $2 per share. If the stock price is $50 or higher at expiration, the put expires and the $2-per-share maximum profit is realized. If the price is below $50 at expiration, the short put is assigned, and the put writer purchases 100 shares at an effective price of $48 per share. If the stock price is below $48 at expiration, this strategy results in a loss.

FIGURE 9–1   Short put at expiration profit-and-loss diagram for a short 50 put sold for 2

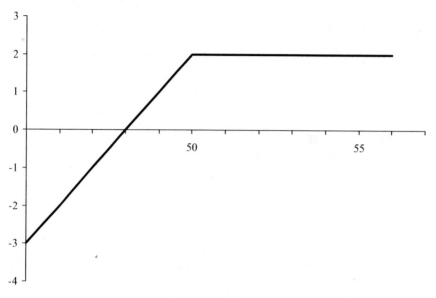

INVESTMENT USES OF SHORT PUTS

One objective of conservative investors stated in the Introduction is to "buy good stocks at good prices." What constitutes a "good stock" and a "good price" are subjective considerations. A common practice, however, is to place a limit-price buy order at a specified price below the current market price. Investors who employ this technique have decided that this stock is a "good stock" and that the price they have specified is a "good price." In these situations, the question becomes, Can writing puts help conservative investors? The answer is a resounding yes. Here's how.

THE STOCK BUYER WITH A NEUTRAL MARKET VIEW

Consider Alex, a young investor who wants to buy Spider Industries, which is currently trading at $36. Alex, however, is in no rush to buy Spider, since he forecasts that the stock will trade sideways or decline in price slightly in the near term. In this example, assume that the 35 put with 75 days to expiration is trading at $1.25 and that Alex has $3,375 in a money market account with which he hopes to purchase Spider stock. For simplicity, commissions and margin account minimum balance requirements are not included.

Rather than placing an order to buy 100 shares of Spider at $33.75, Alex's strategy is to sell one 75-day 35 put at $1.25 and hope that the stock price is below $35 at expiration. Alex's brokerage firm will require him to make a minimum deposit of cash or marginable securities in his margin account. This is known as a *margin deposit*, and its purpose is to help protect the firm in the event that stock purchased as a result of assignment of the short put must be sold at a loss. Among the reasons that a firm may find it necessary to liquidate the stock are that an investor fails to deposit the margin required or that the firm has determined that the stock has become too risky for margin loans. Alex may keep the balance of his $3,375 in a money market account.

If Alex's forecast is accurate, the short put will be assigned, and he will buy 100 shares of Spider at an effective price of $33.75, the $35 strike price less the $1.25 put premium received. If the stock price remains above $35, the put will expire worthless, but Alex will keep the premium.

Has Alex taken an unreasonable risk by selling the put? No.

The maximum risk of Alex's short put is the equivalent of buying 100 shares at $33.75, and this is something that Alex is willing to do. His alternative, remember, was to place a limit-price buy order at $33.75. Rela-

> *Is assignment
> a big risk?*

tive to the limit-price buy order, if the stock price is between $33.75 and $35 at expiration, the short put will be assigned and Alex still gets to buy Spider stock at an effective price of $33.75. Furthermore, if Spider's price is above $35 at expiration, Alex will keep the $1.25 put premium, thus increasing his income. The limit-price buy order offers no such benefit.

THE STOCK BUYER WITH A NEUTRAL-TO-BULLISH MARKET VIEW

Adam is a long-term investor who is seeking to add Mathco, a scientific research company, to his portfolio. However, Adam is only neutral or slightly bullish on Mathco for the next 90 days. With this market forecast, Adam feels that he can do better than buying Mathco at its current price of $68 by selling a 90-day 70 put for $4. If this put

> *When does Adam
> want Mathco
> to rally?*

is assigned, Adam's effective purchase price is $66 (plus transaction costs), the $70 strike price minus the $4-per-share put premium. Adam's maximum theoretical risk is equal to the purchase of stock at $66, and his maximum profit potential from the short put is $4 per share. Adam is hoping for assignment so that he can buy the stock, and he is forecasting that Mathco will stay below $70 for 90 days and rise after that.

THE "AVERAGE-IN" STOCK BUYER

Matthew is considering the purchase of 200 shares of Serviceco, an auto repair franchiser, which is currently trading at $62. Matthew is neutral to bearish on Serviceco for the next two months, and, ideally, he would like to buy 200 shares at $60. But he does not want to miss a rally, so he is considering buying 100 shares now and entering a limit-price buy order for another 100 shares at $58. If that limit-price buy order is filled, his average purchase price for the 200 shares will be the desired $60 per share.

As an alternative, Matthew could buy 100 shares at the current price of $62 and, simultaneously, sell a 55-day 60 put for $2. If that short put is assigned, it would result in an effective purchase price of $58 per share for the second 100 shares. The average price for Matthew's 200 shares would then be the desired $60. If Serviceco is above $60 at expiration, the 60 put expires and Matthew keeps the $2-per-share put premium. If he chooses to buy 100 shares of Serviceco at the market price at that time, the put premium will effectively reduce his purchase price by $2 per share.

SELLING THE "RIGHT" PUT

As with other strategies, which option is "right" depends on the market forecast. A stock buyer who is totally neutral and is willing to buy stock slightly below the current market price might be most inclined to sell an at-the-money put. A stock buyer who is willing to buy only at a much lower price might prefer an out-of-the-money put. A third stock buyer with a neutral-to-bullish forecast might be inclined to sell an in-the-money put. As long as there is a time premium in the price of the put when it is sold, assignment means that stock is purchased at an effective price that is lower than the current market price.

SHORT PUT VERSUS LIMIT-PRICE BUY ORDER
BELOW THE CURRENT MARKET PRICE

Neither the short put nor the limit-price buy order is "better" in an absolute sense. Rather, there is a trade-off. In Matthew's case, both strategies have a maximum theoretical risk of buying the second 100 shares at $58. The short put has the relative advantages of buying stock if the price is *Limit-price buy orders are price-dependent.* between $58 and $60 at expiration and earning the $2-per-share premium if the price is above $60 at expiration. The limit-price buy order does not result in the purchase of stock unless the stock trades at $58 in sufficient quantity to fill Matthew's order and whatever orders at that price may have been ahead of his. Also, the limit-price buy order earns nothing if the price is higher and the order is not filled. The limit-price buy order, however, is only price-dependent, rather than being time- *and* price-dependent like the short put. This means that if the price of Serviceco trades below $58 and then rallies to above $60 prior to expiration, then the limit-price buy order would buy stock

> *Short puts are time- and price-dependent.*

at $58 and earn the corresponding profit, which could be substantial. The short put, however, would most likely not be assigned in these circumstances and would earn, at most, the premium received. Table 9–1 summarizes the differences between short puts and limit-price buy orders.

A COMPARISON TO COVERED WRITING

Many readers will have observed that the profit-and-loss diagrams for the short put (Figure 9–1) and the covered write (Figure 6–1) are similar. This observation is correct and occurs because of the put-call parity concept introduced in Chapter 8. One put-call-parity-related concept is that puts and calls with the same strike price and expiration date can be combined with the underlying stock to create theoretically identical profit-and-loss diagrams. Covered call writing, when the stock is fully paid for, and put writing, when cash is available to buy the underlying stock, are two strategies that, in theory, are identical.

TABLE 9–1   Short Put Versus Limit-Price Buy Order

Stock Price at Expiration	Short Put	Limit-Price Buy Order (limit price is below current market price)	Which is "Better"?
Above Strike	Put Expires Keep Premium	Nothing Happens	Short Put
Between Strike and Strike Minus Premium	Put Assigned Buy Stock	Nothing Happens	Short Put
Below Strike Minus Premium	Put Assigned Buy Stock	Buy Stock	Equal

To emphasize the need for sufficient cash to purchase the underlying stock, this strategy will be referred to as writing *cash-secured* puts.

Whatever the stock price is at expiration, the covered call writer and the cash-secured put writer will end up with the same position. If the stock is above the strike price at expiration, the covered writer will be assigned, will sell stock, and will be left with the cash proceeds from the stock sale. The put writer will also end up with cash, since the sold put will expire worthless.

If the stock price is below the strike price at expiration, the covered call writer will see the short call expire worthless and will be left owning the stock. The cash-secured put writer will also be left owning the stock, because the short put will be assigned, and stock will be purchased.

If the stock price is exactly at the strike price, both the covered call writer and the cash-secured put writer will have cash or stock in an amount equal to the strike price and can buy or sell stock to end up with the preferred position. Consequently, these strategies are identical, ignoring commissions and assuming that the two investors manage their capital in the same manner, i.e., that the covered call writer pays cash for the stock and the put writer has readily available cash to purchase the stock.

CALCULATING RETURNS FOR CASH-SECURED PUT WRITERS

In the first case presented above, Alex is a cash-secured put writer. If Alex's 35 put expires worthless, his income is increased. Alex's income can be calculated as an annual percentage of his capital of $3,375 using the formula in Table 9–2.

TABLE 9–2   Short Puts Calculation of Annual Rate of Return

$$\text{Annual Rate of Return} = \frac{\text{Income}}{\text{Investment}} \times \frac{\text{Days per year}}{\text{Days to Expiration}}$$

$$\text{Annual Rate of Return} = [(\text{interest} + \text{put premium}) \div \$3,375] \times (365 \div 75)$$
$$= [(35 + 125) \div \$3,375] \times (365 \div 75)$$
$$= 23\%$$

where:

Income   = Put Premium + Interest on Funds in Money Market Account

Investment = Cash Available to Purchase Stock (Strike Price – Put Premium)

Note: commissions not included

In the formula in Table 9–2, *income*—for *cash-secured* put writing—consists of the put premium plus the interest earned, if any, on the margin account deposit and on the money market account balance. The *investment* is Alex's capital of $3,375. In this example, Alex's capital is assumed to earn 5 percent interest (annual rate), or approximately $35 for 75 days. If the put expires worthless, Alex's total annualized rate of return, not including commissions, is 23 percent, as shown in Table 9–2.

The 23 percent annualized rate of return is 18 percent greater than the assumed 5 percent annual rate of interest, but this return is earned only if the put expires worthless. One must not forget that the short put position is an obligation to purchase stock at an effective price of $33.75 in this example. If the stock price is below $33.75 at expiration, this strategy will result in a loss.

RISK

The maximum theoretical risk of writing a put is the purchase of 100 shares of stock at the strike price less the put premium received. The percentage of capital at risk varies depending on whether the stock is purchased for cash or on margin. Theoretically, the cash purchaser of stock risks 100 percent of the capital invested. The margin purchaser, however, risks more than 100 percent, because the margin purchaser is theoretically risking all her invested capital plus the amount of the margin loan. Graphically, the slope of the line in the profit-and-loss diagram represents the level of a strategy's risk.

To demonstrate how the amount of capital supporting a position changes the level of risk, Figure 9–2 and Table 9–3 illustrate put writing under three different leverage assumptions. In all three cases, *$4,800 of capital is assumed.*

Line 1 in Figure 9–2 assumes that one 50 put is sold at $2, Line 2 assumes that two 50 puts are sold at $2 each, and Line 3 assumes that three 50 puts are sold. Table 9–3 has columns that correspond to the lines in Figure 9–2 and present the profit-or-loss calculations. The slopes of the lines are different, because the amount of risk is different.

The risk of writing puts, quite simply, depends on an investor's *willingness* and *ability* to purchase the underlying stock. In Figure 9–2, the slope of Line 1 is 1 × 1, equal to the cash purchase of stock. The maximum theoretical risk of Line 1 is $4,800, 100 percent of the assumed capital of $4,800, if the stock falls to zero.

The slope of Line 2 is 2 × 1, equal to a fully margined purchase of stock. The maximum theoretical risk of Line 2 is $9,600, which is 200 percent of the assumed capital of $4,800, if the stock price falls to zero.

FIGURE 9-2 Put writing under three different leverage assumptions

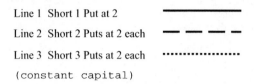

Line 1 Short 1 Put at 2

Line 2 Short 2 Puts at 2 each

Line 3 Short 3 Puts at 2 each

(constant capital)

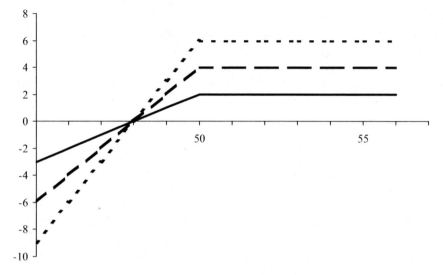

The slope of Line 3 is 3 × 1, steeper than a fully margined purchase of stock. The maximum theoretical risk of Line 3 is $14,400, 300 percent of assumed capital, if the stock price falls to zero. Assignment of the _three_ short puts _cannot_ be met with the amount of capital required to buy 100 shares for cash or 200 shares on margin. Consequently, if assignment of the three short puts occurs, then at least some of the stock would be sold immediately because the assumed capital of $4,800 is insufficient to support the purchase of 300 shares.

MARGIN ACCOUNTS AND SHORT PUTS

Brokerage firms require short put positions to be carried in a margin account, even if the full purchase price of the underlying stock is readily available in

TABLE 9–3 Profit-and-Loss Calculations for Short 1, 2, and 3 Puts

Short 1 Stock Price at Expiration	Short 2 50 Put at $2 P/(L)	Short 3 50 Puts at $2 P/(L)	50 Puts at $2 P/(L)
$52	+200	+400	+600
$51	+200	+400	+600
$50	+200	+400	+600
$49	+100	+200	+300
$48	-0-	-0-	-0-
$47	(100)	(200)	(300)
$46	(200)	(400)	(600)
$45	(300)	(600)	(900)
$44	(400)	(800)	(1,200)
$43	(500)	(1,000)	(1,500)

cash. This is required because cash is easy to transfer and there are technical problems with matching cash availability to potential assignment risk. Brokerage firms also have minimum margin requirements. If a put writer wishes to maintain more than the minimum margin requirement, the put writer, not the brokerage firm, needs to monitor the account or the ready availability of sufficient cash.

Brokerage firms also require investors to meet established minimum financial requirements before they are allowed to trade in margin accounts and even stricter requirements before they are allowed to write put options. These requirements include minimum net worth and minimum account balance criteria. There are also account application and risk disclosure forms that must be read carefully and signed. Investors must be fully informed about a firm's requirements and fulfill them before engaging in the put-writing strategies discussed in this chapter.

SUMMARY

The maximum theoretical risk of writing puts is the purchase of stock at a price equal to the strike price minus the put premium received. As long as there is a time premium in the price of the put at the time of its sale, assignment results in a lower effective purchase price than buying stock at the current market price. Stock buyers can use this strategy as an alternative to a limit-price buy order. A short put performs better than a limit-price buy order if the stock price, at expiration, is above the strike price or between the strike price and a price equal to the strike price minus the premium. If the stock price is below the strike price minus the premium, then the two strategies are equal. Both strategies purchase stock at the same price, effectively. Limit-price orders are time-dependent, while short puts are time- and price-dependent.

Theoretically, according to the concept of put-call parity, if the two strategies are supported by the same amount of capital, then writing cash-secured puts and writing covered calls are identical strategies. Calculating the returns of put writing involves adding the interest earned on the available cash to the put premium and analyzing the sum as an annualized percentage of the available cash.

Cash-secured put writing is equal in risk to buying stock at the price implied by the short put, which is the strike price minus the premium. Selling two puts for one unit of capital is equal in risk to buying stock on margin. Selling three or more puts increases risk even more and means that, if assignment occurs, at least some shares must be sold for lack of equity capital to support the stock position. Thus, selling puts can be risky or conservative, depending on how you manage your capital.

10

LEAPS HAVE MANY APPLICATIONS

INTRODUCTION

PRIOR TO **1990,** LISTED OPTIONS HAD A MAXIMUM LIFE OF NINE MONTHS. In that year, the Chicago Board Options Exchange acted on the perceived demand for longer-term options and started trading what became one of the fastest growth markets of the 1990s. Today, LEAPS® options account for nearly 12 percent of total option-trading volume. Initially, long-term options were traded on 14 large-cap stocks. Since then, the list has grown to over 600 names. This chapter first describes the unique technical aspects of these options and then explains four strategies that are suited for investors with a longer-term investment outlook.

BACKGROUND

LEAPS is an acronym for Long-term Equity AnticiPation Securities. That's a fancy name for what are simply long-term call and put options. These options have expirations of up to three years from the time they are listed.

Are LEAPS just options with longer-dated expirations? Yes and no. While LEAPS are similar to standard options, there are differences in contract specifications and in dynamics.

DIFFERENCES IN CONTRACT SPECIFICATIONS

Fewer strike prices and expiration months. LEAPS are initially listed with only three strike prices available. One is at-the-money, one is approximately 20 percent out-of-the-money, and one is approximately 20 percent in-the-money. Additional strike prices are added as the price of the underlying stock changes and the highest or lowest strike becomes at-the-money. LEAPS also have only one expiration month, January, but there are always two expiration years available.

Different symbols. Standard options have fixed root symbols. The root symbol for short-term options on Microsoft stock, for example, is MSQ. LEAPS options on Microsoft, however, have different root symbols for different years. For example, WMF is the root symbol for Microsoft LEAPS expiring in January 2006, and VMF is the root symbol for Microsoft LEAPS expiring in January 2007. A complete list of LEAPS options and their root symbols can be found in the "Directory of Exchange Listed Options," which is available on the Web site of the Chicago Board Options Exchange at www.cboe.com.

DIFFERENCES IN DYNAMICS

Generally, the longer the time to an option's expiration, the lower the cost of the option's time premium on a unit-of-time basis. Table 10–1 compares the premium of a six-month at-the-money call to the premium of a two-year at-the-money LEAPS call.

In Table 10–1, the cost per month of the two-year LEAPS call is approximately half that of the six-month call. The conclusion is that LEAPS options

TABLE 10–1   Comparison of Two-Year and Six-Month Premiums

	Six-Month 50 Call	Two-Year 50 Call
Premium	5.40	11.40
Total dollar cost (not including commissions)	$540	$1,140
Cost per month	$90	$48

Note: Prices are estimated using a standard binomial options-pricing model assuming a $50 stock price, a $50 strike price, volatility of 35%, interest rates of 4%, zero dividends, and days to expiration of 180 (six months) and 730 (two years).

FIGURE 10–1   Time decay of LEAPS options

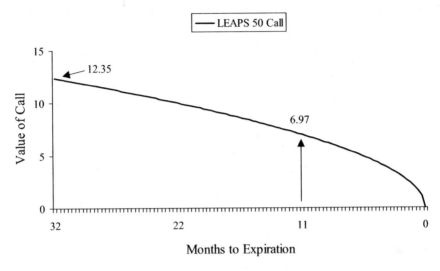

hold their time value relative to traditional short-term options. This concept is illustrated graphically in Figure 10–1, which shows that less than half of an option's initial value erodes during the first two-thirds of its life. Initially, with 33 months to expiration, the LEAPS call has a value of 12.35. With 11 months to expiration, the value is 6.97.

COMMENCEMENT OF TRADING FOR NEW LEAPS EXPIRATIONS
New LEAPS options begin trading in May, June, or July, depending on the quarterly expiration cycle of the short-term options on the underlying security. When LEAPS are first listed, the expiration dates are approximately two years and seven months in the future.

There are three quarterly expiration cycles for short-term options. The first cycle has expiration dates in January, April, July, and October; the second cycle has expirations in February, May, August, and November; and the third cycle has expirations in March, June, September, and December. If a stock's options are on the second cycle, then new LEAPS expirations begin trading at the end of May. For options on the first cycle, new LEAPS begin trading at the end of June, and LEAPS on third-cycle options begin trading at the end of July. For example, if this year is 2007, then LEAPS that expire in January of 2010 will begin trading at the end of May, June, and July for options on the second cycle, the first cycle, and the third cycle, respectively.

LEAPS BECOME SHORT-TERM OPTIONS

As stated earlier, there are a maximum of two LEAPS expirations available for trading. Consequently, when a new LEAPS series is about to be added, the nearest-term LEAPS options are converted to short-term options. Converting LEAPS options to short-term options involves a change of ticker symbol, and your brokerage firm will notify you when this happens. If, for example, you own an IBM LEAPS 90 call, then it might have the symbol WIBAR. The "WIB" stands for "IBM LEAPS options," the "A" stands for "January call," and the "R" stands for "90 strike price." When these LEAPS are converted to short-term options, the new ticker symbol will be IBMAR. "IBM" stands for "IBM short-term options," and "AR," as before the conversion, stands for "January call with a 90 strike price."

USING LEAPS TO PLAN MULTIYEAR GIFTS

Annual giving is a common estate-planning tactic. Typically, funds are invested as they are received, but a creative use of LEAPS calls makes it possible to get market exposure today that is approximately equal to three years of gifts. As an added benefit, risk is substantially less than if the total three-year sum were invested all at once.

The following example illustrates how LEAPS calls might be used to get market exposure that exceeds the investment funds available. Assuming the funds are accumulated during the time period of the LEAPS option's life, then the results will approximate investing the full three years' gifts in the stock today if the market rises and will limit risk if the market declines.

For this example, assume that Laura plans to give $10,000 per year for three years to her daughter Grace, who plans to purchase Growthco stock with the funds. Also assume that the price of Growthco is $90 per share and that the $2\frac{1}{2}$-year 70-strike LEAPS call is trading at $30 per share. Laura would like to give Grace $30,000 today, but such a gift exceeds both the per-year limit and the funds she has available. Table 10–2 illustrates how LEAPS calls might be used to get market exposure today that can be funded over three years, rather than investing the funds each year as they are received.

As Table 10–2 shows, Step 1, in Year 1, is for Laura to give the first year's gift to Grace, which Grace deposits in her brokerage account. Grace then proceeds, in Step 2, to purchase three of the 70-strike LEAPS calls that expire in January of Year 4. Grace must, of course, be approved for options trading by her broker. Note also that the number of LEAPS calls purchased in Step 2 represents only the amount of Growthco stock that Grace plans to purchase, i.e., one LEAPS call for each 100 shares of stock. Remember, the owner of a

TABLE 10–2   Using LEAPS Calls in a Multiyear Gifting Program

Step 1:	Day 1, Year 1. Grace receives a $10,000 gift from Laura
Step 2:	Day 2, Year 1. With Growthco stock at $90 per share, Grace purchases 3 Growthco 70 LEAPS calls expiring in January, Year 4, at a cost of $30 per share ($9,000). $1,000 is deposited in a money market account.
Step 3:	Any time during Year 2. Grace receives a $10,000 gift from Laura and deposits the full amount in a money market account. The money market account balance is now $11,000, not including interest or taxes.
Step 4:	Any time during Year 3. Grace receives a $10,000 gift from Laura and deposits the full amount in a money market account. The money market account balance is now $21,000.
Step 5A:	On or before option expiration of January, Year 4, if Growthco stock is above $70 per share, and if Grace believes that Growthco is still a good investment, then the LEAPS calls can be exercised. Exercising three 70 calls requires payment of $21,000 to purchase the underlying stock. This amount is equal to the money market account balance. At any time prior to the expiration in January, Year 4, if Grace does not want to purchase Growthco stock, then the calls can be sold at the prevailing market price. A professional should be consulted on taxes.
Step 5B:	If the price of Growthco stock is below $70 at option expiration in January, Year 4, then the 70 calls expire worthless. If Grace thinks Growthco stock is still an attractive investment at the lower price, then it may be possible to purchase more than 300 shares with the funds in the money market account. If Growthco stock is no longer deemed to be a good investment, then there is no obligation to purchase shares. If the calls expire worthless, the maximum loss of this strategy is incurred. The maximum potential loss is the full cost of the calls plus commissions. It should be noted, however, that this risk is substantially less than purchasing 300 shares of stock at $90 per share.

LEAPS call does not have the right to receive dividends or to vote in corporate affairs. Also, since a portion of the price of a LEAPS call is time value, the amount of stock value that can be controlled is less than the full amount of funds anticipated. In this example, $30,000 is anticipated, but options on only

$27,000 of Growthco stock are purchased (300 shares at $90 per share). Funds in excess of the cost of the calls can be invested in a money market account.

Steps 3 and 4 involve Laura giving Grace the annual gifts as planned, and the funds should be invested in a money market account. The second gift can be given any time during Year 2, and the third gift can be given any time in Year 3. The expiration date of the calls is in the third week of January of Year 4, so consider the possible outcomes.

THREE SCENARIOS

Scenario 1, Step 5A

Growthco stock has advanced $60 at expiration (in 2 $\frac{1}{2}$ years). If Growthco stock has risen to $150, then the LEAPS 70-strike calls can be exercised. Grace will have benefited from appreciation of 300 shares of Growthco stock from an effective price of $100. This price is calculated by adding the strike price of $70 and the $30 cost of the LEAPS calls. It is impossible to say what the results would be or even if 300 shares could have been purchased if $10,000 had been invested in each of three years.

With the price of Growthco stock above the strike price at expiration, Grace has two choices: She can exercise her LEAPS calls, or she can sell them and realize the profit or loss. Exercising a call means purchasing the underlying stock at the strike price. In this example, the strike price is $70 per share, or $21,000 for 300 shares, which is the balance in the money market account in this example. After exercising, the former call owner becomes a stockowner and assumes all the risk that a long stock position entails. If Grace decides to sell her call, she must consider the tax implications of the realized profit or loss. She also faces the decision of how to invest her funds, which include the money in the money market account and the proceeds from selling her calls.

Scenario 2, Step 5B

The stock has declined $60 at expiration. If Growthco stock has fallen to $30, then the LEAPS 70 calls will expire worthless, and Grace will have a loss of $9,000, or 100 percent of the cost of the calls. However, there will still be $21,000 in the money market account. Had Grace purchased 300 shares of Growthco stock at $90 per share, she would have a loss of $60 per share, or $18,000, twice the loss of the LEAPS position in this example.

Scenario 3, Variation of Step 5A

The stock price is unchanged at $90 at expiration. With Growthco stock at $90 at option expiration, a 70-strike LEAPS call would have a value of $20 per share, and Grace would have a $10-per-share loss and a decision to make. Should the LEAPS calls be sold and the loss realized? Or should they be exercised? This is a personal decision that Grace must make individually.

GIVE TO YOURSELF!

In the previous example, it was assumed that Grace was using LEAPS calls in planning for three years of gifts. The same strategy can be used for saving and personal financial planning. If you plan to save $10,000 per year or some other amount, larger or smaller, you can use LEAPS calls to gain market exposure equal to two or more years of savings. And don't forget, when you're giving to yourself, there is no limit.

A VARIATION ON COVERED WRITING USING LEAPS CALLS

Some aggressive investors and traders are making the shift from traditional covered writing to covered writing with LEAPS, a spread strategy. This has prompted several questions about how the strategy works, what the differences are, and what the risks are. Each of these questions will be answered here.

Traditional covered writing involves the purchase of stock and the sale of calls on a share-for-share basis. For a detailed review of this strategy, please refer to Chapter 6. A variation on traditional covered writing is to substitute an in-the-money LEAPS call for the stock position. This strategy must be done in a margin account, and your account must be approved for trading spreads. First, check with your broker to make sure your paperwork is in order.

As an example, consider Amit, a conservative investor with experience with traditional covered writing. Amit has been studying the stock of Publico, a distributor of books, and he predicts that it will trade sideways for the next 60 days. Rather than initiate a traditional covered write position, however, Amit feels that he is ready for a different strategy. Publico stock is trading at $52 per share, the 18-month 40-strike LEAPS call is trading at $15 per share, and the 60-day 55-strike call is trading at $1.75. Instead of buying Publico stock and selling the 60-day call, Amit decides to purchase the LEAPS call and sell the 60-day call. Table 10–3 illustrates this position.

The net cash investment in Amit's position is $1,325 plus commissions. He paid $1,500 for the purchased LEAPS call, and he received $175 for selling the short-term 55 call. Since an in-the-money call typically has a higher price correlation with the underlying stock than either an at-the-money or an out-of-the-money call, the position in Table 10–3 will have a high price correlation with a traditional covered write.

TABLE 10–3 Covered Writing with LEAPS

		Per Share	$ Cost
Long 1 18-month	40-Strike LEAPS Call	@ $15.00 × $100 =	$1,500
Short 1 60-day	55-Strike Call	@ 1.75 × $100 =	175
	Net Investment	$13.25	$1,325

POSITIVE ASPECTS

The first positive aspect is obvious. The net investment is less, $1,325 per contract for the LEAPS covered write versus $5,025 for the traditional covered write on 100 shares (buying 100 shares at $52 per share and selling one 55 call at $1.75 per share). Even if stock were purchased on minimum margin, the net investment required for the traditional covered write would be approximately $25 per share, or $2,500, in this example, or nearly twice the amount required for the LEAPS covered write.

The second positive aspect is that the LEAPS covered write has a lower maximum risk than the traditional covered write. If the stock price declines sharply, then the most that can be lost in either position is the net amount invested. That is $50.25 per share, not including commissions, for the traditional covered write and $13.25 per share for the LEAPS covered write.

Third, if all goes according to plan, which means that the stock price remains between $52 and $55, then the annualized percentage return from the LEAPS covered write is higher than that from the traditional covered write. With the stock price unchanged on the expiration date of the short option, the traditional covered write earns $175 on the $5,025 net investment. The LEAPS covered write, however, earns nearly the same amount on a $1,325 investment. (The actual profit on the LEAPS covered write will be less than $175 per contract, because time erosion will reduce the price of the LEAPS call.)

NEGATIVE ASPECTS

First and foremost, a LEAPS covered write will incur a loss if the price of the underlying stock declines sharply. Although the maximum potential loss on a LEAPS covered write is less in absolute dollars than the potential loss on a traditional covered write, the percentage loss may be larger.

The second negative aspect occurs if the stock price rises "too much." With a traditional covered write, if an assignment notice is received, then the obligation to sell the underlying stock is easily met. The stock you own is simply delivered to the exerciser of the call. Equity options can be exercised at any time prior to expiration, so the possibility of an early assignment must be considered.

The situation is different, however, with a LEAPS covered write. Since you own no stock with a LEAPS covered write, assignment of the short call means that your broker must borrow stock on your behalf and deliver it. The result is that a short stock position replaces the short call. You must then choose between three courses of action. First, you can cover the short stock and keep the long LEAPS call; second, you can cover the short stock and sell another call; and third, you can close the position by covering the short stock and selling the long LEAPS call. Although it is also possible to exercise the LEAPS call to cover the short stock, this is generally not desirable because the time premium in the price of the LEAPS call will be lost.

Regardless of which action is chosen, there will be extra transactions and extra costs. Depending on the price of the LEAPS call when assignment of the short call occurs, it is also possible that a loss may result from the entire strategy, even though the stock price is higher than when the position was initiated. These potential complications explain why a LEAPS covered write is appropriate only for experienced options users.

IMPLEMENTATION

The goal of a LEAPS covered write is to earn higher annualized percentage rates of return than from traditional covered writing. The risk is incurring higher percentage losses. Investors should focus on finding high-quality stocks and should accept the risk of having a net long exposure to those stocks. Losses occur if the stock price declines sharply, and extra transactions and extra costs are involved if the stock rises too much, so that the short call is assigned. If all goes according to plan, then the price of the underlying stock will remain unchanged or rise slightly, and the short call will expire. LEAPS covered writing is not simply a buy-and-hold strategy, however. It involves thinking ahead about appropriate action if a stock price decline occurs or if an assignment notice is received.

USING A LEAPS COLLAR TO ENTER THE
MARKET WITH LIMITED RISK

Investors sometimes find themselves in the following predicament: They have funds ready to invest, and they are inclined to invest those funds; nevertheless, they are worried that the market will "pull back" or, worse, start a new bear market. A three-part strategy consisting of a market-based exchange-traded fund (ETF) and a LEAPS collar might be just what the investment doctor ordered.

The upcoming example will explain the collar strategy used with Diamonds, an exchange-traded fund that is designed to provide investment returns corresponding generally to the price and yield performance, before fees and expenses, of the Dow Jones Industrial Average (DJIA) as compiled by Dow Jones Corporation.

A collar, as described in Chapter 8, is a two-part option strategy that involves the purchase of an out-of-the-money put and the sale of an out-of-the-money call. When initiated on a dollar-for-dollar basis with a position in Diamonds, a collar provides low-cost insurance and allows some upside participation. Note that the ticker symbol for Diamonds is DIA, and this will be used in the next example.

With the DJIA at 10,000 and the Diamonds trading at 100.00, a DIA 95–115 collar with LEAPS options might be created by the three-part position described in Table 10–4. First, 100 shares of the Diamonds ETF are purchased at $100 per share, or $10,000 total, not including commissions. Second, one 18-month DIA LEAPS 95 put is purchased for $4.50 per share, or $450. Third, one 18-month DIA LEAPS 115 call is sold for $2.50, or $250. The net cost of the collar, therefore, is $2.00, or $200, and the total cost of the three-part strategy is $10,200, 2 percent more than simply buying the Diamonds position alone.

The possible profit-and-loss outcomes of the three-part position at expiration are presented in Table 10–5 and Figure 10–2. The table and chart do not include transaction costs, but you should be sure to include them when analyzing a real strategy.

DIA options are deliverable options, just like regular stock options, so the Diamonds will be sold if either the call is assigned or the put is exercised. At the expiration of the LEAPS options, if the DJIA is above 11,500 and the Diamonds are above 115.00, then the puts will expire worthless, but the short calls

TABLE 10–4   Entering the Market With Limited Risk

	Per Share	$ Cost
Long 100 Diamonds	@ 100.00 × $100	$10,000
Long 1 DIA 18-month 95 Put	@ 4.50 × $100 =	450
Short 1 DIA 18-month 115 Call	@ (2.50) × $100 =	(250)
Net Investment	102.00	$10,200

TABLE 10–5   Diamonds with DIA Collar Profit and Loss at Expiration

DIA % Change	DIA @ Exp.	Long Diamond @ 100.00	Short 115 Call @ 2.50	Long 95 Put @ 2.50	Combined Profit or Loss
−10%	90	−10.00	+2.50	+0.50	− 7.00
− 5%	95	− 5.00	+2.50	−4.50	− 7.00
−0−	100	−0−	+2.50	−4.50	− 2.00
+ 5%	105	+ 5.00	+2.50	−4.50	+ 3.00
+10%	110	+10.00	+2.50	−4.50	+ 8.00
+15%	115	+15.00	+2.50	−4.50	+13.00
+20%	120	+20.00	−2.50	−4.50	+13.00

FIGURE 10–2   Long Diamonds with a DIA collar

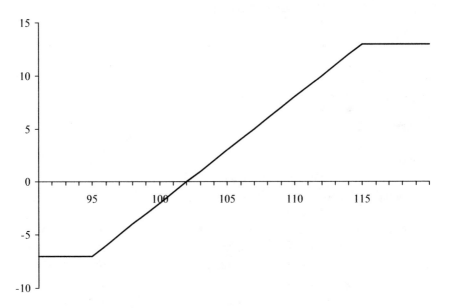

will probably be assigned. Assignment of a short DIA call means that the underlying Diamonds shares must be delivered. Above the strike price, 115 in this example, the rise in value of the short calls will offset the rise in value of the long Diamonds. Therefore, in this example, profit is limited to $15.00 per

Diamonds share less the $2.00 cost of the collar, or $13.00 net per share in 18 months plus dividends.

If the DJIA is below 9,500 and the Diamonds are below 95.00 at expiration, then the short call expires worthless and the put is exercised. Exercise of a DIA put means that the Diamonds shares are sold at the strike price. Below the strike price of the put, the rise in value of the put offsets the loss from the long Diamonds position. In this example, the maximum loss is $7.00 per Diamonds share, which is equal to the purchase price of $100.00 minus the strike price of the put of $95.00 plus the $2.00 cost of the collar.

If the DJIA is between 9,500 and 11,500 at expiration, then both options expire worthless, and the profit or loss is equal to the rise or fall of the Diamonds shares, plus dividends and minus the cost of the collar.

MOTIVATION

A long Diamonds position with a DIA collar is appropriate for investors who are forecasting modestly rising prices and do not want to bear the full risk of a significant market decline. The distance between the purchase price of the Diamonds and the strike price of the put should be viewed as the risk that the investor is willing to assume. The strike price of the short calls should be viewed as the level above which the market is not expected to rise.

AN END-OF-YEAR TAX STRATEGY INVOLVING LEAPS

Investors sometimes find themselves with a loss on a stock that they want to keep. Selling the stock to realize the loss causes some mixed emotions. On the one hand, they would like to realize the loss, perhaps because they have some gains that the loss would partially offset. On the other hand, they still consider the underlying stock to be a good investment that belongs in their portfolio. What to do?

Unfortunately, it is not possible to recognize a loss for tax purposes if the stock is sold today and repurchased tomorrow. According to "Taxes and Investing," a publication of the Options Industry Council, "The wash-sale rule prevents taxpayers who are not dealers from selling stock or securities (including options) at a loss and reacquiring 'substantially identical' stock or securities (or options to acquire substantially identical stock or securities) within a 30-day period before or after the loss."

Prior to the existence of options, investors had two choices to attempt to deal with their conflicting emotions. First, they could sell their losing stock position today, wait 31 days, and then repurchase the stock. Second, they could acquire an identical position to the stock they currently owned, wait 31 days, and then sell the stock they currently owned. Both of these strategies involve trade-offs.

The first alternative, selling now, waiting, and repurchasing, has the advantage that the investor is out of the market and, therefore, has no downside risk during the waiting period. The disadvantage is that, if the price rises during the waiting period, the investor does not own the stock and so does not get the benefit. Furthermore, the cost required to reacquire the position might be substantially higher than the amount received from the sale 31 days earlier.

The second alternative, doubling up today and waiting to sell, has the advantage of the investor's being in the market and able to participate in a stock price rise. The disadvantages, however, are that the risk is twice that of the original position if the stock price declines and that the purchase price of the new position must be financed today.

Options offer a third alternative that, while similar to the second choice just discussed, mitigates some of its disadvantages. The strategy is as follows. First, buy LEAPS calls today. Second, wait 31 days and sell the original stock position. Third, wait 31 days more, then repurchase the original stock position and sell the LEAPS call. If these steps are taken at the appropriate time intervals, then the loss on the stock can be recognized for tax purposes, according to "Taxes and Investing." Be sure to check with a professional tax advisor to make sure that this strategy fits your personal situation and that IRS regulations have not changed.

This strategy has two advantages. First, it keeps you in the market so that you do not miss a rally. Second, it requires less additional investment and less risk than purchasing an equal position in the stock. However, it also has two disadvantages. The first is that there is still an increased risk if the stock price declines. The second is that the time premium in the LEAPS calls means that participation is less than 100 percent if the stock price rises.

Consider Marty, an investor in Downco, a feather-bedding manufacturer. Marty originally purchased 100 shares of Downco at $50 per share on June 10. It is now November 10, and the price of Downco has fallen to $30. Marty has conflicting thoughts on what to do. On the one hand, Marty would like to keep his Downco stock, because he still believes in the long-term growth prospects of the company. On the other hand, Marty would like to realize a $2,000 tax loss this year. Marty confirms with his professional tax advisor that the following course of action is appropriate for him and consistent with IRS regulations in the current year. Here are the steps in his plan.

Today is November 10 of Year 1. Step 1 of Marty's plan is to purchase a 14-month Downco LEAPS 30 call for $4.80 per share, or $480, not including commissions. Marty will continue to hold his Downco shares, so purchasing this call increases his maximum risk by $480. Step 2 is to wait at least 31 days and then sell his Downco shares at the prevailing market price. In this example, Marty plans to sell his shares on December 15 of Year 1, which is 35 days after November 10. It is, of course, impossible to predict what the prices of Downco stock and Marty's LEAPS call will be, but that is part of the risk that Marty is taking when he employs this strategy. Step 3 is to wait at least another 31 days and then repurchase 100 shares of Downco stock and simultaneously sell his call. Both transactions will be executed at the prevailing market price. In this example, Marty plans to purchase stock and sell his call on January 20 of Year 2, which is 34 days after December 15 of Year 1.

After Step 2 is completed, as long as Step 3 is not taken until after 30 days, it is likely that the sale of Marty's Downco shares will qualify as a tax loss in Year 1.

Table 10–6 analyzes the possible real costs and opportunity costs of this strategy for three scenarios. The estimated changes in price of Marty's LEAPS 30 call are consistent with the change in stock price and time to expiration, according to the Op-Eval4 software, explained in Chapter 11. In the first scenario, Marty sells his Downco shares at $30 and repurchases them at the same price, experiencing only the loss from time erosion of his LEAPS call. In the second scenario, Marty sells his Downco shares at $30, but repurchases them at $35. In this scenario, his LEAPS call increases in price. The third scenario assumes that Marty sells his Downco shares at $30 and repurchases them at $25. However, he also loses money on his LEAPS call. Each of these scenarios will be discussed briefly.

Table 10–6 makes three assumptions. First, it is assumed that a LEAPS 30 call with 420 days to expiration, or approximately 14 months, is purchased for $4.80 per share on November 10. The stock price is assumed to be $30, and the assumptions about interest rates, dividends, and volatility are stated at the bottom of the table. The second assumption is that shares of the underlying stock are sold on December 15 of Year 1 at $30 per share. Although it is unlikely that the stock price would have remained unchanged for 35 days, the actual price behavior of the stock between Step 1 and Step 2 does not affect the price of the option between Step 1 and Step 3, which determines the option's portion of the cost of the strategy. The third assumption is that interest rates, dividends, and implied volatility are unchanged between Step 1 and Step 3. Readers should follow the reasoning presented here first, then work through other scenarios assuming changes in these factors to assess their impact.

In Scenario 1, Marty purchases a Downco LEAPS 30 call on November 10 of Year 1 at $4.80 per share, or $480. He then sells his Downco shares on

TABLE 10–6   End of Year Tax Strategy Involving LEAPS

Beginning position: Own 100 shares at $50, current price $30

Step 1: November 10 of Year 1:   Purchase 1 30-Strike LEAPS Call at 4.80

Step 2: December 15 of Year 1:   Sell 100 shares at $30

Step 3: January 20 of Year 2:   Buy 100 shares and sell LEAPS Call

	Step 1	Step 3 Scenario 1 Stock Unchanged	Step 3 Scenario 2 Stock Up $5	Step 3 Scenario 3 Stock Down $5
	Day 1 Nov 10	Day 3 Jan 20	Day 3 Jan 20	Day 3 Jan 20
Stock Price	$30	$30	$35	$25
Days to Exp	420	351	351	351
Price of LEAPS Call	4.80	4.40	7.70	1.90

Scenario #1: LEAPS Call purchased at 4.80 and sold at 4.40
             Stock sold at $30 and repurchased at $30
             Real cost* of strategy is 40-cent loss from option
             Benefit is realized tax loss on stock sale

Scenario #2: LEAPS Call purchased at 4.80 and sold at 7.70
             Stock sold at $30 and repurchased at $35
             Net opportunity cost* is 2.10 plus real cost of tax on option profit
             Benefit is realized tax loss on stock sale

Scenario #3: LEAPS Call purchased at 4.80 and sold at 1.90
             Stock sold at $30 and repurchased at $25
             Net benefit* is 2.10 plus tax deduction on option loss
             Benefit is realized tax loss on stock sale plus lower repurchase cost

Assumptions: Strike Price, 30; No Dividends; Volatility, 35%; Interest Rates, 2%.
* Does not include commissions, taxes, or bid-ask spreads. Consult a professional tax advisor about tax implications.

December 15 at $30 per share. Finally, on January 20 of Year 2, he repurchases 100 Downco shares at $30 and sells the LEAPS call at $4.40. If his tax advisor agrees, Marty has a $20-per-share tax loss on Downco shares purchased and sold in Year 1 and a 40-cent tax loss on his LEAPS call in Year 2. Moving forward, Marty also owns 100 shares of Downco stock with a cost basis of $30 per share, purchased on January 20 of Year 2. The benefits of this strategy are that Marty keeps a position in Downco stock, and he gets a tax loss in Year 1. The cost, in this scenario, is the 40-cents-per-share loss on the LEAPS call. The call, however, was Marty's protection against missing a price rise in Downco stock during that 30-day-plus time period when he did not own any Downco shares.

In Scenario 2, Marty is not so lucky as to buy back the Downco shares at the same price at which he sold them. This time, the shares rise in price by $5, to $35. Although Marty repurchased his Downco shares at a price $5 above his selling price, this "opportunity loss" is partially offset by the profit of $2.90 on his LEAPS call. The result is that Marty gets his tax loss in Year 1, and, moving forward, he owns 100 Downco shares purchased at $35 per share on January 20. Marty also has a taxable short-term profit of 2.90 per share on his LEAPS call, realized in Year 2.

In Scenario 3, Marty is able to repurchase 100 Downco shares at $25, $5 below his $30 selling price. Unfortunately, his LEAPS call also declined in price to $1.90, for a short-term loss of $2.90 per share, or $290. Again assuming that his tax advisor agrees, Marty gets a $20-per-share tax loss in Year 1. Moving forward, he owns 100 shares of Downco purchased for $25 per share on January 20. He also has a short-term tax loss on his LEAPS call, realized in Year 2.

To summarize Marty's strategy, purchasing a LEAPS call has some advantages and some disadvantages relative to purchasing an identical position in his Downco shares. The advantages are that LEAPS calls require less of an investment and have less risk than purchasing Downco shares. LEAPS calls also are likely to experience less time erosion in both percentage and absolute terms than short-term calls. The disadvantage is that, if the stock price rises when he does not own the shares, Marty's calls will rise less in dollar terms than the underlying shares. Is there a place for a LEAPS tax strategy in your investing and trading activities? First, check with your professional tax advisor, and, second, consider the trade-offs.

SUMMARY

LEAPS, or simply long-term options, are a fast-growing segment of the financial markets. They are available on over 600 stocks. They always have a January expiration and a ticker symbol that differs from the symbol for short-term options on the same stock. When the time to expiration approaches nine months, a LEAPS option series is converted to a short-term series and a new

LEAPS series is listed. This occurs every May, June, and July, depending on the expiration cycle of the short-term options. Four possible strategies involving LEAPS options are to use them as part of a multiyear gifting program, in a variation on covered writing, to enter the market with limited risk, and in year-end tax planning. These strategies are only a small sampling of the many potential uses of LEAPS options.

Trading Strategies

11

OPERATING THE OP-EVAL4 SOFTWARE

INTRODUCTION

COMPUTER PROGRAMS PROVIDE VALUABLE ASSISTANCE TO OPTION TRADERS. They perform calculations quickly and improve analysis; however, *they do not make decisions!* The computer program Op-Eval4, which accompanies this text, calculates option theoretical values given inputs from the user, and it graphs many strategies involving options only or options and stock. This chapter explains how to install and operate the program.

OP-EVAL4

Enclosed with this book is a computer CD labeled "Op-Eval4™ Setup Disk." This disk is designed to work on computers with WindowsXP operating systems. Although the installation procedures are straightforward, if you have little experience with computers, you may want the assistance of someone who is experienced in installing computer programs. Once the program is installed, you will find that it is easy to use.

The installation instructions are as follows:

1. Insert the setup CD in the CD drive
2. If the setup program does not start automatically, click on "Start," then click on "Run." Type "e:\setup" (or "f:\setup"), press "Enter," and follow instructions.

To run the program, click on the "Op-Eval4" icon. Alternatively, you can click on "Start," then on "Programs," then on "Op-Eval Programs," and finally on "Op-Eval4."

The first page you will see when you start the program is shown in Figure 11–1. This page, "Disclosures and Disclaimers," contains important information about the assumptions made by the program. You should scroll through this entire section and read everything carefully. Only with a thorough understanding of the limitations of this program (or any program) can you make informed decisions. If you proceed on your own intuition and uninformed perceptions, you are not likely to do well in any area of investing or trading, let alone with options. After you have read all the disclosures and disclaimers carefully, you can choose "Yes" if you accept the conditions and limitations of the program or "No" to exit the program. Then click "OK."

A complete discussion of operating Op-Eval4 will now be presented. Even experienced options traders and computer users should read this section to learn the full range of capabilities of the program.

FIGURE 11–1   Op-Eval4 disclosures and disclaimers

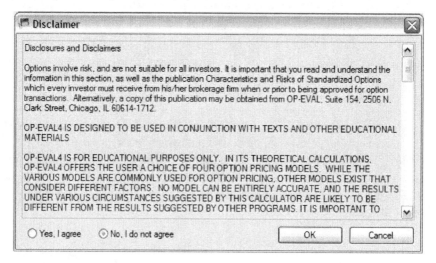

FEATURES OF OP-EVAL4

This program has the following eight features, each of which is explained in detail in the sections that follow:

Single Option Calculator
Spread Calculator
Graphing
Theoretical Table Generator
Print Preview
Print
Save Spread
Open Spread

DIFFERENT OPTIONS USE DIFFERENT PRICING FORMULAS

Option contract specifications vary by exercise style, type of underlying security, and method of dividend payment. Op-Eval4 has the capability to apply four option-pricing formulas that analyze options on individual stocks, options on indexes, options that are subject to American-style exercise, and options that are subject to European-style exercise. The following explanations detail how to choose the underlying type and the exercise style of the option you are analyzing.

THE SINGLE OPTION CALCULATOR

Figure 11–2 shows the single option calculator page. This feature calculates theoretical values, delta, gamma, theta, and vega for a call and put with the same strike price, same expiration, and same underlying security. Definitions of all terms appear in the HELP feature of the program, and later chapters will explain how information in the program can be used to analyze option prices and to estimate how those prices might change given your forecast, but this chapter describes only how the various aspects of the program work.

MOVING AROUND THE SINGLE OPTION CALCULATOR PAGE

The highlighted rectangle can be changed either by clicking on a desired rectangle or by pressing the arrow keys. The down arrow (↓) and the right arrow (→) move the highlighted rectangle down the inputs column first, then over to the "Call" rectangle, then to the "Put" rectangle, and, finally, back to the "Stock Price" rectangle. The up arrow (↑) and the left arrow (←) move the high-

FIGURE 11–2   Op-Eval4 single option calculator

EQUITY	AMERICAN		CALL	PUT
STOCK PRICE	50.0000	VALUE	3.1912	2.7435
STRIKE PRICE	50.0000	DELTA	0.5557	-0.4533
VOLATILITY %	30.0000	GAMMA	0.0539	0.0556
INTEREST RATE %	4.0000	VEGA	0.0976	0.0975
DIVIDEND	0.0000	7-THETA	-0.1351	-0.1008
DAYS TO EX-DIV	0.0000	RHO	0.0606	-0.0491
DAYS TO EXPIRY	90.0000			

lighted rectangle in the opposite direction. The rectangles below the call and put values cannot be highlighted, as they are "output only."

After familiarizing yourself with movement around the single option calculation page, highlight the "Stock Price" rectangle, and make sure the settings appear as in Figure 11–2. These are 50.0000 for "Stock Price," 50.0000 for "Strike Price," 30.0000 for "Volatility %," 4.0000 for "Interest Rate %," 0.0000 for "Dividend," 0.0000 for "Days to Ex-Div," and 90.0000 for "Days to Expiry." Also, at the top-left corner of the single option calculator, "Equity" and "American" should appear.

"Equity" indicates that it is an option on a stock that is being analyzed, and "American" indicates that the option is subject to American-style exercise. If "Index" or "European" appears, simply left-click on that cell with your mouse, and "Equity" or "American" will appear. Finally, in the lower-right corner of your screen, "Dividend: Quarterly" and "Steps=50" should appear. The dividend information is unimportant for this specific exercise, as it is assumed that the stock pays no dividend, but "Steps=50" must appear or you will not get exactly the same results as the examples presented in this chapter. To change either of these features, simply double left-click on the desired item and type in the appropriate information on the pop-up box that appears, then left-click on "OK" to save the information.

Given the inputs described above, Op-Eval4 calculates the theoretical value of the 50 call as 3.1912, which appears on the top line of the right-hand side of the single option calculator page under the "Call" rectangle and to the right of the "Value" rectangle.

CHANGING "STOCK PRICE"

With the "Stock Price" rectangle highlighted, you can input any price from 0.0000 to 99,999.99. If a whole number, such as 50, is entered, Op-Eval4 assumes that all four numbers to the right of the decimal point are zeros. After 50 (or some other number) is entered, then, when the "Enter" key or an arrow key is pressed or when another rectangle is highlighted by clicking on it, the number 50.0000 appears in the "Stock Price" rectangle, and all output values are recalculated.

You can now practice with the different input rectangles and observe how Op-Eval4 calculates option theoretical values, given your inputs.

CHANGING "STRIKE PRICE"

In option markets in the United States, option strike price intervals vary by underlying security and by the price of the underlying security. For options on stocks, it is common to have strike prices every $2.50 for stock prices from zero to $25. For stock prices from $25 to $200, strike price intervals are frequently $5, and for stock prices above $200, strike price intervals are usually $10. These are only guidelines, however. Some actively traded stocks with prices under $25 have $1 intervals between strike prices. Also, some stocks have strike prices at intervals of $2.50 up to a stock price of $50. Options on exchange-traded funds (ETFs) and similar products also have varying intervals for strike prices.

Op-Eval4 has the flexibility to set the strike price at any number between 0 and 9,999. This feature allows Op-Eval4 to be used for options on a wide variety of underlying instruments.

CHANGING "VOLATILITY %"

Volatility, as discussed in Chapter 3, is a statistical measure of potential price changes in an option's underlying instrument. If other factors remain constant, a wider range of possible stock prices (i.e., higher volatility) means that options have a higher theoretical value. It is common practice to express volatility as a percentage, and this practice is used in Op-Eval4. When the "Volatility %" rectangle is highlighted, it is possible to enter any number from 1.0000 to 999.99. If all inputs appear as in Figure 11–2, then changing the volatility to "31" and pressing "Enter" results in 31.0000 appearing in the "Volatility %" rectangle and 3.2888 and 2.8410, respectively, appearing under

"Call" and "Put." Experiment with the volatility input and develop a feel for how changes in volatility affect option prices.

CHANGING THE "INTEREST RATE %"

Interest rates are a factor in the values of options, because time and the cost of money directly affect purchasing decisions. Experiment with this input and observe that changes in interest rates have a very small impact on option prices relative to any of the other inputs. This is consistent with the discussion in Chapter 3.

CHANGING "DAYS TO EXPIRY"

The effect of time on option values was explained in Chapter 4. Tables 4–3 and 4–5 illustrate how the time value portion of option prices erodes as expiration approaches. Chapter 4 also explains how changes in time affect at-the-money options differently from in-the-money and out-of-the-money options.

When counting the days to expiration, include the current day if you are doing it before or during market hours, but do not include the current day if you are doing it after the market close. Also, be sure to use the day after the correct last day of trading as the expiration day. For options on individual stocks and for American-style index options, such as OEX options, the correct expiration day is the Saturday following the third Friday of the expiration month. (Even though expiration is technically on the Saturday following the third Friday of the month, Friday is the last trading day.) For European-style index options, such as SPX or XMI options, the correct day is one day earlier, the third Friday of the expiration month, with the last trading day being the Thursday preceding the last Friday.

DIVIDEND INPUT DEPENDS ON OPTION TYPE

Op-Eval4 has different formulas for options on stocks and for cash-settled options on indexes. If "Index" appears on the single option calculator, or if the "IsIndex" box is checked on the spread calculator (explained further on in the text), the program assumes that the underlying is an index and that the option is cash-settled. If "European" appears or the "IsEuropean" box is checked, the program assumes that early exercise is prohibited.

If the underlying security is a stock that is traded in the United States, then the option is American-style. This means that two inputs are required, the amount of the dividend and the ex-dividend date. The amount entered in this cell must be in dollars and cents per share, like 0.50 for 50 cents. Dividends are frequently listed in daily financial newspapers, but they also are usually available from a company's Web site.

Securities valuation involves a process known as *discounting cash flows*, so the number of "Days to Ex-Div," or the ex-dividend date, is required in order to calculate the timing of the dividend payment.

CORRECT INPUTS ARE ESSENTIAL

If you attempt to analyze an option without the proper inputs, there is likely to be a significant difference between the value calculated by Op-Eval4 and the prices observed in the real marketplace. Improper settings are also likely to lead to incorrect estimates of option price changes and inaccurate conclusions about strategy selection. This is one of the risks you assume in using the program, as explained in the "Disclosures and Disclaimers" section of the program.

If the options are cash-settled and the underlying is an index, then only a "Dividend Yield" is required. Index dividend yield numbers are frequently presented in the *Wall Street Journal, Investor's Business Daily,* and *Barron's*.

CHANGING CALL AND PUT PRICES—ESTIMATING
IMPLIED VOLATILITY

Given the inputs in Figure 11–2, the "Value" rectangle under the "Call" rectangle reads 3.1912. Highlight the "Call" rectangle, type in "4," and press "Enter." The first change you will notice is the number in the "Value" rectangle is now 4.0000. But another change is far more important. Can you tell what it is?

Look at the "Volatility %" rectangle. You will observe that the volatility number has been recalculated from 30.0000 to 38.2906. Figure 11–3 shows the computer screen with a call price of 4.0000 and volatility of 38.2906, and this is the implied volatility of this call. How implied volatility can be used in making trading decisions and estimating results will be discussed in Chapter 12.

When the value in the "Call" rectangle is changed, Op-Eval4 not only recalculates the volatility, but also recalculates the put value using the new volatility percentage and all other outputs as well. Op-Eval4 will also calculate an "implied volatility" percentage given a new put value. A new call value is then calculated using the new volatility percentage, and all other outputs are also recalculated.

THE SPREAD POSITIONS PAGE

Clicking on the "Spread" item on the menu bar at the top of the screen brings up a new screen that looks like Figure 11–4.

FIGURE 11–3   Op-Eval4 calculating implied volatility

Input call value of "4," and get output of volatility of "38.2906"

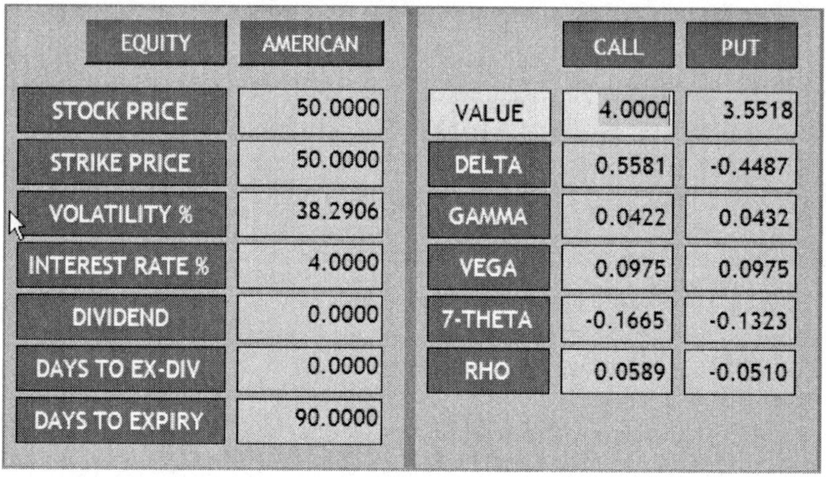

EQUITY	AMERICAN		CALL	PUT
STOCK PRICE	50.0000	VALUE	4.0000	3.5518
STRIKE PRICE	50.0000	DELTA	0.5581	-0.4487
VOLATILITY %	38.2906	GAMMA	0.0422	0.0432
INTEREST RATE %	4.0000	VEGA	0.0975	0.0975
DIVIDEND	0.0000	7-THETA	-0.1665	-0.1323
DAYS TO EX-DIV	0.0000	RHO	0.0589	-0.0510
DAYS TO EXPIRY	90.0000			

FIGURE 11–4   Op-Eval4—spread positions page

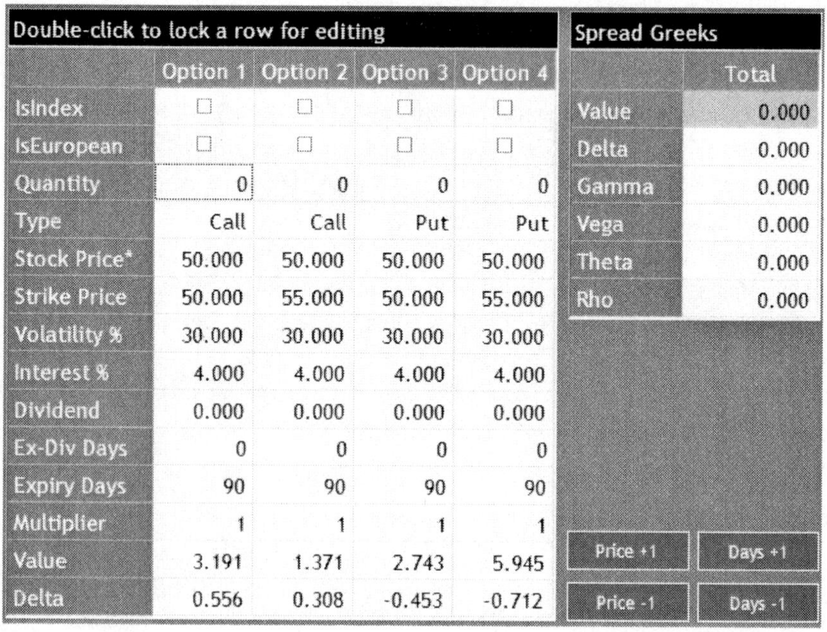

Double-click to lock a row for editing					Spread Greeks	
	Option 1	Option 2	Option 3	Option 4		Total
IsIndex	☐	☐	☐	☐	Value	0.000
IsEuropean	☐	☐	☐	☐	Delta	0.000
Quantity	0	0	0	0	Gamma	0.000
Type	Call	Call	Put	Put	Vega	0.000
Stock Price*	50.000	50.000	50.000	50.000	Theta	0.000
Strike Price	50.000	55.000	50.000	55.000	Rho	0.000
Volatility %	30.000	30.000	30.000	30.000		
Interest %	4.000	4.000	4.000	4.000		
Dividend	0.000	0.000	0.000	0.000		
Ex-Div Days	0	0	0	0		
Expiry Days	90	90	90	90		
Multiplier	1	1	1	1		
Value	3.191	1.371	2.743	5.945	Price +1	Days +1
Delta	0.556	0.308	-0.453	-0.712	Price -1	Days -1

The purpose of the spread positions page is to analyze and graph multiple-option positions and stock and option positions. The spread positions page operates in a way similar to the single option calculator. Left-clicking highlights rectangles, and highlighted rectangles can have their values changed. Arrow keys can also be used to change the highlighted rectangle and recalculate outputs. Pressing the "Enter" key recalculates the outputs while leaving the highlighted rectangle unchanged. The following features on this page do not appear on the single option calculator page.

USING THE ASTERISK (*) TO LOCK A ROW

The spread positions page can be used to analyze two or more options with the same volatility or different volatilities or two or more options with the same number of days to expiration or different numbers of days to expiration. It is also possible to analyze spreads involving calls only, puts only, and options with stock. The asterisk (*) facilitates the analysis of some spreads.

If an asterisk appears next to an item in the leftmost column ("IsIndex," "IsEuropean," "Quantity," "Stock Price," "Strike Price," etc.), then all items will lock to the item in the first input column if a change is made.

An asterisk indicates that all inputs in that row are set to the input in the "Option 1" column and that a change in the contents of one rectangle will change the contents of the other rectangles in that row. For example, if the spread positions page is set to the settings shown in Figure 11–4 and an asterisk appears next to "Quantity," then a change in the "Quantity" of "Option 1" will also change the "Quantity" of "Option 2."

The absence of an asterisk indicates that the numbers in that row are set individually. A change in the contents of one rectangle will not change the contents of the other rectangles in that row.

Adding and Removing an Asterisk—Double Left-Click

To add or remove an asterisk, simply double left-click when the mouse pointer is over the desired rectangle. If an asterisk was in the cell initially, it will disappear. If an asterisk did not appear initially, then it will.

CHOOSING "CALL," "PUT," OR "STOCK"

When a cell in the "Type" row is highlighted, a drop-down arrow will appear. Left-clicking on this arrow opens a drop-down box that contains the items "Call," "Put," and "Stock." Clicking on one closes the drop-down box and changes the content of the "Type" cell to the item that was clicked on. If the "Type" cell in the leftmost column contains an asterisk, then changing any cell in that row will change the contents of every cell in that row to the new setting.

If an asterisk does not appear, then changing one cell will not change the others.

ANALYZING A HYPOTHETICAL SPREAD

The spread positions page can be used to analyze a wide variety of positions, including one-to-one vertical spreads with only calls or only puts, ratio spreads, time spreads, spreads with calls and puts, and stock and option spreads.

An example of a one-to-one vertical call spread is the simultaneous purchase of one 50 call and sale of one 55 call. Both calls are assumed to have the same expiration and the same underlying stock. The following example illustrates how this vertical call spread might be analyzed.

Setting Up the Spread Positions Page

The first step in estimating the value of a hypothetical 50–55 call spread is entering all of the inputs: the stock price, days to expiration, volatility, and so on. An example of how this might be accomplished is presented in Figure 11–5.

FIGURE 11–5   Op-Eval4—calculation of 50–55 call spread on a per-share basis

Spread Positions					Spread Greeks	
	Option 1	Option 2	Option 3	Option 4		Total
IsIndex	☐	☐	☐	☐	Value	1.820
IsEuropean	☐	☐	☐	☐	Delta	0.247
Quantity	1	-1	0	0	Gamma	0.006
Type	Call	Call	Put	Put	Vega	0.014
Stock Price*	50.000	50.000	50.000	50.000	Theta	-0.024
Strike Price	50.000	55.000	50.000	55.000	Rho	0.026
Volatility %	30.000	30.000	30.000	30.000		
Interest %	4.000	4.000	4.000	4.000		
Dividend	0.000	0.000	0.000	0.000		
Ex-Div Days	0	0	0	0		
Expiry Days	90	90	90	90		
Multiplier	1	1	1	1	Price +1	Days +1
Value	3.191	1.371	2.743	5.945		
Delta	0.556	0.308	-0.453	-0.712	Price -1	Days -1

To start, since the underlying security is assumed to be a stock, there must *not* be a check mark in either the "IsIndex" row or the "IsEuropean" row. Second, the basic specifications must be entered. This includes such information as the "Stock Price," assumed to be $50 in this example; days to expiration, assumed to be 90 days; the volatility, assumed to be 30 percent; and other inputs, as indicated in Figure 11–5. Finally, the position must be entered.

The "Quantity" Row

To enter a position, the "Quantity" row is used. The "1" in the "Option 1" column of Figure 11–5 indicates that one of these options, the 50 call, was purchased. The "−1" in the "Option 2" column indicates that one 55 call was sold. The result is a position consisting of one long (or purchased) 50 call at 3.191 and one short (or sold) 55 call at 1.371.

Value and Multiplier Rows

For the simple 50–55 call spread position in Figure 11–5, one might be able to calculate the net spread value of 1.820 mentally by subtracting the 55 call value from the 50 call value. But for more complicated positions, it is nice to have the help of the computer.

The number that appears in the "Value" rectangle in the upper-right portion of the spread positions page is calculated from the quantity of options in the "Quantity" row and the number in the "Multiplier" row. The multiplier indicates the number of underlying units per option contract. This feature makes it possible to analyze positions on either a "per-share" basis or a "dollar" basis.

For example, if "1" appears in the "Multiplier" row, as in Figure 11–5, then the spread value is, as stated above, 1.820, which is 1.820 per share. If the "Multiplier" row contains "100," however, then the value of the 50–55 call spread would be 182.042. This indicates a value of approximately $182 for a spread with real options, each of which has 100 shares of stock as its underlying security.

A positive number in the "Value" rectangle indicates a debit, i.e., the position is established for a net payment, or cost, not including transaction costs. In the example in Figure 11–5, the 50 call is purchased for 3.191 and the 55 call is sold for 1.371. The net cost, therefore, is 1.820 per share, and this is what the number in the "Value" rectangle indicates.

A negative number in the "Value" rectangle indicates a credit, i.e., the position is established for a net receipt of money, as opposed to a net payment. Some traders speak of this as "selling a spread." Suppose, for example that the 50 call had been sold for 3.191 and the 55 call had been purchased for 1.371.

In this case, a "−1" would appear in the "Quantity" row under "Option 1," indicating that this option was sold, and a "1" would appear under "Option 2," indicating that this option was purchased. The "Value," in this case, would then be −1.820, indicating this net amount was received.

Spread Delta

Another feature of the spread positions page is the "Delta" rectangle, which presents the "position delta." The following comments about "Delta" also apply to "Gamma," "Vega," "Theta," and "Rho."

A position delta is the sum of the deltas of "Option 1" and "Option 2." Just as the delta of an individual option is an estimate of how much that option will change in price for a one-point change in the underlying instrument, the *spread delta* is an estimate of how much a multiple-part option position will change in price when the underlying instrument changes by one point, assuming all other inputs remain constant.

The spread delta of 0.247 in Figure 11–5 indicates that the value of the 50–55 call spread will increase by approximately 0.247 if the underlying stock price is raised by 1.00 and that the value will decrease by a like amount with a one-point decrease in the stock price.

The "Multiplier" affects the calculation of delta just as it affects the calculation of value. If the multiplier is 1, as it is in Figure 11–5, then the result indicates how a one-share spread is estimated to change, by approximately 25 cents. If the multiplier is 100, then the delta of "24.700" indicates that a one-option spread could be expected to change by approximately $25, not including commissions.

Plus One and Minus One Button

In the lower right corner of the spread positions page are four command buttons. Click on one and see what happens. As expected, a click on the "Price +1" button raises all numbers in the "Stock" row by one full point and recalculates the option values, their deltas, the spread value, and the spread delta. Click on one of the other three buttons and a one-unit change in either the stock price or days to expiration, as indicated, will occur and all outputs will be recalculated.

These "+1" and "−1" buttons make it easy to estimate how a position will change in value given a change in the underlying security (in whole points) and/or a change in the number of days to expiration. For example, a trader might want to know how much the value of the 50–55 call spread illustrated in Figure 11–5 will change if the stock price rises $4 in five days. To answer this question, just click on the "Price +1" button four times (raising the stock price from 50 to 54), then click on the "Days −1" button five times (decreasing the days from 90 to 85). The result is that the spread value has increased to 2.936.

CHANGING "THEORETICAL VALUE"— ESTIMATING IMPLIED VOLATILITY

The implied volatility of an option can be calculated on the spread positions page just as on the single option calculator page. First, highlight a rectangle in the "Value" row; second, type in the market price of the option; and third, press the "Enter" key. "Volatility" now becomes a calculated output, and this is the implied volatility of the option whose price was entered. If an asterisk appears next to "Volatility %," then calculating an implied volatility for one option in one column does not affect the values of options in other columns. However, a change in any number in the "Volatility %" row will change all the numbers in that row.

GRAPHING PROFIT-AND-LOSS DIAGRAMS

As explained earlier, profit-and-loss diagrams are valuable for educational purposes and for strategy analysis. The graphing capability of Op-Eval4 makes it possible to quickly prepare and print diagrams such as the ones that appear throughout this book. The graphing capability is available only from the spread positions page.

Check Figure 11–5 to make sure all the information is correct. Are the "Volatility %" and other inputs correct? Is the "Quantity" of each option correct? Be careful, because it is easy to make mistakes until you become familiar with the layout of the spread positions page. When all the inputs are correct, you are ready to graph the call spread.

If you click on the "Graph" item on the menu bar at the top of the screen, the screen will look like Figure 11–6.

THE GRAPH PAGE

This feature creates two different types of graphs. First, it creates graphs of single- or multiple-part strategies consisting of one to four options or up to three options and one stock. Second, it creates graphs of strategy sensitivities known as the "Greeks": delta, gamma, theta, and vega. Definitions of these terms appear in the "Help" file. To select the type of graph you want, right-click on the graph and select from the list of choices. The legend at the bottom of the graph will contain the strategy characteristic depicted.

FIGURE 11–6   Op-Eval4—theoretical graph page

Op-Eval4: Theoretical Graph

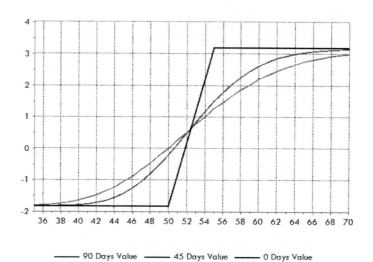

———— 90 Days Value   ———— 45 Days Value   ———— 0 Days Value

Name	Quantity	Description	Value	Position
Option 1	1	50 Call	3.191	3
Option 2	-1	55 Call	1.371	-1
Option 3	0	50 Put	2.743	0
Option 4	0	55 Put	5.945	0

Underlying at 50

P&&L at 90 days	P&&L at 45 days	P&&L at 0 days
0	0	-2

Total Spread Value: -2

All positions must have the same underlying price ("Stock Price"), the same expiration date ("Expiry Days"), the same dividend, the same "Ex-Div Days" (if applicable) and the same interest rate. If these inputs are not consistent, a graph cannot be created. Option specifications (underlying price, strike price, volatility, and so on) must be entered on the spread positions page. Only the number of long or short contracts can be entered or changed on either the theoretical graph page or the spread calculator page. There must be a non-zero number in the "Quantity" row for a position to be graphed. The quantity of an option in a position may be changed on the spread calculator page by clicking on the appropriate quantity, typing a new number, and pressing the "Enter" button. On the theoretical graph page, the quantity of an option can be changed by clicking on the appropriate quantity, typing a new number, and pressing the "Enter" button.

Time spreads cannot be graphed; all options must have the same expiration ("Expiry Days").

Up to four options or three options and one underlying instrument in the same position may be graphed. A "+" indicates a long position, and a "−" indicates a short position. The quantity must also be set. The program allows the user to set the multiplier. Therefore, care should be taken in setting a quantity to be sure that the number of units and the multiplier are consistent among the options and the underlying stock. The graph page shows three lines. The line with straight segments is a graph of the strategy at expiration. The middle line is a graph of the strategy at half of the days to expiration indicated on the spread positions page in the "Expiry Days" row. The middle line may be recalculated by clicking on the "−1" or "+1" in the middle box in the lower right corner of the graph page. The third line is a graph of the strategy at the number of days prior to expiration indicated on the spread positions page.

"QUICK CHANGE" TO GRAPH

At the bottom left of the graph page are four lines that describe the strike price and quantity of Options 1, 2, 3, and 4 from the spread positions page. Changing the quantity of a particular option in a position will, of course, change the total position; and Op-Eval4 will immediately graph the new position.

GRAPHING A POSITION IN THE UNDERLYING INSTRUMENT

Op-Eval4 has the capability to graph a position in an underlying stock. When the "Type" on the spread positions page is set to "Stock," the "Description" on the graph page will change to "Stock," and the "Value" will be equal to the stock price. If "1" is in the "Quantity" row of the "Underlying" column and the other rectangles in the "Quantity" row are set to zero, then clicking on the "Graph" item on the menu bar brings up a screen like Figure 11–7. This is a graph of a long position in an underlying stock.

GRAPHING STRATEGY SENSITIVITIES
(DELTA, GAMMA, THETA, VEGA)

Right-click over a graph with the mouse pointer and a box containing "Value, Delta, Gamma, Theta, Vega, Rho" appears. To graph one of these items, simply left-click on that item.

BE SURE THAT MULTIPLIERS ARE CONSISTENT

Op-Eval4 allows the user to adjust the multiplier for all parts of a position. This allows positions to be valued and graphs to be drawn on either a per-unit basis or a dollar basis. For individual stocks and options on those stocks, this

FIGURE 11–7   Op-Eval4—graph of a long stock position

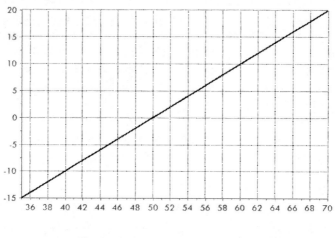

Op-Eval4: Theoretical Graph

——— 90 Days Value   ——— 45 Days Value   ——— 0 Days Value

Name	Quantity	Description	Value	Position
Option 1	1	Stock	50.000	50
Option 2	0	55 Call	1.371	0
Option 3	0	50 Put	2.743	0
Option 4	0	55 Put	5.945	0

Underlying at 50

P&&L at 90 days	P&&L at 45 days	P&&L at 0 days
0	0	0

Total Spread Value: -50

is either on a per-share basis or a dollar value basis. As a result of this feature, however, care must be taken in setting the "Quantity" and "Multiplier" rows to be sure that the numbers are consistent between the options and the underlying instrument.

Consider, for example, a covered call position consisting of 100 shares of stock and one short call on that stock. One way to graph this position would be to set the quantity of the stock at "100," for 100 shares, and to set the quantity of the option as "−1," for one short call. The "Multiplier" row, therefore, would have a "1" for the stock and a "100" for the call. The number in the "Value" row would then reflect the total dollar value of this position. To show the same long stock and short call position on a per-share basis would require a "1" in the "Quantity" row for the stock and a "−1" in the "Quantity" row for the option. The "Multiplier" row would then contain a "1" for both the stock and option, and the number in the "Value" row would indicate the per-share price of the position.

THEORETICAL-VALUE TABLE

This feature creates a table of theoretical values or sensitivities (delta, gamma, theta, vega) for the net position in the spread positions page. To select the type of table you want, right-click on the table and select from the list of choices. The upper-left cell in the table will contain the strategy characteristic being calculated. All limitations of the theoretical graph feature apply to this feature.

Figure 11–8 contains values for the bull call spread created in the spread positions page in Figure 11–5 and graphed in Figure 11–6. A table of theoretical values makes it easy to estimate the change in price of a position if the stock price rises or falls or if time passes to expiration. It would be much more time-consuming to enter the necessary specific inputs into the spread posi-

FIGURE 11–8   Op-Eval4—theoretical table for 50–55 call spread

Values on a per-share basis with "Precision" set to two decimal places

Op-Eval4: Theoretical Table

Value	90 days	80 days	70 days	60 days	50 days	40 days	30 days	20 days	10 days	0 days
70	4.80	4.85	4.88	4.92	4.94	4.97	4.98	4.99	4.99	5.00
66	4.62	4.67	4.74	4.80	4.86	4.91	4.96	4.98	4.99	5.00
63	4.38	4.44	4.52	4.61	4.69	4.79	4.87	4.95	4.99	5.00
60	4.02	4.08	4.15	4.25	4.36	4.50	4.63	4.80	4.95	5.00
56	3.27	3.32	3.37	3.45	3.54	3.64	3.79	4.01	4.35	5.00
52	2.32	2.31	2.31	2.31	2.32	2.32	2.28	2.24	2.18	2.00
49	1.61	1.57	1.52	1.44	1.36	1.26	1.11	0.90	0.57	0.00
46	0.93	0.87	0.81	0.72	0.62	0.49	0.36	0.20	0.05	0.00
42	0.34	0.30	0.24	0.18	0.13	0.07	0.03	0.01	0.00	0.00
38	0.08	0.06	0.04	0.02	0.01	0.00	0.00	0.00	0.00	0.00

Name	Quantity	Description	Value	Position
Option 1	1	50 Call	3.191	3
Option 2	-1	55 Call	1.371	-1
Option 3	0	50 Put	2.743	0
Option 4	0	55 Put	5.945	0

Volatility   30.00

Precision   2

tions page to estimate the outcomes of several market scenarios. The "Table" feature makes it easy to quickly estimate potential profit-and-loss results of a strategy over a range of possible market changes.

A table is created from the same information in the spread positions page that is used to create a graph. Consequently, you must be sure that all inputs are consistent in the same way that you must for the graph feature. The numbers of days in the columns (90, 80, 70, and so on) are fixed and cannot be changed by the user. The stock prices in the leftmost column are also determined by the program based on the stock price in the spread positions page and cannot be changed by the user. However, it is possible to change the volatility assumption. Also, the user can set the desired number of decimal places in the output calculation. This makes it easy to analyze both low-priced and high-priced strategies.

Note that the values in the theoretical table are calculated assuming the volatility percentage in the first column of the "Volatility" row on the spread positions page. This percentage also appears in the "Volatility" box in the lower-right corner of the theoretical table, and it can be changed by left-clicking on the box and typing in a new number or using the up or down arrows. Even if different options in the spread positions page have different volatility assumptions, the theoretical table will recalculate all option values and the resulting position value with the volatility percentage in the first column of the "Volatility" row. This means that values in the theoretical table will differ from values calculated using specific volatility percentages and from prices observed in the marketplace. Care should be taken when using values in the theoretical table to analyze multiple-part option strategies in which different options have different volatility assumptions.

SUMMARY

Computer programs such as Op-Eval4 are designed to perform calculations and draw diagrams quickly and to improve the analytic process. They are not designed to take over the decision-making process.

After installing the program, you must read carefully and thoroughly understand the Disclosures and Disclaimers before you attempt to use the program to analyze individual options or multiple-part option strategies.

The single option calculator presents the theoretical values of a call and put with the same strike price, underlying security, and expiration, along with their respective deltas, gammas, thetas, and vegas.

If the "Value" is changed on any page, Op-Eval4 recalculates the volatility percentage; this is known as the implied volatility.

The graphing and table features require consistent inputs in the spread positions page. The line with straight segments is a graph of the strategy at expiration. The middle line is a graph of the strategy at half of the days to expiration and may be recalculated. The third line is a graph of the strategy at the number of days prior to expiration indicated on the spread positions page.

It is important to practice using the many features of Op-Eval4 because it is easy to make mistakes in inputting information if you are not familiar with the layout of the various pages. However, once you get to know the many features of Op-Eval4, you will find it to be a valuable tool for analyzing option prices and strategies.

12

TRADING OPTIONS

INTRODUCTION

BUYING OPTIONS IS A POPULAR STRATEGY. It seems simple enough: Buying options is generally low in cost even after commissions, the risk is limited, and profits can be substantial if the forecast works out. Is it really this simple? Unfortunately, speculating with options involves a number of nuances. The purpose of this chapter is to discuss those nuances.

Options traders typically want to know first, "How do I find the right option?" Then there are other questions, such as, "How should I measure results?" "How should I manage my capital?" and "What do I need to know about volatility?"

This chapter will go through the steps of making a market forecast, analyzing several potential options, and using the results of the analysis to select a particular option. Op-Eval4 will be used to estimate the results of several forecasts. Capital management will be discussed, and a three-part market forecasting technique will be introduced.

STARTING THE ANALYSIS

The trader in this example is a training manager in Cincinnati named Greg. He traded stocks for several years before starting with options, which he has been trading for four years now. Greg subscribes to a weekly stock market charting service, and he spends from one to three hours each week analyzing charts and planning trades. He typically makes one to four trades per month. His preferred trading strategy is buying options because the risk is limited.

Recently, Greg has been following a stock named Teckco, which is currently trading at $37. Today is 60 days before October expiration, and Greg believes that Teckco is ready for a rally into the low 40s. He is considering whether to buy some October 35 calls for $3.70 or some October 40 calls for $1.65. Greg has $1,500 to commit to this trade, so he can buy either four of the 35 calls ($370 × 4 = $1,480) or nine of the 40 calls ($165 × 9 = $1,485). Greg wants to determine which strategy will produce the largest profits if his forecast is correct. We will follow Greg as he thinks through this decision.

Step 1 is making a market forecast, and Greg has made one: He forecasts that Teckco will rise approximately 10 percent, from $37 to $41, in 10 days. Today is nine days before Teckco's earnings announcement, and Greg expects the stock price to rise the day after the announcement. He wants to position himself now in case the stock price rises in anticipation of the announcement. The topic of market forecasting is beyond the scope of this book, so Greg's forecast will be taken as presented and the validity of the thinking behind it will not be addressed. However, the biggest risk of any trading decision is that the forecast is wrong. The result, if that is the case, would undoubtedly be a loss. Greg is well aware of this risk. He is financially capable of bearing the risk, and he is ready to move forward.

Step 2 is setting up Op-Eval4 to analyze the October 35 and 40 calls. Greg gathers the available information and creates Figure 12–1, which is the spread positions page of Op-Eval4. Greg is not contemplating trading a spread, but this page allows him to analyze the potential price behavior of two options at the same time. It saves time over using the single option calculator page to make two estimates. The inputs to the spread positions page in Figure 12–1 show that the stock price is 37, the strike prices are 35 and 40, the interest rate is 2 percent, there are no dividends, and there are 60 days to expiration.

INCLUDING "BID" AND "ASK" PRICES

Note that the strike prices in columns 1 and 2 are "35," and the strike prices in columns 3 and 4 are "40." Also note that the "Value" entries in columns 1 and 2 are "3.60" and "3.70," respectively. These are the current "bid" and "ask" prices for the Teckco October 35 call. Columns 3 and 4 show that the bid price for the 40 call is 1.55, and the ask price is 1.65. It is important to know an

FIGURE 12–1   **Greg's spread positions page analyzing the Teckco October 35 and 40 calls**

Spread Positions	Option 1	Option 2	Option 3	Option 4	Spread Greeks	Total
IsIndex	☐	☐	☐	☐	Value	3.600
IsEuropean	☐	☐	☐	☐	Delta	0.669
Quantity	1	0	0	0	Gamma	0.059
Type*	Call	Call	Call	Call	Vega	0.053
Stock Price*	37.000	37.000	37.000	37.000	Theta	-0.139
Strike Price	35.000	35.000	40.000	40.000	Rho	0.035
Volatility %	41.245	43.138	44.105	45.852		
Interest %*	2.000	2.000	2.000	2.000		
Dividend*	0.000	0.000	0.000	0.000		
Ex-Div Days*	0	0	0	0		
Expiry Days*	60	60	60	60		
Multiplier*	1	1	1	1	Price +1	Days +1
Value	3.600	3.700	1.550	1.650		
Delta	0.669	0.665	0.372	0.379	Price -1	Days -1

option's bid and ask prices because nonprofessional traders buy options at the ask price and sell them at the bid price. Consequently, this difference should be included in the comparison of trading strategies.

A final observation to be made from Figure 12–1 is that the implied volatility for all four prices has been calculated by Op-Eval4. The bid and ask prices for the 35 call have implied volatilities of 41.2 percent and 43.1 percent, respectively. For the 40 call, the implied volatilities are 44.1 percent and 45.8 percent, respectively. Note that, although Op-Eval4 calculates the numbers to three decimal places, most traders do not find it necessary to go out more than one.

As explained in Chapter 4, implied volatility is the volatility percentage used in an option-pricing formula with the known inputs of time to expiration, interest rates, and so on, that will return the current market price of an option as the theoretical value. The current level of implied volatility is the basis for creating the theoretical-value tables that are used to estimate strategy results. The current level of implied volatility will also be compared to historic levels so that a volatility forecast can be included in estimating strategy results.

Step 3 is using Op-Eval4 to estimate the prices of the October 35 and 40 calls assuming that Greg's forecast is correct. Greg's forecast is that the price of Teckco stock will rise to approximately $41 in 10 days, or 50 days prior to expiration. Figure 12–2 is Greg's spread positions page with the "Stock Price" changed to 41and the "Expiry Days" changed to 50. As one would expect, there are also new numbers in the "Value" row. The new bid price of the 35 call is 6.532, and the new bid price of the 40 call is 3.235.

Real option prices, of course, trade in 5-cent increments up to $3 and in 10-cent increments above $3, so Greg must take the estimates from Op-Eval4 and adjust them to what he thinks the actual bids in the marketplace might be. Given the price estimates of 6.532 and 3.235, Greg rounds down to $6.50 for the 35 call and to $3.20 for the 40 call. Greg now has the first necessary information to make a choice.

Table 12–1 shows the analysis that Greg has done so far.

Table 12–1 shows that, if Greg's forecast is correct, then the 35 call will rise 75 percent, to $6.50, and the 40 call will rise 93 percent, to $3.20. This is a powerful argument in favor of buying the 40 call rather than the 35 call, but Greg's analysis is not yet complete.

FIGURE 12–2　New option prices assuming that Greg's forecast is correct

Double-click to lock a row for editing					Spread Greeks	
	Option 1	Option 2	Option 3	Option 4		Total
IsIndex	☐	☐	☐	☐	Value	6.532
IsEuropean	☐	☐	☐	☐	Delta	0.871
Quantity	1	0	0	0	Gamma	0.034
Type*	Call	Call	Call	Call	Vega	0.034
Stock Price*	41.000	41.000	41.000	41.000	Theta	-0.112
Strike Price	35.000	35.000	40.000	40.000	Rho	0.040
Volatility %	41.245	43.138	44.105	45.852		
Interest %*	2.000	2.000	2.000	2.000		
Dividend*	0.000	0.000	0.000	0.000		
Ex-Div Days*	0	0	0	0		
Expiry Days*	50	50	50	50		
Multiplier*	1	1	1	1	Price +1	Days +1
Value	6.532	6.595	3.235	3.339		
Delta	0.871	0.862	0.599	0.597	Price -1	Days -1

TABLE 12–1   Greg's Preliminary Analysis

		Initial Inputs		Inputs Changed to Greg's Forecast
Inputs:	Stock Price	37.00	→	41.00
	Strike Prices	35 / 40		
	Dividend Yield	0%		
	Volatility	43.1 / 45.8	→	41.2 / 44.1
	Interest Rates	2%		
	Days to Expiration	60	→	50
Outputs:	35 Call Price	3.70	→	6.50 (+75%)
	40 Call Price	1.65	→	3.20 (+93%)

Greg started with a very specific forecast: The stock price would be up approximately 10 percent in 10 days. It is unlikely that such a forecast will be exactly right, so Greg wants to explore results over a range of outcomes. Suppose the stock price rises more or less than 10 percent or rises over a longer period than 10 days. The tool that will help with this analysis is the theoretical table in Op-Eval4.

SETTING THE MULTIPLIER AND THE QUANTITY

The analysis in Table 12–1 compares the percentage changes in price, and that is helpful. Trading strategies, however, involve dollars and quantities of options. It is therefore necessary to set up the spread positions page correctly to assist in the analysis.

A per-share price of $6.50 for each 35 call has a value of $650 per option, not including commissions, and four of them amount to $2,600. At $3.20, each 40 call has a value of $320, and nine of them amount to $2,880 in total. Obviously, Greg would prefer to end up with the larger amount, given that the investment and the risk are the same. If he makes sure that the quantities and multipliers are correct, the percentage results will match the dollar results on the spread positions page. Since each option has 100 shares of stock as the underlying security, the "Multiplier" should be set to 100.

Figure 12–3 shows a spread positions page with the first column of the "Quantity" row set to "4" and all columns of the "Multiplier" row set to "100." The value in the first column has also been set to "6.50" in an attempt to more realistically estimate how four of the 35 calls will perform. Note that "2,600" appears in the "Value" row under "Total" in the upper-right corner of the spread positions page. This indicates that four calls have a value of $650 each, for a total value of $2,600. Remember, Greg will have to sell his options at the bid price.

If a "9" were entered in the third column of the "Quantity" row in Figure 12–3 (and the "4" were removed from the first column), that would indicate that nine 40 calls have a value of $320 each, for a total value of $2,880.

CREATING THEORETICAL-VALUE TABLES

Step 4 is creating theoretical-value tables so that results over a range of stock prices and days to expiration can be compared. Figures 12–4 and 12–5 are tables that Greg might create for the 35 and 40 calls, respectively. The table in Figure 12–4 was created from the spread positions page shown in Figure 12–3. The spread positions page for Figure 12–5 is not shown, but it had a "9" in column 3.

FIGURE 12–3   **Spread positions page setup for the theoretical table. Column 1: "Quantity" set to "4" and "Multiplier" set to "100"**

Spread Positions					Spread Greeks	
	Option 1	Option 2	Option 3	Option 4		Total
IsIndex	☐	☐	☐	☐	Value	2,600.000
IsEuropean	☐	☐	☐	☐	Delta	350.481
Quantity	4	0	0	0	Gamma	13.442
Type*	Call	Call	Call	Call	Vega	13.430
Stock Price*	41.000	41.000	41.000	41.000	Theta	-42.399
Strike Price	35.000	35.000	40.000	40.000	Rho	16.123
Volatility %	40.307	43.138	43.504	45.852		
Interest %*	2.000	2.000	2.000	2.000		
Dividend*	0.000	0.000	0.000	0.000		
Ex-Div Days*	0	0	0	0		
Expiry Days*	50	50	50	50		
Multiplier*	100	100	100	100		
Value	6.500	6.595	3.200	3.339	Price +1	Days +1
Delta	0.876	0.862	0.599	0.597	Price -1	Days -1

FIGURE 12–4   Theoretical table analyzing four 35 calls

Value	90 days	80 days	70 days	60 days	50 days	40 days	30 days	20 days	10 days	0 days
55	8,081	8,069	8,058	8,048	8,039	8,031	8,023	8,015	8,008	8,000
52	6,895	6,880	6,865	6,852	6,841	6,831	6,823	6,815	6,808	6,800
48	5,345	5,316	5,293	5,271	5,252	5,237	5,225	5,215	5,208	5,200
44	3,852	3,815	3,775	3,733	3,699	3,665	3,637	3,619	3,608	3,600
41	2,823	2,764	2,712	2,658	2,600	2,543	2,489	2,441	2,410	2,400
38	1,908	1,843	1,774	1,700	1,620	1,541	1,455	1,356	1,258	1,200
34	945	879	810	735	654	565	464	348	205	0
30	343	294	248	204	157	108	65	27	3	0
27	119	93	70	50	31	16	6	1	0	0
24	28	18	12	7	3	1	0	0	0	0

Name	Quantity	Description	Value	Position
Option 1	4	35 Call	6.500	2,600
Option 2	0	35 Call	6.595	0
Option 3	0	40 Call	3.200	0
Option 4	0	40 Call	3.339	0

Volatility	40.31
Precision	0

How does Greg use the theoretical tables in Figures 12–4 and 12–5? He starts by comparing the cells in the table that are above, below, and next to the cell that contains his forecast. He predicts that the stock price will be $41 with 50 days to expiration. In Figure 12–4, which analyzes four 35 calls, the number "2,600" appears in the highlighted cell, which is a stock price of $41 and 50 days to expiration. Similarly, the number "2,880" appears in the highlighted cell in Figure 12–5.

Note that the Op-Eval4 software determines the range of stock prices and days to expiration in the theoretical table. It will not always be possible, therefore, to exactly match a cell in the table with the forecast. Nevertheless, the table can offer some valuable and easy-to-use information, and it is preferable to repeatedly entering stock prices and days to expiration in the spread positions table and then manually calculating which position has the greatest profit in dollar or percentage terms.

FIGURE 12–5   Theoretical table analyzing nine 40 calls

Value	90 days	80 days	70 days	60 days	50 days	40 days	30 days	20 days	10 days	0 days
55	13,941	13,864	13,783	13,717	13,653	13,605	13,567	13,540	13,520	13,500
52	11,435	11,331	11,221	11,125	11,034	10,955	10,890	10,845	10,820	10,800
48	8,268	8,133	7,993	7,844	7,683	7,549	7,409	7,296	7,224	7,200
44	5,487	5,306	5,115	4,909	4,701	4,490	4,251	3,995	3,736	3,600
41	3,709	3,522	3,324	3,111	2,880	2,625	2,337	1,996	1,571	900
38	2,270	2,091	1,901	1,702	1,498	1,272	1,017	716	361	0
34	975	842	703	584	454	312	193	81	9	0
30	300	228	177	122	76	37	13	2	0	0
27	91	63	41	23	11	4	1	0	0	0
24	18	11	6	2	1	0	0	0	0	0

Name	Quantity	Description	Value	Position
Option 1	0	35 Call	6.500	0
Option 2	0	35 Call	6.595	0
Option 3	9	40 Call	3.200	2,880
Option 4	0	40 Call	3.339	0

Volatility	43.50
Precision	0

USING THE THEORETICAL TABLE

Starting with the highlighted cells, Greg compares the cells to the right in the same row and the cells up and down and to the right. The cells to the right in the same row estimate the position value if the targeted stock price rise takes longer than expected. The cells up and to the right estimate the position value if the stock price rise is greater than expected but takes longer than expected. The cells down and to the right estimate the position value if the stock price rise is not as great as expected and takes longer than expected. If one strategy is better in all outcomes, then that strategy is the clear preference. However, if different strategies perform better in different cells, as is frequently the case, then close attention to the forecast is required.

Looking at the cells immediately to the right of the highlighted cells, Greg sees that, at 40 days to expiration, the nine 40 calls (Figure 12–5) still outperform the four 35 calls (Figure 12–4), as there is a value of $2,625 for the 40 calls versus $2,543 for the 35 calls. Moving right one more cell, at 30 days to expiration, however, the situation reverses. With a stock price of $41 and 30 days to expiration, the position of four 35 calls has a value of $2,489 versus $2,337 for the 40 calls.

Comparing Figures 12–4 and 12–5 also reveals that, if the stock price rises to $44 or higher, then nine 40 calls always outperform four 35 calls. However, if the stock price rises to only $38, then four 35 calls are always preferable to nine 40 calls.

What can Greg conclude from these observations? His forecast for a 10 percent stock price rise in 10 to 20 days is crucial to the success of buying nine 40 calls over buying four 35 calls. If these were the only considerations, then Greg would have to think hard about his forecast for Teckco stock and then choose to purchase either four 35 calls or nine 40 calls. But Greg has one more factor to consider.

CHANGING THE IMPLIED VOLATILITY

Experienced options traders are aware that implied volatility sometimes rises in anticipation of an earnings report and then declines after the report. Why does this happen? Think of options as insurance policies. If you live on an ocean coast and a hurricane is forecast for this weekend, then it would be reasonable to expect the cost of insurance to rise. After the weekend, whether or not there was a storm, it would be reasonable to expect the cost of insurance to go back down. In the options market, an earnings report is like a hurricane. It may or may not cause the price of the underlying stock to move sharply, but option writers want higher premiums to protect themselves against the increased risk. After the earnings report, it is possible that the volatility component of option prices returns to its former level.

What this means for Greg is that, to make a complete forecast, he should consider the possibility of a decrease in implied volatility. His analysis in Figures 12–1 and 12–2 indicated that the volatility of the bid prices of the 35 and 40 calls was 41.2 percent and 44.1 percent, respectively. Greg's experience tells him that a decrease of 10 percent in implied volatility is possible. Therefore, Greg creates the spread positions page in Figure 12–6, in which the stock price is $41, the days to expiration is 50, and the implied volatility of the bid prices for the 35 and 40 calls is 31.0 percent and 34.0 percent.

FIGURE 12–6   Spread positions page with implied volatility down 10 percent

Double-click to lock a row for editing					Spread Greeks	
	Option 1	Option 2	Option 3	Option 4		Total
IsIndex	☐	☐	☐	☐	Value	2,374.878
IsEuropean	☐	☐	☐	☐	Delta	549.620
Quantity	0	0	9	0	Gamma	67.330
Type*	Call	Call	Call	Call	Vega	53.127
Stock Price*	41.000	41.000	41.000	41.000	Theta	-139.025
Strike Price	35.000	35.000	40.000	40.000	Rho	27.616
Volatility %	31.000	43.138	34.000	45.852		
Interest %*	2.000	2.000	2.000	2.000		
Dividend*	0.000	0.000	0.000	0.000		
Ex-Div Days*	0	0	0	0		
Expiry Days*	50	50	50	50		
Multiplier*	100	100	100	100		
Value	6.252	6.595	2.639	3.339	Price +1	Days +1
Delta	0.929	0.862	0.611	0.597	Price -1	Days -1

With the new—and lower—implied volatility level, the estimated price for the 35 call is $6.20, an increase of 67 percent from $3.70. The estimated price for the 40 call is $2.60, an increase of 57 percent from $1.65. This information definitely has an impact on Greg's thinking. With lower implied volatility, four 35 calls result in a higher profit than nine 40 calls.

To complete his analysis, Greg creates the theoretical tables in Figures 12–7 and 12–8 to compare the two strategies with the lower implied volatility. It is interesting to observe that if Greg's stock price and time forecast are correct, but implied volatility decreases, then purchasing four 35 calls is preferred over purchasing nine 40 calls.

At Greg's target price, for example, a stock price of $41 and 50 days, Figure 12–7 shows that four 35 calls have a value of $2,501. Figure 12–8, however, shows that nine 40 calls have a value of $2,216. Looking at all the cells near Greg's target price, the same thing is true: Four 35 calls have a higher value than nine 40 calls. If the stock price rises to $44, then nine 40 calls outperform four of the 35 calls, but that exceeds Greg's forecast by 75 percent.

FIGURE 12–7   Theoretical table—four 35 calls with implied volatility of 31 percent

Value	90 days	80 days	70 days	60 days	50 days	40 days	30 days	20 days	10 days	0 days
55	8,070	8,062	8,054	8,046	8,038	8,031	8,023	8,015	8,008	8,000
52	6,872	6,863	6,855	6,846	6,838	6,831	6,823	6,815	6,808	6,800
48	5,285	5,272	5,260	5,249	5,240	5,231	5,223	5,215	5,208	5,200
44	3,736	3,713	3,690	3,671	3,652	3,637	3,625	3,616	3,608	3,600
41	2,643	2,605	2,569	2,536	2,501	2,470	2,442	2,421	2,408	2,400
38	1,666	1,615	1,568	1,518	1,463	1,403	1,343	1,280	1,225	1,200
34	692	641	587	528	465	396	323	238	127	0
30	177	147	116	91	65	41	20	6	0	0
27	37	28	19	11	6	2	1	0	0	0
24	4	2	1	1	0	0	0	0	0	0

Name	Quantity	Description	Value	Position
Option 1	4	35 Call	6.252	2,501
Option 2	0	35 Call	6.595	0
Option 3	0	40 Call	2.639	0
Option 4	0	40 Call	3.339	0

Volatility	31.00
Precision	0

A THREE-PART FORECAST

What Greg's analysis has shown is that trading options is different from trading stocks or futures, because there are more factors to consider. When making a forecast, options traders start with a price forecast for the underlying stock or index, but then there are two more elements to include. Since option prices decrease as expiration approaches, options traders must be precise in their opinion about time.

With stocks, the only consideration is direction. Futures contracts have expirations, so time is a consideration, but time is not as important in futures trading as it is with options. Neither stocks nor futures have a volatility component in the price as options do.

FIGURE 12–8   Theoretical table—nine 40 calls with implied volatility of 34 percent

Value	90 days	80 days	70 days	60 days	50 days	40 days	30 days	20 days	10 days	0 days
55	13,718	13,684	13,654	13,626	13,602	13,580	13,559	13,539	13,520	13,500
52	11,077	11,034	10,989	10,949	10,914	10,885	10,860	10,840	10,820	10,800
48	7,703	7,627	7,546	7,468	7,401	7,336	7,283	7,244	7,220	7,200
44	4,675	4,560	4,438	4,307	4,166	4,034	3,893	3,757	3,643	3,600
41	2,821	2,684	2,539	2,384	2,216	2,030	1,821	1,591	1,296	900
38	1,434	1,313	1,186	1,049	901	738	557	372	155	0
34	406	330	268	205	137	87	41	10	0	0
30	62	40	27	15	7	2	0	0	0	0
27	7	5	2	1	0	0	0	0	0	0
24	0	0	0	0	0	0	0	0	0	0

Name	Quantity	Description	Value	Position
Option 1	0	35 Call	6.252	0
Option 2	0	35 Call	6.595	0
Option 3	9	40 Call	2.639	2,375
Option 4	0	40 Call	3.339	0

Volatility	31.00
Precision	0

VOLATILITY

How does a trader forecast volatility? There is no proven method, but one can gain insights by tracking the history of implied volatility. When forecasting anything, a starting point is to gather historical information. There is, of course, no guarantee that this information, or any information, will lead to an accurate forecast, but it is the nature of trading to gather information, to make forecasts, and to act on those forecasts.

GREG'S DECISION

Greg has done a lot of work to arrive at this point of making a decision. If he believed that implied volatility would remain constant, he would choose to buy nine of the 40 calls. However, his belief that implied volatility could drop as much as 10 percent changes his choice to buying four of the 35 calls.

Not all traders, of course, would interpret this information the same way or make the same decision that Greg did. But that is not the point. The point is to demonstrate the analysis and decision-making process that Greg used.

SUMMARY

Buying options is different from buying stocks or futures contracts, because option prices behave differently from stock prices and futures prices. The forecasting process is also different. For options, a three-part forecast is essential. Options traders should start with a specific forecast for the underlying security. Second, a specific forecast for time is required. The third element is a forecast for the level of implied volatility after the change in stock price occurs.

13

VERTICAL SPREADS

INTRODUCTION

*S*PREAD* IS A LOOSELY USED TERM THAT DESCRIBES MANY MULTIPLE-PART OPTION STRATEGIES.* Some spreads involve both long and short options. Others involve only long or only short options. Therefore, having an understanding of how individual options change in price does not automatically lead to an intuitive understanding of how spread strategies change in price.

The goal of this chapter is to explain the unique aspects of vertical spreads, how to analyze them, and how to determine when they are appropriate for a particular market forecast and when they are not. The topics in this chapter include defining some specific spreads, analyzing their mechanics, and then discussing the motivations for choosing a spread, the market forecast, and some alternatives. In the process, many aspects of vertical spreads and the required thinking will be explained.

The examples in this chapter do not include transaction costs or margin requirements. Since spreads involve more than one option position, transaction costs and margin requirements can be higher than for single option positions, and they must be included in the analysis of any real strategy involving real options.

VERTICAL SPREAD DEFINED

A *vertical spread* involves the purchase of one option and the sale of a second option of the same type with the same underlying security and the same expiration, but with a different strike price. The term *vertical* describes the relationship of the strike prices, with one being higher, or over, or "vertical to," the other. Also, unless stated otherwise, the term *vertical spread* refers to one-to-one vertical spreads, in which one option is purchased and one is sold. *Ratio spreads*, as the name implies, involve the purchase (or sale) of one option and the sale (or purchase) of more than one of a second option.

BULL CALL SPREAD

The purchase of one call and simultaneous sale of a second call with the same underlying and same expiration but with a higher strike price is known as a bull call spread. Figure 13–1 illustrates a 70–80 bull call spread, in which one 70 call is purchased for $5.50, and one 80 call is sold for $1.50. The net cost of this spread, therefore, is $4, or $400, not including commissions.

The name *bull call spread* describes three aspects of the position. First, this is a *bull* call spread because the position has a tendency to profit if the underlying stock rises in price. In Figure 13–1, for example, the bull call spread achieves its maximum profit potential at expiration only if the stock is at or above $80. Second, this is a bull *call* spread because only call options are involved. Third, this is a *spread* because two different options are involved. In this example, *spread* refers to the $10 difference, or spread, between the strike prices of the 70 and 80 calls.

Bull call spreads are sometimes referred to as *debit call spreads* because they are established for a net cost, or net debit. The spread in Figure 13–1, for example, is purchased for a net cost, or net debit, of $4, or $400. Also, it is common practice to describe a spread using the lower strike first regardless of whether calls or puts are involved; hence the name for the position in Figure 13–1 is a 70–80 bull call spread.

PROFIT OR LOSS AT EXPIRATION—BULL CALL SPREAD

At expiration, there are three possible outcomes: The stock can be at or below the lower strike price, above the lower strike price but not above the higher strike price, or above the higher strike price. The straight line in Figure 13–1 illustrates these possibilities. If the stock level is at or below the lower strike price of a bull call spread at expiration, then both calls expire worthless, and

FIGURE 13–1   Bull call spread: long one 70 call @ $5.50 and short one 80 call @ $1.50

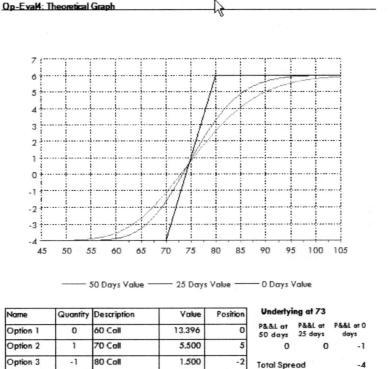

Op-Eval4: Theoretical Graph

——— 50 Days Value ——— 25 Days Value ——— 0 Days Value

Name	Quantity	Description	Value	Position
Option 1	0	60 Call	13.396	0
Option 2	1	70 Call	5.500	5
Option 3	-1	80 Call	1.500	-2
Option 4	0	90 Call	0.245	0

Underlying at 73

P&&L at 50 days	P&&L at 25 days	P&&L at 0 days
0	0	-1

Total Spread Value: -4

the full amount paid for the position, $400 plus commissions in this example, is lost.

If the stock is above the lower strike price but not above the higher strike price, then the long call (with the lower strike price) is exercised, and the short call (with the higher strike price) expires worthless. As a result, a long stock position is created. The stock price at expiration at which a bull call spread breaks even is equal to the lower strike price plus the net premium paid for the position. In Figure 13–1, for example, the breakeven stock price at expiration is $74, the lower strike price of $70 plus the net cost of $4.

If the stock price is above the higher strike price at expiration, then the long call is exercised and the short call is assigned. If the stock price is above $80 at expiration, for example, then exercising the 70 call creates a stock purchase transaction at $70, and assignment on the 80 call causes a stock sale transaction at $80, for a net receipt of $10 per share, or $1,000 per spread. The cost of the position, $400 in this example, is subtracted from the $1,000 received, and the result is a net profit of $6 per share, or $600, not including commissions.

Note that the maximum profit potential of a bull call spread is equal to the difference between the strike prices less the net cost of the spread. Also, the maximum profit is realized at expiration if the underlying stock is at or above the higher strike price.

BEAR CALL SPREAD

The sale of one call and the simultaneous purchase of a second call with the same underlying security and the same expiration, but with a higher strike price is known as a *bear call spread*. Figure 13–2 illustrates a 70–80 bear call spread in which one 70 call is sold for $5.50 and one 80 call is purchased for

FIGURE 13–2   **Bear call spread: short one 70 call @ $5.50 and long one 80 call @ $1.50**

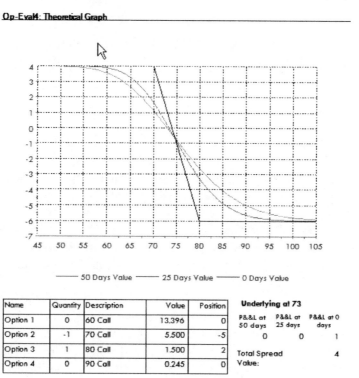

Op-Eval: Theoretical Graph

——— 50 Days Value ——— 25 Days Value ——— 0 Days Value

Name	Quantity	Description	Value	Position
Option 1	0	60 Call	13.396	0
Option 2	-1	70 Call	5.500	-5
Option 3	1	80 Call	1.500	2
Option 4	0	90 Call	0.245	0

Underlying at 73

	P&&L at 50 days	P&&L at 25 days	P&&L at 0 days
	0	0	1

Total Spread Value:	4

$1.50. The term *bear* means that the position has a tendency to profit as the underlying instrument declines in price. In Figure 13–2, the bear call spread achieves its maximum theoretical profit at expiration only if the stock is at or below $70 at expiration.

Bear call spreads are sometimes referred to as *credit call spreads* because they are established for a net receipt of premium or net credit. The spread in Figure 13–2, for example, is established for a net credit of $4, or $400.

PROFIT OR LOSS AT EXPIRATION—BEAR CALL SPREADS

At expiration, there are three possible outcomes: The stock can be at or below the lower strike price, above the lower strike price but not above the upper strike price, or above the upper strike price. The straight line in Figure 13–2 illustrates these possibilities. If the stock price is at or below the lower strike price of a bear call spread at expiration, then both calls expire worthless, and the net premium received, $400 in this example, is kept as income.

If the stock price is above the lower strike price but not above the upper strike price, then the short call (with the lower strike price) is assigned, and the long call (with the higher strike price) expires worthless. The net result is that a short stock position is created. The stock price at expiration at which a bear call spread breaks even is equal to the lower strike price plus the net premium received. In Figure 13–2, the breakeven stock price at expiration is $74, the lower strike price of $70 plus the net premium received of $4.

If the stock price is above the higher strike price at expiration, then the short call is assigned and the long call is exercised. In this example, if the stock price is above $80 at expiration, then assignment of the 70 call causes a stock sale transaction at $70, and exercise of the 80 call creates a stock purchase transaction at $80. The result is a net cash payment of $10 per share, or $1,000. The net cash payment at expiration, $1,000 in this example, is subtracted from the $400 net received when the position was established, and the result is a net loss of $6, or $600, not including commissions.

Note that the maximum potential loss on a bear call spread is equal to the difference between the strike prices less the net premium received for establishing the position. Also, this maximum loss is realized at expiration if the stock is at or above the higher strike price.

BEAR PUT SPREAD

The purchase of one put and the simultaneous sale of a second put with the same underlying security and the same expiration but with a lower strike price

FIGURE 13–3   Bear put spread: short one 60 put @ $1 and long one 70 put @ $5

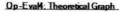

Op-Eval: Theoretical Graph

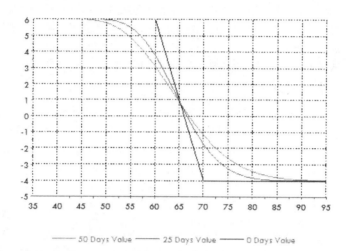

———— 50 Days Value ———— 25 Days Value ———— 0 Days Value

Name	Quantity	Description	Value	Position
Option 1	0	50 Put	0.026	0
Option 2	-1	60 Put	1.000	-1
Option 3	1	70 Put	5.000	5
Option 4	0	80 Put	13.248	0

Underlying at 67

P&&L at 50 days	P&&L at 25 days	P&&L at 0 days
0	0	-1

Total Spread Value: -4

is known as a *bear put spread*. Figure 13–3 illustrates a 60–70 bear put spread in which one 70 put is purchased for $5 and one 60 put is sold for $1.

Bear put spreads are sometimes referred to as *debit put spreads* because they are established for a net cost or net debit. The spread in Figure 13–3, for example, is established for a net cost, or net debit, of $4, or $400, not including commissions. Remember, it is common practice to describe a vertical spread using the lower strike price first regardless of whether calls or puts are involved; hence the name for the position in Figure 13–3 is a 60–70 bear put spread.

PROFIT OR LOSS AT EXPIRATION—BEAR PUT SPREAD

At expiration, there are three possible outcomes: The stock can be at or above the higher strike price, below the higher strike price but not below the lower strike price, and below the lower strike price. The straight line in Figure 13–3 illustrates these possibilities. If the stock price is at or above the upper strike price of a bear put spread at expiration, then both puts expire worthless, and the full amount paid for the position, $400 in this example, is lost.

If the stock is below the higher strike price but not below the lower strike price, then the long put (with the higher strike price) is exercised, and the short put (with the lower strike price) expires worthless. The net result is that a short stock position is created. The stock price at expiration at which a bear put spread breaks even is equal to the higher strike price minus the net premium paid for the position. In Figure 13–3, the breakeven stock price at expiration is $66, the higher strike price of $70 minus the net cost of $4.

If the stock is below the lower strike price at expiration, then the long put is exercised and the short put is assigned. The net result is a receipt of $10 per share in this example. The cost of the position, $400 in this example, is subtracted from the $1,000 received, and the result is a net profit of $6, or $600, not including commissions.

Note that the maximum potential profit on a bear put spread is equal to the difference between the strike prices less the net cost of the position. Also, this maximum profit is realized at expiration if the stock is at or below the lower strike price.

BULL PUT SPREAD

The sale of one put and the simultaneous purchase of a second put with the same underlying security and the same expiration but with a lower strike price is known as a *bull put spread*. Figure 13–4 illustrates a 60–70 bull put spread in which one 60 put is purchased for $1 and one 70 put is sold for $5.

Bull put spreads are sometimes referred to as *credit put spreads* because they are established for a net receipt, or net credit. The spread in Figure 13–4, for example, is established for a net receipt, or net credit, of $4, or $400, not including commissions. Once again, it is common practice to describe a vertical spread using the lower strike price first regardless of whether calls or puts are involved; hence the name for the position in Figure 13–4 is a 60–70 bull put spread.

PROFIT OR LOSS AT EXPIRATION—BULL PUT SPREAD

At expiration, there are three possible outcomes: The stock can be at or above the higher strike price, below the higher strike price but not below the lower strike price, and below the lower strike price. The straight line in Figure 13–4 illustrates these possibilities. If the stock price is at or above the upper strike

FIGURE 13–4   Bull put spread: long one 60 put @ $1 and short one 70 put @ $5

Op-Eval: Theoretical Graph

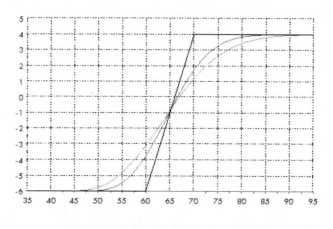

──────── 50 Days Value ──────── 25 Days Value ──────── 0 Days Value

Name	Quantity	Description	Value	Position
Option 1	0	50 Put	0.026	0
Option 2	1	60 Put	1.000	1
Option 3	-1	70 Put	5.000	-5
Option 4	0	80 Put	13.248	0

Underlying at 67

P&&L at 50 days	P&&L at 25 days	P&&L at 0 days
0	0	1

Total Spread Value: 4

price of a bull put spread at expiration, then both puts expire worthless, and the full amount received, $400 less commissions in this example, is kept as income.

If the stock price is below the higher strike price but not below the lower strike price, then the short put (with the higher strike price) is assigned, and the long put (with the lower strike price) expires worthless. The result is that a long stock position is created. The stock level at expiration at which a bull put spread breaks even is equal to the higher strike price minus the net premium received. In Figure 13–4, the breakeven stock price at expiration is $66, the higher strike price of $70 minus the $4 received.

If the stock price is below the lower strike price at expiration, then the short put is assigned and the long put is exercised. The net result is a payment of $10 per share, or $1,000 per spread. The credit received for initiating the spread, $400 in this example, is subtracted from the $1,000 paid at expiration, and the result is the net loss of $6, or $600, not including commissions.

Note that the maximum potential loss of a bull put spread is equal to the difference between the strike prices less the net credit received. Also, this maximum loss is realized at expiration if the stock is at or below the lower strike price.

TRADING CASE STUDY—SPREADS VERSUS LONG OPTIONS

Frank is an active trader who has a quote machine on his desk at work and who trades options regularly. Frank has a typical holding period of 30 to 60 days, but he is not averse to taking profits (or losses) if the market moves faster than he initially predicts. Recently, Frank has been paying close attention to Riser Industries, a blue chip type of company with slow, but steady and predictable earnings growth. Riser is currently trading at $31 per share. Earnings announcements have passed without the stock price moving, but Frank thinks that the time for a 10 percent stock price advance is close. How close Frank cannot say for sure, but 30 to 60 days is his guess, and he is willing to invest $2,500 on his forecast. Frank is considering taking a bullish position on Riser.

CAPITAL MANAGEMENT AND STRATEGY ALTERNATIVES

Let's see how Frank can choose between alternatives with approximately the same maximum theoretical risk. Although Frank has many alternatives involving calls and puts with different strike prices and expiration dates, for the sake of simplicity, we will examine only two strategies, buying 60-day Riser 30 calls and buying 60-day Riser 30–35 bull call spreads. The purpose of this example is to demonstrate how the price behavior of vertical spreads differs from the price behavior of long options. Although this example uses call options to illustrate several points, the concepts apply equally to puts.

IDENTIFYING THE ALTERNATIVES

Given that Frank has allocated $2,500 to this trade, two strategies that he can evaluate are the purchase of ten 60-day 30 calls and the purchase of fourteen 60-day 30–35 bull call spreads. The 30 calls are trading at $2.50, and the 35 calls are trading at $0.75. Dividing the capital available by the cost of the strategy and then rounding to the nearest whole number determines the maximum number of units for each strategy.

The number of 30 calls that can be purchased is 10. This is calculated by dividing the capital of $2,500 by the 30 call price of $2.50, or $250. By the same process, it is calculated that 14 of the 30–35 bull call spreads can be purchased for $2,450 (14 × $175). Both strategies cost approximately $2,500, not including commissions.

ESTIMATING RESULTS

To help him decide, Frank uses Op-Eval4 to create Figures 13–5 and 13–6 to estimate the results of these strategies under different market forecasts. Since Frank does not have a specific time period in his forecast, other than 30 to 60 days, the tables will make it easy for him to estimate the profits from the predicted 10 percent price rise over a range of time periods.

FIGURE 13–5   Frank's analysis of the Riser 30 call long 10 calls at $2.50 each, $2,500 total

Value	90 days	80 days	70 days	60 days	50 days	40 days	30 days	20 days	10 days	0 days
50	20,155	20,135	20,117	20,099	20,082	20,066	20,049	20,033	20,016	20,000
46	16,175	16,149	16,124	16,103	16,084	16,066	16,049	16,033	16,016	16,000
42	12,246	12,203	12,160	12,127	12,096	12,071	12,050	12,033	12,016	12,000
39	9,385	9,317	9,256	9,192	9,142	9,095	9,059	9,034	9,016	9,000
35	5,847	5,730	5,627	5,516	5,397	5,285	5,174	5,081	5,021	5,000
31	2,947	2,808	2,659	2,500	2,327	2,137	1,927	1,692	1,388	1,000
27	1,024	914	806	689	564	425	295	156	37	0
23	195	153	115	75	47	23	8	1	0	0
20	30	18	11	5	2	1	0	0	0	0
16	1	0	0	0	0	0	0	0	0	0

Name	Quantity	Description	Value	Position
Option 1	0	27.5 Call	4.152	0
Option 2	10	30 Call	2.500	2,500
Option 3	0	32.5 Call	1.446	0
Option 4	0	35 Call	0.750	0

Volatility	38.53
Precision	0

**FIGURE 13–6   Frank's analysis of the Riser 30–35 bull call spread long 14
spreads at $1.75 each, $2,450 Total**

Value	90 days	80 days	70 days	60 days	50 days	40 days	30 days	20 days	10 days	0 days
50	6,933	6,948	6,962	6,971	6,979	6,984	6,988	6,992	6,996	7,000
46	6,835	6,869	6,907	6,935	6,960	6,977	6,987	6,992	6,996	7,000
42	6,520	6,587	6,666	6,754	6,822	6,895	6,950	6,983	6,996	7,000
39	5,952	6,054	6,173	6,305	6,430	6,570	6,725	6,871	6,977	7,000
35	4,607	4,679	4,756	4,858	4,981	5,127	5,320	5,586	5,981	7,000
31	2,592	2,566	2,528	2,465	2,397	2,329	2,217	2,053	1,778	1,400
27	860	783	688	585	474	361	229	108	18	0
23	111	84	59	36	18	7	2	0	0	0
20	9	5	2	1	0	0	0	0	0	0
16	0	0	0	0	0	0	0	0	0	0

Name	Quantity	Description	Value	Position
Option 1	0	27.5 Call	4.205	0
Option 2	14	30 Call	2.500	3,500
Option 3	0	32.5 Call	1.446	0
Option 4	-14	35 Call	0.750	-1,050

Volatility	40.00
Precision	0

Frank believes that Riser's stock price will move from $31 to $34 or $35 sometime in the next 30 to 60 days. The highlighted cells in the tables in Figures 13–5 and 13–6 are the starting point for both strategies. If the price rise takes 30 days, then the results of buying 10 Riser 30 calls are shown in Figure 13–5 in the cell that is one row above and three cells to the right of the highlighted cell. The table shows that 10 of the 30 calls are estimated to have a value of $5,174. The same cell in Figure 13–6, however, indicates that 14 of the 30–35 bull call spreads will have a value of $5,320.

The difference between the two strategies is not significant at 30 days to expiration, so look over three more cells to the right to find the estimated results if Riser stock is at $35 at option expiration in 60 days. Figure 13–5 indicates that 10 of the 30 calls will have a value of $5,000, and Figure 13–6 indicates that 14 of the 30–35 bull call spreads will have a value of $7,000. This difference is significant.

At this point, assuming that these estimates are accurate, the conclusion is that purchasing 14 of the Riser 30–35 bull call spreads will yield the highest profit.

A DIFFERENT FORECAST LEADS TO A DIFFERENT STRATEGY

Suppose that Frank believes that a 10 percent price rise is conservative and that a 20 percent price rise is possible. A look at the estimated values in the cells two rows above the highlighted cell indicate that, with a stock price of $39 at any time prior to expiration, the position of 10 of the 30 calls has a higher value than the position of 14 of the 30–35 bull call spreads. With the new forecast, the bull call spread fell to second place.

The conclusion is that, when choosing between purchasing calls outright and purchasing bull call spreads, assuming a constant amount of capital, short, sharp price rises favor the purchase of calls outright. Smaller price rises over a longer time period favor the bull call spreads.

CHANGING THE VOLATILITY

What should traders do when they have a strong opinion about market direction but are worried about an adverse change in volatility? Such a situation might arise when an earnings report is eagerly awaited, as Greg experienced in Chapter 12.

Space does not permit a detailed explanation of the impact of changing volatility on vertical spreads relative to outright long or short options, but one-to-one vertical spreads can be much less sensitive to changes in volatility than single option positions. When traders think that volatility risk is high, one-to-one vertical spreads may be the strategy of choice.

CREDIT SPREADS VERSUS SELLING UNCOVERED OPTIONS

Many traders ask which is better, selling vertical spreads or selling uncovered options? Unfortunately, there is no simple answer to this question because the strategies involve different short-term risks and different maximum theoretical risks. Uncovered short stock options involve substantial or unlimited risk, and this strategy is suitable only for experienced traders who are financially and psychologically able to assume such a risk.

Which is better? There is no "better." Short uncovered options and credit spreads are strategies that offer a choice between two sets of trade-offs. Choosing between them is a personal decision that can be made only by traders themselves based on their market forecast and tolerance for risk. This may be an unsatisfying answer to those who want a clear choice. Unfortunately, there are rarely clear choices in trading, whether what is being traded is options, stocks, or futures. One advantage of options is that they provide traders with a wide range of alternatives. But only a trader can decide which alternative is "best" for a particular forecast. And, of course, the risk is that the forecast is wrong and a loss will be incurred.

SUMMARY

There are four basic one-to-one vertical spreads. Assuming the same underlying security and expiration date, a bull call spread consists of a long call with a lower strike price and a short call with a higher strike price. A bear call spread consists of a short call with a lower strike price and a long call with a higher strike price. A bear put spread consists of a long put with a higher strike price and a short put with a lower strike price. A bull put spread consists of a short put with a higher strike price and a long put with a lower strike price. Regardless of whether calls or puts are involved, it is common practice to refer to vertical spreads using the lower strike price first.

The prices of vertical spreads behave differently from the prices of at-the-money or out-of-the-money single options. Consequently, the same three-part forecasting technique, including a price forecast, a time forecast, and a volatility forecast, used for individual options must be used with vertical spreads. Different forecasts will lead to the selection of different strategies.

Vertical spreads tend to be less sensitive to changes in implied volatility than single option positions. This means that vertical spreads may be a preferred choice when a forecast calls for a decrease in implied volatility.

Selling vertical spreads and selling uncovered options are not directly comparable because they involve different risks and different profit potentials. There are no "better" strategies. Traders must make individual judgments about their level of confidence in their forecasts and their tolerance for risk when choosing between alternative strategies.

C H A P 14 E R

STRADDLES AND STRANGLES

INTRODUCTION

THE NAMES *STRADDLE* AND *STRANGLE* MAY SOUND EXOTIC, BUT THEY ARE NO DIFFERENT FROM OTHER OPTION STRATEGIES. They are not "better" than other strategies; they simply offer a unique set of trade-offs. Understanding the trade-offs of any strategy is key to knowing when to use that strategy. In a format similar to that of the previous chapter, on vertical spreads, this chapter will present four strategies by starting with a profit-and-loss diagram, then explaining the mechanics and price behavior of the strategy, and, finally, discussing the motivation that would lead to the choice of that strategy.

LONG STRADDLE DEFINED

A long straddle involves the simultaneous purchase of one call and one put with the same strike price, the same expiration, and the same underlying security. Figure 14–1 illustrates a long 50 straddle that is established by purchasing one 50 call for $3.50, or $350, and simultaneously purchasing one 50 put for $3, or $300. The total cost, therefore, is $6.50, or $650. It is common practice to describe a straddle using the strike price, because the strike price is the same

FIGURE 14–1   Long straddle: long one 50 call @ $3.50 and long one 50 put @ $3

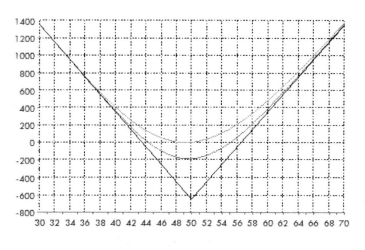

Name	Quantity	Description	Value	Position
Option 1	0	45 Put	0.867	0
Option 2	1	50 Put	3.000	300
Option 3	1	50 Call	3.500	350
Option 4	0	55 Call	1.164	0

Underlying at 50

P&&L at 60 days	P&&L at 30 days	P&&L at 0 days
0	-190	-650

Total Spread Value: -650

for both the call and put. Hence the name for the position in Figure 14–1 is a long 50 straddle. *Long* indicates that both options are purchased.

  Straddle is an appropriate name, because it means taking both sides at the same time, and this strategy has the potential of profiting from either up or down movements in the underlying stock.

LONG STRADDLE—PROFIT OR LOSS AT EXPIRATION
At expiration, there are three possible outcomes. The stock can be above the strike price, below the strike price, or at the strike price. The straight line in Figure 14–1 illustrates these possibilities. If the stock price is above the strike price at expiration, then the call is exercised and the put expires worthless. The result is that a long stock position is created. The effective price is the strike

price plus the total premium paid for the straddle. If the stock price is above the strike price but below the upper breakeven point at expiration, then the result is a loss. In Figure 14–1, the upper breakeven stock price at expiration is $56.50.

If the stock price is below the strike price at expiration, then the put is exercised and the call expires worthless. The result is that a short stock position is created. The effective price is the strike price minus the total premium paid for the straddle. If the stock price is below the strike price but above the lower breakeven point at expiration, then the result is a loss. In Figure 14–1, the lower breakeven stock price at expiration is $43.50.

Expiration profit-and-loss analysis is beneficial, because it reveals the stock prices at which the best possible and worst possible outcomes occur. Such analysis, however, does not help short-term traders understand how the strategy behaves prior to expiration. The following discussion addresses pricing issues that short-term traders should consider.

BUYING STRADDLES

Lisa is confident and unsure at the same time!

She is confidently predicting that the price of Gonzo, Inc. will move sharply in response to its earnings report this week, but she is unsure about the direction. She is thinking, "News good, Gonzo up; news bad, Gonzo down; but which will it be?" Consequently, she is considering the purchase of a 60-day Gonzo 50 straddle. "As long as Gonzo moves," Lisa says, "I'll make a profit."

Figure 14–2 tends to confirm Lisa's logic, but a loss can still result if the market does not move sufficiently in either direction. Figure 14–2 contains a table of theoretical values created using Op-Eval4. The value in each box is the dollar value of one 50 straddle, assuming the indicated stock price and days to expiration. Lisa's starting position is the highlighted cell, a 50 straddle value of 650 with the stock price at $50 and 60 days to expiration.

The table in Figure 14–2 estimates how the value of the 50 straddle changes over a range of stock prices at different numbers of days prior to expiration, assuming that volatility, interest rates, and dividends remain constant. If, for example, the stock rises $4 in 10 days to a price of $54 at 50 days prior to expiration, then the value of the straddle is estimated to be $706. That would amount to a profit of $56, not including commissions. If, however, it takes 30 days for the stock price to rise $4, then the value of the straddle is estimated to be $588, for a loss of $62.

The table in Figure 14–2 makes an important point about straddles. If the stock price is at the strike price when a straddle is purchased, down moves gen-

FIGURE 14–2   Gonzo 50 straddle theoretical table

Value	90 days	80 days	70 days	60 days	50 days	40 days	30 days	20 days	10 days	0 days
70	2,066	2,053	2,041	2,029	2,020	2,014	2,009	2,006	2,003	2,000
66	1,706	1,686	1,668	1,648	1,634	1,621	1,612	1,606	1,603	1,600
62	1,379	1,347	1,322	1,294	1,266	1,244	1,224	1,209	1,203	1,200
58	1,103	1,064	1,022	985	946	904	866	830	806	800
54	901	857	811	761	706	647	588	518	445	400
50	796	750	702	650	594	531	460	376	266	0
46	830	790	747	702	652	605	552	491	431	400
42	983	958	931	903	875	850	827	809	800	800
38	1,257	1,243	1,232	1,220	1,212	1,205	1,202	1,200	1,200	1,200
34	1,610	1,606	1,604	1,602	1,601	1,600	1,600	1,600	1,600	1,600

Name	Quantity	Description	Value	Position
Option 1	0	45 Put	0.867	0
Option 2	1	50 Put	3.000	300
Option 3	1	50 Call	3.500	350
Option 4	0	55 Call	1.164	0

Volatility	40.43
Precision	0

erally have to be larger than up moves in order for a profit to be realized. An $8 rise in the stock price in 10 days, for example, is estimated to result in a straddle value of $946. However, an $8 stock price decline to $42 causes the straddle to rise to only $875. The reason for this asymmetrical price action is the assumption about stock prices in the option pricing formula. Stock prices are assumed to be "log normally distributed." This means that there is a slightly greater chance that stock prices will rise than that they will fall. A result of this assumption is that time premiums in puts erode more quickly than time premiums in calls, especially as an option becomes in-the-money.

How much of a change in the stock and over what period of time justify the purchase of a straddle? Unfortunately, there is no objective answer to this question. Lisa must consider her forecast and make a personal assessment of the potential profits and risks. The creation of value estimates such as the table in Figure 14–2 is helpful in making this decision.

TESTING SCENARIOS

The spread positions feature in Op-Eval4 can be used to "test" various scenarios that do not appear in the theoretical-value table. Suppose, for example, that Lisa forecasts that the Gonzo stock will be $10 higher or lower in 20 days and that volatility will decline 5 percent. As mentioned earlier, Lisa's forecast for the change in the stock is based on her belief that the earnings reports will be good or bad and that the market will react strongly. Her forecast for a decrease in implied volatility could be based on her knowledge that implied volatility has risen in recent days, perhaps in anticipation of the report, and on her belief that implied volatility will "return to normal" after the report. Figure 14–3 shows how Op-Eval4 might be used to test this forecast.

Figure 14–3 contains a spread positions page from Op-Eval4 in which columns 1 and 2 analyze Lisa's straddle if the stock price rises and columns 3 and 4 analyze the outcome if the stock price falls. The "Value" row in column

FIGURE 14–3   Lisa's specific forecast: stock price up or down $10 in 20 days with volatility down 5 percent

Spread Positions	Option 1	Option 2	Option 3	Option 4	Spread Greeks	Total
IsIndex	☐	☐	☐	☐	Value	0.000
IsEuropean	☐	☐	☐	☐	Delta	0.000
Quantity	0	0	0	0	Gamma	0.000
Type	Put	Call	Put	Call	Vega	0.000
Stock Price	40.000	40.000	60.000	60.000	Theta	0.000
Strike Price	50.000	50.000	50.000	50.000	Rho	0.000
Volatility %	35.000	35.000	35.000	35.000		
Interest %*	2.000	2.000	2.000	2.000		
Dividend*	0.000	0.000	0.000	0.000		
Ex-Div Days*	0	0	0	0		
Expiry Days*	40	40	40	40		
Multiplier*	1	1	1	1	Price +1	Days +1
Value	10.012	0.055	0.151	10.260		
Delta	-0.982	0.031	-0.049	0.951	Price -1	Days -1

1 indicates that the 50 put will be trading at $10 if the stock price is $40 with 40 days to expiration and volatility of 35 percent, down 5 percent from the initial estimate. In column 2, the 50 call is estimated to be trading at 5 cents, so the 50 straddle is estimated to be trading at $10.05 with Gonzo stock trading at $40.

Columns 3 and 4 estimate that with a stock price of $60, the 50 call will be $10.26 and the 50 put will be $0.15, for a total 50 straddle value of approximately $10.40.

What can Lisa conclude from this information? If Lisa believes in this forecast, then Figure 14–3 indicates that she should buy the 60-day 50 straddle! Both the up-market scenario and the down-market scenario result in a profit. A different scenario, however, might lead to a different conclusion. Should Lisa believe her forecast? That is a subjective decision that only she can make, based on her conviction and her tolerance for risk. The important lesson for all traders to learn is that the analysis involved a three-part forecast: for the change in the stock price, for the timing of the expected change, and for the implied volatility. When trading straddles, the second and third parts of this analysis are especially important, because straddles involve two options.

SHORT STRADDLE DEFINED

A short straddle involves the simultaneous sale of one call and one put with the same strike price, the same expiration, and the same underlying security. Figure 14–4 illustrates a short 50 straddle that is established by selling one 50 call for $3.50 and one 50 put for $3, for a total amount received of $6.50.

SHORT STRADDLE—PROFIT OR LOSS AT EXPIRATION

At expiration, there are three possible outcomes: The stock can be above the strike price, below the strike price, or at the strike price. The straight line in Figure 14–4 illustrates these possibilities. If the stock price is above the strike price at expiration, then the call is assigned and the put expires worthless. The result is that a short stock position is created. The effective price is the strike price plus the total premium received for the straddle. If the stock price is above the upper breakeven point at expiration, then the result is a loss. In Figure 14–4, the upper breakeven stock price at expiration is $56.50.

If the stock price is below the strike price at expiration, then the put is assigned and the call expires worthless. The result is that a long stock position is created. The effective price is the strike price minus the total premium

FIGURE 14–4   Short straddle: short one 50 call @ $3.50 and short one 50 put @ $3

Op-Eval4: Theoretical Graph

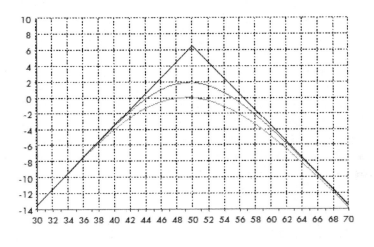

———— 60 Days Value   ———— 30 Days Value   ———— 0 Days Value

Name	Quantity	Description	Value	Position
Option 1	0	45 Put	1.200	0
Option 2	-1	50 Put	3.000	-3
Option 3	-1	50 Call	3.500	-3
Option 4	0	55 Call	1.500	0

Underlying at 50

	P&&L at 60 days	P&&L at 30 days	P&&L at 0 days
	0	2	6
Total Spread Value:			6

received for the straddle. If the stock price is below the lower breakeven point at expiration, then the result is a loss. In Figure 14–4, the lower breakeven stock price at expiration is $43.50.

If the stock is exactly at the strike price at expiration, then both the call and the put expire worthless, and the full amount received initially, $650 in this example, is kept as income.

SELLING STRADDLES

Selling straddles is, essentially, the opposite of buying straddles. Whereas the straddle buyer hopes for a "big" move in either direction and an increase in implied volatility, the straddle seller hopes for no movement at all and a decrease in implied volatility.

Short straddles involve two uncovered short options, so the risk is unlimited. Consequently, the use of this strategy with stock options is suitable only for experienced traders who are financially and psychologically capable of assuming this level of risk and who receive approval from their brokerage firm to use this strategy. Many beginning options traders are drawn to strategies that involve selling options. Frequently, their logic goes like this, "Look how much I can make from time decay!" This potential benefit, however, is balanced by the risk of an increase in implied volatility and the risk of a large move in either direction.

Traders who sell options in general and straddles in specific are well advised to have as much information as possible about the underlying stock and the level of the implied volatility of the options they are selling. They should be confident that they are selling options when implied volatility is high, in their opinion. There are no guarantees that this knowledge will avoid a loss, but the purpose of gathering as much information as possible is to reduce risk as much as possible.

LONG STRANGLE DEFINED

A long strangle involves the simultaneous purchase of one call with a higher strike price and one put with the same expiration and the same underlying security but with a lower strike price. Figure 14–5 illustrates a long 45–55 strangle that is established by purchasing one 45 put for $1.15 and one 55 call for $1.50, for a total cost of $2.65. It is common practice to describe a strangle using the lower strike price first. Hence the name for the position in Figure 14–5 is a long 45–55 strangle. *Long* indicates that both options are purchased. The origin of the term *strangle* is unknown, but it starts with the same letters as *straddle* and may have been coined for convenience.

LONG STRANGLE—PROFIT OR LOSS AT EXPIRATION

At expiration, there are four possible outcomes: The stock can be above the higher strike price, below the lower strike price, at one of the strike prices, or between the strike prices. The straight line in Figure 14–5 illustrates these possibilities. If the stock price is above the higher strike price at expiration, then the call is exercised and the put expires worthless. The result is that a long stock position is created. The effective price is the higher strike price plus the total premium paid for the strangle. If the stock price is above the higher strike price but below the upper breakeven point at expiration, then the result is a loss. In Figure 14–5, the upper breakeven stock price at expiration is $57.65.

FIGURE 14–5   Long strangle: long one 45 put @ $1.15 and long one 55 call @ $1.50

Op-Eval4: Theoretical Graph

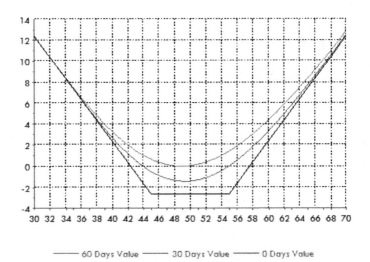

Name	Quantity	Description	Value	Position
Option 1	1	45 Put	1.150	1
Option 2	0	50 Put	3.000	0
Option 3	0	50 Call	3.500	0
Option 4	1	55 Call	1.500	2

Underlying at 50

P&&L at 60 days	P&&L at 30 days	P&&L at 0 days
0	-1	-3

Total Spread Value:		-3

If the stock price is below the lower strike price at expiration, then the put is exercised and the call expires worthless. The result is that a short stock position is created. The effective price is the lower strike price minus the total premium paid for the strangle. If the stock price is below the lower strike price but above the lower breakeven point at expiration, then the result is a loss. In Figure 14–5, the lower breakeven stock price at expiration is $42.35.

If the stock price is at either strike price or between the strike prices at expiration, then both the call and the put expire worthless, and the full amount paid for the strangle is lost.

SHORT STRANGLE DEFINED

A short strangle involves the simultaneous sale of one call with a higher strike price and one put with the same expiration and the same underlying security, but with a lower strike price. Figure 14–6 illustrates a short 45–55 strangle that is established by selling one 45 put for $1.15 and one 55 call for $1.50, for a total amount received of $2.65.

SHORT STRANGLE—PROFIT OR LOSS AT EXPIRATION

At expiration, there are four possible outcomes: The stock can be above the higher strike price, below the lower strike price, at one of the strike prices, or between the strike prices. The straight line in Figure 14–6 illustrates these possibilities. If the stock price is above the higher strike price at expiration, then

FIGURE 14–6   Short strangle: short one 45 put @ $1.15 and short one 55 call @ $1.50

Op-Eval4: Theoretical Graph

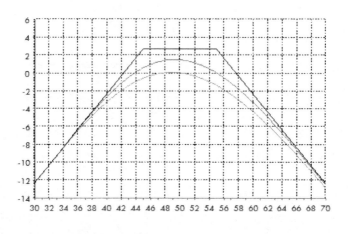

Name	Quantity	Description	Value	Position
Option 1	-1	45 Put	1.150	-1
Option 2	0	50 Put	3.000	0
Option 3	0	50 Call	3.500	0
Option 4	-1	55 Call	1.500	-2

Underlying at 50

P&&L at 60 days	P&&L at 30 days	P&&L at 0 days
0	1	3

Total Spread Value: 3

the call is assigned and the put expires worthless. The result is that a short stock position is created. The effective price is the higher strike price plus the total premium received for the strangle. If the stock price is above the upper breakeven point at expiration, then the result is a loss. In Figure 14–6, the upper breakeven stock price at expiration is $57.65.

If the stock price is below the lower strike price at expiration, then the put is assigned and the call expires worthless. The result is that a long stock position is created. The effective price is the lower strike price minus the total premium received for the strangle. If the stock price is below the lower breakeven point at expiration, then the result is a loss. In Figure 14–6, the lower breakeven stock price at expiration is $42.35.

If the stock is exactly at either strike price or between the strike prices at expiration, then both the call and the put expire worthless, and the full amount received initially is kept as income.

STRADDLES VERSUS STRANGLES

A comparison of the expiration profit-and-loss diagrams reveals that straddles and strangles offer different sets of trade-offs. This discussion will focus on long, or purchased, straddles and strangles, but similar reasoning applies to short straddles and strangles.

First, compare the expiration profit-and-loss diagrams in Figures 14–1 and 14–5. The straddle is purchased for $6.50, and the strangle is purchased for $2.65. The straddle is more expensive, a disadvantage, but its breakeven points are $56.50 and $43.50, closer together than the strangle's breakeven points of $57.65 and $42.35. The relative closeness of the straddle's breakeven points is an advantage.

Also, consider the chances that the result of buying a straddle will be a total loss of the premium paid. In order for this to occur, the stock price must be exactly at the strike price at expiration. For the strangle to incur its maximum loss, however, the stock can be at or between the two strike prices. In the examples in this chapter, that is a $10 range. Whatever the chances are that the long straddle will incur its maximum loss, the chances that the long strangle will do so are greater.

The conclusion is that neither strategy is better in an absolute sense. A long straddle costs more than a comparable long strangle, but its breakeven points at expiration are closer together and there is less of a chance that the maximum loss will be incurred. Now consider the profit and risk potential of the two strategies for short-term traders.

PRICE BEHAVIOR—STRADDLES VERSUS STRANGLES

The table in Figure 14–7 contains the values of a 45–55 strangle that are comparable to the values of the 50 straddle in the table in Figure 14–2. Assuming an initial stock price of $50 and 60 days to expiration, which is the highlighted cell in both tables, an $8 rise or fall in the stock in any time frame yields a higher absolute profit for the straddle. At 50 days with a stock price of $58, for example, the straddle value is $944, up $296, compared to the strangle value of $526, up $261. In this case, the larger investment in the straddle earned a higher profit. However, the profit as a percentage was higher for the strangle. Over a longer time period, the same holds true. At 20 days to expiration with a stock price of $62, for example, the straddle value is $1,209, up $559 and 86 percent. In comparison, the strangle value of $731, while up only $466 in

FIGURE 14–7   Lisa's evaluation of a 45–55 strangle

Value	90 days	80 days	70 days	60 days	50 days	40 days	30 days	20 days	10 days	0 days
70	1,594	1,578	1,561	1,547	1,534	1,523	1,513	1,507	1,503	1,500
66	1,247	1,225	1,203	1,180	1,161	1,141	1,125	1,111	1,103	1,100
62	934	905	877	847	817	788	759	731	708	700
58	672	635	600	564	526	487	444	397	347	300
54	485	447	406	362	318	270	220	164	100	0
50	390	348	307	265	221	172	120	68	19	0
46	407	373	337	298	259	218	174	127	76	0
42	542	516	491	464	437	409	380	352	320	300
38	786	772	759	745	732	721	710	703	700	700
34	1,117	1,113	1,108	1,104	1,102	1,100	1,100	1,100	1,100	1,100

Name	Quantity	Description	Value	Position
Option 1	1	45 Put	1.150	115
Option 2	0	50 Put	3.000	0
Option 3	0	50 Call	3.500	0
Option 4	1	55 Call	1.500	150

Volatility	39.90
Precision	0

absolute dollars, is up 182 percent. As before, the straddle value increased more in absolute terms, but the strangle value increased more in percentage terms.

The situation is different, however, in unprofitable outcomes. If the stock price is 44 at 10 days to expiration, then both strategies incur a loss. The straddle value has declined to $445, an absolute loss of $205 and a 31 percent loss on the initial investment. In comparison, the strangle value declined to $100, a lower absolute loss of $165, but a higher percentage loss of 62 percent.

This difference in profit measurement when absolute results are compared to percentage results is significant, because it emphasizes the need for traders to define their profit goals in advance of a trade. Any forecast will tend to favor one strategy over another depending on how the profit target is stated.

SUMMARY

Long straddles involve the purchase of a call and a put with the same underlying security, the same expiration, and the same strike price. Short straddles involve the sale of both. Strangles are different from straddles in that they involve calls and puts with different strike prices. When considering these strategies, it is important to draw an expiration profit-and-loss diagram first so that the best and worst possible outcomes are fully understood. Short straddles and strangles involve unlimited risk and are suitable only for experienced traders who are financially and psychologically capable of assuming this risk and who receive approval from their brokerage firm to use these strategies.

Studying straddles and strangles involves the same method of analysis presented in previous chapters. First, have a three-part forecast: a target for the underlying stock, a prediction for the time period, and an outlook for implied volatility. Second, estimate the price of each option in a position and then calculate the estimated profit or loss. Third, evaluate a number of alternative strategies and select the one that best fits your personal risk/reward parameters.

Advanced Topics

15

RATIO SPREADS FOR INVESTORS AND TRADERS

INTRODUCTION

A *RATIO SPREAD* INVOLVES THE PURCHASE OF ONE QUANTITY OF AN OPTION AND THE SALE OF A DIFFERENT QUANTITY OF ANOTHER OPTION. This chapter focuses on one-by-two (1 × 2) ratio spreads in which the one option is purchased and the two options are sold. The options are of the same type, have the same underlying security and the same expiration date, but have different strike prices. This type of ratio spread is commonly known as a *ratio vertical spread* because of the relationship of the strike prices: One strike price is higher than, or vertical to, the other. The strategy of purchasing two options and selling one option is frequently described as a *ratio volatility spread*.

This chapter will present four examples of how ratio spreads might be used, three for conservative investors and one for aggressive traders. As with the examples in previous chapters, commissions, margin requirements, and taxes are not included. Since ratio spreads involve two or more option positions, transaction costs and margin requirements can be higher than for single option positions. Also, some uses of ratio spreads involve uncovered short options, which means that these strategies are suitable only for experienced options traders who receive the specific approval of their brokerage firms.

ADDING LEVERAGE WITHOUT INCREASING RISK

Adding a ratio spread with calls to a long stock position has three parts that are usually implemented simultaneously. First, stock is purchased. Second, one at-the-money call is purchased for each 100 shares that are purchased. Third, two out-of-the-money calls are sold for each 100 shares that are purchased. Consider how Britton, a conservative investor, uses a ratio spread to improve the profit potential of his forecast for Tailorco, a men's wholesale clothing chain.

Today is April 5. Tailorco is currently trading at $70, and the June 70 and 75 calls are trading at $5 and $2.50, respectively. Given his forecast for a modest price rise in the stock by June expiration, Britton believes that the purchase of Tailorco stock at $70, the purchase of one June 70 call for $5 and the sale of two 75 calls at $2.50 each will outperform the stock alone. Britton creates

TABLE 15–1   Profit and Loss at Expiration: Long Stock @ $70, Long 1 70 Call and Short 2 75 Calls

Stock Price at Expiration	Long Stock @ $70 Profit/(Loss)	Long 1 70 Call @ $5 Profit/(Loss)	Short 2 75 Calls @ $2.50 each Profit/(Loss)	Combined Profit/(Loss)
77.00	+7.00	+2.00	+1.00	+10.00
76.00	+6.00	+1.00	+3.00	+10.00
75.00	+5.00	0.00	+5.00	+10.00
74.00	+4.00	(1.00)	+5.00	+8.00
73.00	+3.00	(2.00)	+5.00	+6.00
72.00	+2.00	(3.00)	+5.00	+4.00
71.00	+1.00	(4.00)	+5.00	+2.00
70.00	0.00	(5.00)	+5.00	0.00
69.00	(1.00)	(5.00)	+5.00	(1.00)
68.00	(2.00)	(5.00)	+5.00	(2.00)
67.00	(3.00)	(5.00)	+5.00	(3.00)

FIGURE 15–1   Long stock with ratio call spread compared to long stock

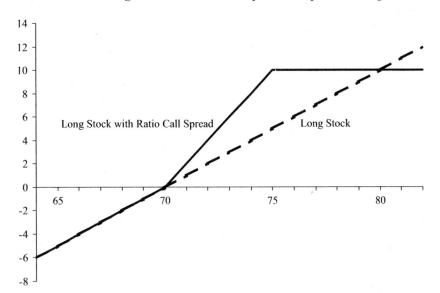

Table 15–1 and Figure 15–1 to show how this strategy will perform on a per-share basis.

ANALYZING THE POSSIBILITIES

At option expiration, the price of Tailorco stock could be (1) at or below $70, (2) between $70 and $75, or (3) above $75. Britton considers each possibility.

If the price of Tailorco stock is at or below $70 at expiration, then all the options expire worthless. The amount of the loss depends entirely on the price of Tailorco stock, because, in this example, the ratio spread was established for a zero net cost, not including commissions. At a stock price of $67, for example, the result is a loss of $3 per share.

If the stock price is between $70 and $75 at expiration, then the profit is twice the stock profit. With Tailorco stock at $72, for example, the profit is $4 per share. Half of this profit comes from the stock price rise from $70 to $72, and the other half comes from the value of the 70 call. Such an outcome, the 70 call being in-the-money, must be planned for. It must be decided whether to exercise the call or sell it. If it is exercised, then the shares must be purchased, which requires the commitment of additional cash.

The third possible outcome is for the price of Tailorco stock to be above $75 at expiration. If this happens, then the owned 70 call is exercised and the short 75 calls are assigned. This exercise and assignment causes another 100 shares to be purchased and all shares (200) to be sold. The net result is that Britton's stock position plus the profit will be converted into cash less transaction costs.

Early assignment of one or both of the short calls is also a possibility. Although an early assignment would not increase the risk of this strategy, it might be confusing to an inexperienced option user. Therefore, before using this strategy, it is important to understand the process and to have a plan in place in case it is necessary to respond.

SOME OBSERVATIONS

There are four observations to be made. First and foremost, there are no uncovered short calls. One short call is covered by the owned stock, and the other is covered by the owned 70 call. Second, the downside risk, in this example, is equal to that of a long stock position. Third, if the price of Tailorco stock rises to $75, profits are greater than those from simply owning the stock. A final observation is that the profit potential is limited. When the stock price is above the strike price of the short options, 75 in this example, the maximum profit potential has been achieved.

TRADE-OFFS

Every strategy has its own advantages and disadvantages, and adding a ratio call spread to a long stock position is no different. The positives are that the profits of owning stock are increased over a limited price range and the risk is not increased. The negatives are limited profit potential and additional transaction costs.

THE STOCK REPAIR STRATEGY

In the previous example, it was assumed that the stock and option positions were initiated simultaneously. Suppose, however, that Britton had purchased shares of Tailorco last year at $70, and that the current price is $60. In this case, Britton is losing $10 per share. He has also become less optimistic about the stock, and he has changed his goal. Britton now believes that Tailorco will rise back toward his purchase price, but he no longer believes that the price will rise significantly above $70. As a result, Britton just wants to break even on this investment. While some investors might be inclined to "double up" on their position, which involves buying more shares, Britton does not want to commit more capital to this position. Instead, he considers a creative use of the ratio call spread to improve his situation.

Table 15–2 and Figure 15–2 show the potential profit and loss of purchasing one 60 call for $4 and selling two 65 calls at $2 each. First, the breakeven stock price is lowered from $70 to $65. Second, no additional capital investment (other than transaction costs) is required. Third, the risk is not doubled, as it would be if an additional 100 shares were purchased.

The potential negative aspect of this strategy is that breaking even is the best possible result. If the stock price rises above $65, then the maximum result has been achieved.

Which is better, doubling up or using the ratio spread? Once again, there is no "better." Each strategy offers a different set of trade-offs. Doubling up lowers the breakeven price and allows unlimited profit potential in return for increased investment and doubling of risk. The ratio call spread, in contrast, lowers the breakeven price without increasing risk and without increased investment, in this example. Upside participation in a stock price rise above $65, however, is forgone. Neither strategy is "better." The selection depends on an investor's forecast, risk tolerance, and available capital.

TABLE 15–2   Profit and Loss at Expiration
Starting Position: Long Stock @ $70, currently $60 ($10 per-share loss)
Strategy: Long 1 60 Call @ $4 and Short 2 65 Calls @ $2 each

Stock Price at Expiration	Long Stock @ $70 Profit/(Loss)	Long 1 60 Call @ $4 Profit/(Loss)	Short 2 65 Calls @ $2 each Profit/(Loss)	Combined Profit/(Loss)
67.00	(3.00)	+3.00	0.00	0.00
66.00	(4.00)	+2.00	+2.00	0.00
65.00	(5.00)	+1.00	+4.00	0.00
64.00	(6.00)	0.00	+4.00	(2.00)
63.00	(7.00)	(1.00)	+4.00	(4.00)
62.00	(8.00)	(2.00)	+4.00	(6.00)
61.00	(9.00)	(3.00)	+4.00	(8.00)
60.00	(10.00)	(4.00)	+4.00	(10.00)
59.00	(11.00)	(4.00)	+4.00	(11.00)
58.00	(12.00)	(4.00)	+4.00	(12.00)
57.00	(13.00)	(4.00)	+4.00	(13.00)

FIGURE 15–2   The stock repair strategy

Starting Position: Long Stock at $70, currently $60
Strategy: Buy 1 60 Call @ $4 and Sell 2 65 Calls @ $2 each

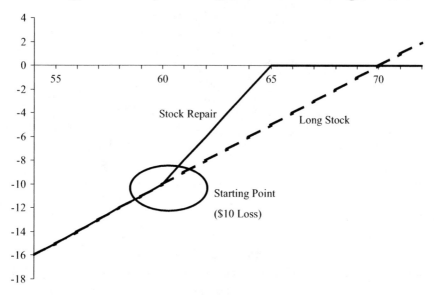

AN ALTERNATIVE TO SIMPLY SELLING PUTS

For an investor who wishes to buy stock below the current market price, a ratio spread with puts is an interesting alternative to selling cash-secured puts. Kyle is another conservative investor. He has been watching Rangeco trade between $45 and $50 for the last few months. The price is currently at $50, but Kyle predicts that it will once again dip to $45. This time, however, Kyle wants to not just buy the stock, but buy it at a price below $45.

Table 15–3 and Figure 15–3 illustrate the strategy of buying one 50 put at $2 and selling two 45 puts at $1 each. It is also assumed that Kyle sets aside $4,000 for each ratio spread. This cash will be used to purchase 100 shares of Rangeco stock if the short puts are assigned, as described next.

ANALYZING THE POSSIBILITIES

Once again, there are three possible outcomes at expiration: The price of Rangeco stock could be at or above $50, between $45 and $50, or at or below $45.

TABLE 15–3   Profit and Loss at Expiration—Ratio Put Spread Long 1 50 Put @ $2 and Short 2 45 Puts @ $1 each

Stock Price At Expiration	Long 1 50 Put @ $2 Profit/(Loss)	Short 2 45 Puts @ $1 each Profit/(Loss)	Combined Profit/(Loss)
35.00	+13.00	(18.00)	(5.00)
40.00	+ 8.00	(8.00)	0.00
45.00	+ 3.00	+2.00	+5.00
50.00	(2.00)	+2.00	0.00
55.00	(2.00)	+2.00	0.00

FIGURE 15–3   Ratio put spread: long one 50 put @ $2 and short two 45 puts @ $1 each

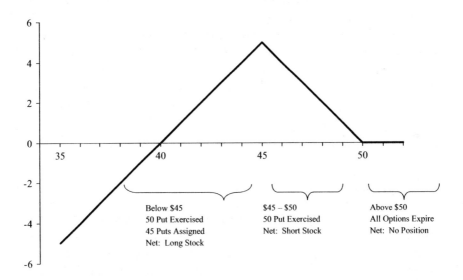

If the price of Rangeco stock is at or above $50 at expiration, then all the options expire worthless. The bad news is that Kyle's forecast was wrong; the stock price rose instead of falling. The good news, however, is that Kyle did not lose. With the stock price above $50, there is no profit or loss, other than commissions, because the ratio spread in this example was established for a net cash outlay of zero.

If the price of Rangeco is between $45 and $50 at expiration, then the profit equals the value of the 50 put. With Rangeco at $47, for example, the 50 put will have a value of $3, or $300. If the put is sold at this price, then the profit will equal $300. Remember, the position was established for zero net cash outlay. If the 50 put is exercised and the 45 puts expire worthless, then a short stock position is created. Even if Kyle does not instruct his broker to exercise his put, an automatic exercise is possible if the stock price is 25 cents or more in the money. Newcomers to options must be aware of this possibility, and they must pay close attention to their options positions as expiration approaches so that appropriate action can be taken.

The third possibility is that Rangeco is below $45 at expiration, an outcome that causes two things to happen. First, Kyle exercises the 50 put that he owns, creating a short position of 100 shares of Rangeco. Second, Kyle's two short 45 puts are assigned. This causes 200 shares of Rangeco stock to be purchased. The short position is covered by 100 of the purchased shares, and the other 100 shares are kept as a long position. This is what Kyle wanted: to purchase 100 shares of Rangeco stock.

Kyle's effective purchase price is $40 per share in this example, not including commissions. Although the strike price of the assigned put was $45, Kyle also had a $5 profit on the 100 shares that were shorted and covered. Subtracting the $5 profit from the $45 strike price yields a net price of $40. Again, the possibility that one or both of the short puts might be assigned early must be considered. An early assignment would not increase the risk of this strategy, but it might sound complicated to an inexperienced options user.

RATIO SPREADS AS A TRADING STRATEGY

Aggressive traders might consider using ratio spreads as a short-term strategy if their short-term price forecast for the underlying stock or index is consistent with the price behavior of the ratio spread. Do not forget that ratio spreads involve uncovered short options, so this strategy is appropriate only for experienced traders who have received special approval from their brokerage firm.

Table 15–4 contains the theoretical values of a ratio spread in which one 60 call is purchased and two 65 calls are sold. Column 1, row 8 in Table 15–4, for example, assumes an underlying stock price of $60, 30 days to expiration, and the assumptions about volatility, interest rates, and dividends given in the table heading. Although the individual call values are not shown, purchasing

TABLE 15–4   Theoretical Values of 60–65 1×2 Ratio Spread with Calls (Long 1 60 Call and Short 2 65 Calls) (Volatility, 40%; Interest Rates, 2%; No Dividends)

		Col. 1	Col. 2	Col. 3	Col. 4	Col. 5	Col. 6	Col. 7
Row	Stock Price	30 Days	25 Days	20 Days	15 Days	10 Days	5 Days	EXP
1	67.00	(0.70)	(0.30)	0.10	0.60	1.25	2.00	3.00
2	66.00	(0.25)	0.10	0.50	1.00	1.55	2.40	4.00
3	65.00	0.00	0.35	0.75	1.20	1.80	2.60	5.00
4	64.00	0.35	0.65	0.95	1.35	1.85	2.55	4.00
5	63.00	0.45	0.75	1.05	1.40	1.80	2.35	3.00
6	62.00	0.65	0.85	1.10	1.35	1.650	1.95	2.00
7	61.00	0.65	0.85	1.05	1.25	1.40	1.45	1.00
8	60.00	0.70	0.85	1.00	1.10	1.15	1.00	0.00
9	59.00	0.65	0.80	0.85	0.90	0.90	0.65	0.00
10	58.00	0.65	0.70	0.75	0.70	0.65	0.35	0.00

Parentheses indicate that a position is established for a credit or closed for a debit.
No parentheses indicate that a position is established for a debit or closed for a credit.

one 60 call at $2.80 and selling two 65 calls at $1.05 each results in a net debit, or payment, of $0.70, or $70, not including commissions, and 0.70 is the number that appears in this cell.

Parentheses in Table 15–4 indicate the strategy could be established for a net credit or closed for a net debit. The number in parentheses appearing in column 1, row 2, for example, indicates that purchasing one 60 call and selling two 65 calls when the stock price is $66 and the time to expiration is 30 days results in a net credit of $0.25, or $25. Conversely, selling one 60 call and buying two 65 calls would cost $25.

Table 15–4 can be difficult to interpret because the calculation of profit or loss involves properly combining the opening debit or credit and the closing debit or credit. Opening a position for a debit is a cash outflow, but opening a position for a credit is a cash inflow. Closing a position at a debit is a cash inflow, and closing a position for a credit is a cash outflow. Consider two examples.

First, assume that the ratio spread is opened in column 1, row 8, and closed in column 6, row 7. The position is opened for a debit of $0.70. This means that $0.70 or $70, is paid. The position is then closed at a debit of $1.45, which means that $145 is received. The final result is $0.70 paid and $1.45 received, for a net received, or profit, of $0.75, or $75.

Second, assume that the ratio vertical spread is opened in column 1, row 2, and closed in column 6, row 7. The position is opened for a credit of $0.25, which means that $25 is received. The position is then closed at a debit of $1.45, which means that $145 is received. The net result is $25 received and $145 received, for a total amount received, or profit, of $170.

The conclusion from Table 15–4 is that ratio spreads perform best when the underlying stock or index trades in a narrow range around the strike price of the short options. A sharp stock price move beyond the strike price of the short options, however, will cause a loss. Furthermore, in the case of ratio spreads with calls, the loss potential is unlimited. Traders must, therefore, forecast that the stock price will trade near the strike price of the short options in order to choose this strategy.

SUMMARY

A 1 × 2 ratio spread consists of buying one close-to-the-money option and selling two options farther from the money. All the options are of the same type, and they all have the same underlying security and the same expiration date, but there are two different strike prices. The strategy can be used in conjunction with a long stock position, either to increase profits over a limited price range without increasing risk or as a "stock repair" strategy. Ratio spreads with puts can be used as an alternative to selling cash-secured puts. The goal is to establish an even lower purchase price for the underlying stock. Finally, aggressive traders can use ratio spreads as a short-term trading strategy if their short-term price forecast for the underlying security is consistent with the price behavior of this strategy. Traders must remember, however, that there is significant risk from the uncovered short option. Ratio spreads are a flexible strategy for advanced options traders.

16

COVERED COMBOS— LONG AND SHORT

INTRODUCTION

ONE THEME OF THE INTRODUCTION WAS THAT "OPTIONS GIVE INVESTORS AND TRADERS MORE ALTERNATIVES." A variation on that theme is that options give you something to do when there seems to be nothing to do. The *covered combination* strategy, or *covered combo*, for short, is appropriate for a neutral market view, i.e., when the stock investor or trader might be inclined to do nothing. This chapter will describe how the strategy works, how investors and traders might think about using it, different ways in which capital can be managed, and alternative courses of action as expiration approaches. A variation is the *covered straddle*, which will also be discussed.

A THREE-PART STRATEGY

A *covered combination* involves the purchase of stock, the sale of an out-of-the-money call, and the sale of an out-of-the-money put with the same expiration. The derivation of the name *combination* is unknown. The strategy of buying (or selling) both a call and a put with the same expiration but different strike prices is sometimes called a "strangle," as described in Chapter 14.

A *covered straddle* involves selling a call and a put with the same strike price and the same expiration.

Writing both a call and a put means that the investor is taking on two obligations: the obligation to sell the owned stock (if the call is assigned) and the obligation to buy more stock (if the put is assigned). Although transaction costs are not included in the examples in this chapter, this strategy involves more transaction costs than typical buy-and-hold strategies. Transaction costs and margin requirements can significantly affect the desirability of this strategy and must be taken into consideration before using real options on real stocks.

NOT NECESSARILY "COVERED"

The short call in this strategy is covered, because calls are sold on a share-for-share basis against owned stock. The short put, however, is not covered unless the investor has sufficient cash, or other liquid assets, available to fulfill the obligation to purchase stock. If margin loans are required to purchase stock, or if the investor has insufficient capital to purchase stock even with margin loans, then the short put is not covered.

PROFIT-AND-LOSS DIAGRAM

For the example presented in Table 16–1 and Figure 16–1, assume $10,000 of cash (equity capital), interest rates of 4 percent (annual rate), 90 days to expiration, a stock price of $52, a 55 call price of $2, and a 50 put price of $2. To establish a covered combination, an investor buys 100 shares at $52 (total $5,200), sells one 90-day 55 call for $2 per share ($200), sells one 90-day 50 put for $2 per share ($200), and invests $5,000 at 4 percent for 90 days (interest equals $50). For the sake of simplicity, the effect of interest on the option premiums is ignored.

Before using this strategy, it is essential to thoroughly understand the mechanics. Only then is it possible to determine whether this strategy has the potential to meet an investor's objectives. To review the mechanics, a stock price at expiration is selected, and then what happens to each component is explained.

STOCK PRICE BETWEEN $50 AND $55 AT EXPIRATION

With a stock price at one of the strike prices or between the strike prices at expiration, both options expire and the long stock position is kept. The profit is equal to the change in the stock price plus the $4 of option premiums plus

**TABLE 16–1   Buy Stock at $52, Sell 55 Call at $2 and Sell 50 Put at $2—
Profit-and-Loss Calculations**

Stock Price at Expiration	Long 100 Shares @ $52 P/(L)	Short 1 55 Call @ $2 P/(L)	Short 1 50 Put @ $2 P/(L)	Invest $5,000 @ 4% for 90 days (Interest = $50)	Total P/(L)
$60	+$800	($300)	+$200	+$50	+$750
$55	+$300	+$200	+$200	+$50	+$750
$54	+$200	+$200	+$200	+$50	+$650
$53	+$100	+$200	+$200	+$50	+$550
$52	-0-	+$200	+$200	+$50	+$450
$51	($100)	+$200	+$200	+$50	+$350
$50	($200)	+$200	+$200	+$50	+$250
$49	($300)	+$200	+$100	+$50	+$50
$48	($400)	+$200	-0-	+$50	($150)
$47	($500)	+$200	($100)	+$50	($350)
$46	($600)	+$200	($200)	+$50	($550)
$45	($700)	+$200	($300)	+$50	($750)
$40	($1,200)	+$200	($800)	+$50	($1,750)

the interest earned on the cash investment. With a stock price of $54, for example, the profit of $6.50 per share is calculated by adding the stock profit of $2 ($54 – $52) to the option premium of $4 and the interest of $0.50. If the stock price declines to $51, there is still a net profit of $3.50, because the $4 per share from the options more than offsets the loss of $1 per share from the stock. The final position is long 100 shares plus $5,450 in cash, as described in Table 16–2A.

STOCK PRICE ABOVE $55 AT EXPIRATION

If the stock price is above the strike price of the call at expiration, the short put expires and the short call is assigned. In this example, as a result of the call assignment, the owned stock is sold at $55, for cash proceeds of $5,500. The $400 option premium is kept as profit, and the final strategy component, the

FIGURE 16–1   The covered combo

Capital:	$10,000
Buy 100 Shares	@ 52.00
Sell 1 55 Call	@ $2.00
Sell 1 50 Put	@ $2.00

Invest $5,000 for 90 days @ 4%

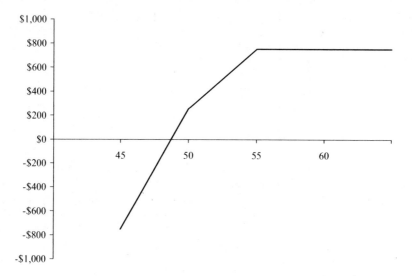

$5,000 cash investment, earns $50 interest. As described in Table 16–2B, the resulting position is a cash balance of $10,950, $950 of which is profit before commissions.

As Table 16–2B shows, at any stock price above the strike price of the call at expiration, the result will be the same profit. The short put expires, the short call is assigned, the stock is sold, and the resulting position is cash. Given this outcome, all capital in cash, the investor is faced with the decision of what to do next. Whatever is decided, a nice profit will have been earned during the 90-day period just ended.

STOCK PRICE BELOW $50 AT EXPIRATION

With the stock price below the strike price of the put at expiration, the short call expires and the short put is assigned. As a result of the put assignment, 100 shares are purchased at $50 per share, which raises the total position to 200 shares. The shares are purchased for cash with the proceeds from the maturing cash investment. The resulting position is long 200 shares and $450 in cash,

TABLE 16–2   Buy Stock and Sell Combination Analysis of Outcomes

16-2A – Stock Price Between the Strikes at Expiration

      Call Expires, Put Expires

      Keep Stock (100 Shares)

      Total P/(L) = P/(L) from Stock + Option Premiums + Interest

      Position: Long 100 Shares

Option Premiums	$ 400
Money Market Balance	5,000
Interest Earned	50
	$5,450 + 100 Shares

16-2B – Stock Price Above the Call Strike at Expiration

      Call Assigned, Put Expires

      Sell Stock (100 Shares)

      Total P/(L) = Call Strike − Purchase Price + Option Premiums + Interest

      Position: Cash from Stock Sale

Cash from Stock Sale	$ 5,500
Option Premiums	400
Money Market Balance	5,000
Interest Earned	50
	$10,950

16-2C – Stock Price Below the Put Strike at Expiration

      Call Expires, Put Assigned

      Buy Stock (100 Shares)

      Total P/(L) = (Current Price − Purchase Price) + [Current Price −
                     (Strike Price − Option Premiums)] + Interest

      Position: Long 200 Shares

Option Premiums	$400
Money Market Balance	0
Interest Earned	50
	$450 + 200 Shares

$400 from the option premiums plus $50 interest. There may be a profit or a loss, depending on the current stock price.

At a stock price of $49 at expiration, this covered combination breaks even, not including the interest of $50. This results because 100 shares were purchased at $52 per share and 100 shares were purchased at an effective price of $46 per share ($50 minus the option premiums). The average price, therefore, is $49. As Table 16–2C illustrates, the final position is long 200 shares plus cash of $450.

SIMILARITY TO COVERED WRITING

Those with experience in options may notice a similarity between Figure 16–1 and Figure 6–1, which depicts a covered call. This similarity is another result of the put-call parity concept discussed in Chapter 8. Rather than focus on an explanation of put-call parity, however, the following examples will illustrate how the covered combo can help both investors and traders. The targeted investment objectives depend on an investor's initial position and market forecast.

Do not proceed through the case study examples that follow until you are thoroughly familiar with the mechanics of this strategy as presented here. If it seems confusing, simply analyze each component before determining the final position.

CASE 1: THE INCOME-ORIENTED STOCK INVESTOR

The first investor, John, does not look at the stock market pages every day, but he likes to buy safe, blue chip stocks that pay nice dividends. John's primary goal is to increase the income from his portfolio. He does not use margin loans to buy stock, but he is not a buy-and-hold investor, either. He is willing to sell stocks at a profit. Right now John has $14,000 in cash and wants to purchase Basic Industries stock, which is trading at $68. The 90-day 70 call is trading at $4, and the 90-day 65 put is trading at $3. John's forecast is neutral to bullish. He expects Basic to remain in a trading range near $68 for the next 90 days. He is debating whether to buy 200 shares now or to buy 100 shares now and wait for a lower price on the second 100 shares. Also, John would be happy to sell 100 shares at $77 and realize a $9-per-share profit in 90 days.

Given John's market forecast and his willingness to assume the risk of owning 200 shares at or near $68, the "buy stock and sell combo" strategy might help John get the best of both worlds. John can establish this strategy by purchasing 100 shares at $68 and simultaneously selling both the 70 call and the 65 put. The remaining $7,200 cash is left on deposit earning interest. To see how this strategy might achieve John's objectives, consider what happens if the price of Basic is above $70, below $65, or in between $65 and $70 at expiration.

BASIC ABOVE $70 AT EXPIRATION

If the price of Basic is above $70 at expiration, the 70 put expires, the 70 call is assigned, and the owned 100 shares are sold at an effective price of $77, not including commissions or the interest earned on the money market deposit. This is calculated as follows: The call assignment requires John to sell his stock at $70 per share, but he keeps both the call premium and the put premium; $70 + $4 + $3 = $77. This was one of John's initial objectives. He was willing to sell the initial 100 shares and realize a $9-per-share profit.

BASIC BELOW $65 AT EXPIRATION

If the price of Basic is below $65 at expiration, the 70 call expires, the 65 put is assigned, and a second 100 shares are purchased at an effective price of $58 (not including commissions or interest). This is calculated as follows: The put assignment requires John to purchase 100 shares at $65 per share, but he keeps both the put premium and the call premium; $65 – $4 – $3 = $58. This was also part of John's initial plan. After purchasing 100 shares initially, his plan was to wait to buy the second 100 shares at a lower price.

BASIC BETWEEN $65 AND $70 AT EXPIRATION

If Basic is between the strike prices at expiration, we can assume that both the 70 call and the 65 put expire worthless and both option premiums are kept as income. This is also consistent with John's original goal of increasing income. If this third possible outcome occurs, John's position is long 100 shares plus $7,700 in cash plus interest from the money market account. He can then choose between buying a second 100 shares, writing another combination, or using some other strategy.

Regardless of the stock price at expiration—above, below, or at $70—John meets one of his original objectives: to increase income, to realize a $9-per-share profit on 100 shares in 90 days, or to buy a second 100 shares at a price below $68.

COMMON OBJECTIONS

As good as all of this sounds, investors learning about this strategy for the first time have some reasonable questions. First, one might ask: "What if the stock price rises to $80 or $90 or higher?" Second, "Suppose the stock price falls to $60 or $50 or lower?" And, finally, "The $9 profit in 90 days sounds attractive, but how do I know I can earn it again three more times this year?" These questions will be addressed in order.

A "LARGE" PRICE RISE

It is true that this strategy, like any strategy involving a covered call, limits participation in a rising market. But remember, John's market forecast and objectives were very specific. Also, what was responsible for the missed rally—the market forecast or the option strategy? Had John forecasted a sharply rising stock price, he undoubtedly would have chosen to buy 200 shares initially rather than 100 shares. Consequently, it is the inaccurate market forecast rather than the option strategy that accounts for the missed opportunity.

A "LARGE" PRICE DECLINE

A similar answer applies to the objection about a sharp price decline. If John had expected the price of Basic stock to decline sharply, he undoubtedly would not have chosen a neutral-to-bullish strategy. Again, any loss must be attributed to an inaccurate stock selection and/or market forecast rather than to the option strategy.

REPEATING THE RETURN

Although there is no guarantee that new 90-day options will have the same price as the ones sold by John in this example, the concern over the possibility of repeating the profit misunderstands an important point. Profit calculations are only one element of the subjective investment selection process, and they should not be overemphasized. The profit potential, remember, is accompanied by the risk of stock ownership. In John's example, he is assuming the risk of owning 200 shares.

BALANCING THE POSITIVES AND NEGATIVES

The most important element of an investment decision is the market forecast. Buying Basic stock and writing the 65–70 combination matches John's forecast, but only John can decide how much confidence he has in his forecast. The objections about potential missed opportunities or negative stock price action should be addressed to the market forecast.

Experienced buy-and-hold stock investors must adapt their style to the two-step thinking required for successful investing with options. The initiation of an option strategy has implications for what happens at option expiration, and that depends on the stock price. Investors who use options must consider all possible outcomes and plan accordingly.

CASE 2: THE INDECISIVE STOCK INVESTOR
WITH A GAIN

Ramona is an investor with a nice problem. Some time ago she purchased 200 shares of Rising Star at $20 per share; the current price is $44. Ramona is bullish and would like to sell her Rising Star at a higher price than $44, but her instincts are telling her that the stock might pull back before rising further. Consequently, she is thinking about taking some profits now. Ramona is considering two alternatives: (1) holding now and selling all 200 shares later, or (2) selling 100 shares now and 100 later. A third alternative that Ramona might consider is a variation on the strategy "buy stock and sell combo."

In John's situation in Case 1, he started with $14,000. His initial trade was the purchase of 100 shares at $68 and the sale of the 90-day 65–70 combination. After this transaction, John's position was long 100 shares, short the 70 call, short the 65 put, and $7,200 on deposit. Ramona can create a similar position by selling 100 shares now and simultaneously selling the 90-day 40–45 combination.

To see how this strategy might meet Ramona's objectives, first consider what happens if Ramona chooses to hold. Second, consider the implications of selling 100 shares now and 100 later, and third, examine what happens if the option strategy is used and the price of Rising Star is above $45, below $40, or between $40 and $45 at expiration.

If Ramona chooses to hold, she is postponing her sell decision; the ultimate selling price will depend on the future performance of Rising Star's stock. It is impossible to say in advance what the results of holding will be, but, as will be seen, the option strategy provides a basis of comparison.

The outcome of the second alternative, selling 100 shares now and 100 shares later, also depends on the stock's future price action. The difference between holding now and selling all shares later and selling 100 now and 100 later is the price movement required to achieve the same average selling price. If, for example, Ramona sells 100 shares now at $44 and 100 shares after a $4 price rise to $48, the average price of $46 is equal to holding now and selling all 200 shares after a $2 price rise to $46.

A two-to-one difference also exists if the stock price declines. Holding now and selling all 200 shares at $41 is equal to selling 100 shares now at $44 and the second 100 shares at $38. It is impossible to know in advance which strategy will perform better, but the scenarios can be described. If the price of Rising Star continues to rise, the strategy of selling 200 shares later is best. However, if the price falls to $41 and then rises to new highs, then selling 100 shares now at $44 and placing a stop-loss sell order for 100 shares at $38 would outperform a 200 share stop-loss sell order at $41.

The strategy of selling 100 shares now at $44 and simultaneously selling one 90-day 45 call and one 90-day 40 put is not just a third alternative. This strategy also provides additional information for making a decision. The short combination establishes two prices: a sell price for the second 100 shares and a price at which the sold 100 shares will be repurchased. In Ramona's case, assume that the 90-day 45 call is trading at $2 and the 90-day 40 put is trading at $1.50.

If the price of Rising Star is above $45 at expiration, then the short call is assigned and the second 100 shares is sold at an effective price of $48.50, the $45 strike price plus the call premium of $2 and the put premium of $1.50. The average selling price for all 200 shares under this scenario is $46.25 (100 shares at $44 and 100 at $48.50).

If Rising Star is below $40 at expiration, the short put is assigned and 100 shares are purchased at an effective price of $36.50 (the strike price of 40 minus the two option premiums). The original 200-share position is reestablished, but Ramona will have bought back the second 100 shares at a price of $36.50, $7.50 lower than the current price of $44. The $7.50-per-share "savings" on 100 shares equals $3.75 on 200 shares.

This strategy, selling 100 shares now, at $44, and simultaneously selling the 90-day 40–45 combination, offers Ramona a third set of trade-offs. If her short call is assigned, Ramona will have sold her 200 shares at an average price of $46.25. If both options expire worthless, she will have an extra profit of $350, and if the short put is assigned, she will have a $7 profit on 100 shares or a $3.75 profit on her 200-share position.

Under what scenario will the covered combo perform best? If the stock stays below $46.25, the option strategy increases results. If the stock trades above $46.25, and if Ramona is able to make optimal trading decisions, then one of the other alternatives will produce better results. By being aware of this option alternative, however, Ramona has a frame of reference, a stock price of $46.25, that she can use as part of her subjective decision-making process in choosing between the three alternatives.

CASE 3: USING THE COVERED STRADDLE
TO CREATE A TRADING RANGE

Floyd is an aggressive trader who watches the market daily and frequently trades on margin. One of the stocks he follows closely is Fluctuation Industries, and Floyd's position in Fluctuation has varied during the past 12 months from a low of zero shares to a high of 600 shares. Floyd has been "trading the range," accumulating shares of Fluctuation near $55 and selling near $65. The stock price is currently $60, and Floyd is long 300 shares. He owns the shares with no margin loans, and he has no surplus cash in his money market account. His current outlook is neutral to bullish. Selling three Fluctuation 60 straddles might assist Floyd's aggressive trading strategy.

Given his current holdings of 300 shares, a stock price of $60, a 30-day 60 call price of $2.50, and a 30-day 60 put price of $2, Floyd can consider three alternatives. First, he can wait for the stock price to rise, at which point he can sell the owned shares. Second, he can wait for the price to fall, at which point he can purchase an additional 300 shares with margin loans. Third, he can write three 30-day straddles; this might achieve similar results, even if the stock price did not change very much.

By writing three 60 calls at 2.50, Floyd is assuming the obligation of selling the 300 shares he owns at an effective price of $62.50. By writing three 60 puts at $2, he is assuming the obligation of buying an additional 300 shares, effectively, at $58.

Writing three straddles, however, brings in both option premiums, thus raising the effective selling price to $64.50 and lowering the effective buying price to $55.50. If the price of Fluctuation is above $60 at expiration, the 60 puts will expire, the 60 calls will be assigned, and the owned shares will be sold at an effective selling price of $64.50 (the $60 strike price plus the call premium plus the put premium). Floyd's position will then be no stock and all cash. If Fluctuation is below $60, the calls will expire, the puts will be assigned, and 300 shares are purchased, effectively, at $55.50 (the $60 strike price minus the call and put premiums). Floyd would then own 600 shares and have a margin loan of $18,000.

If Fluctuation is exactly at $60 at expiration, then we assume that both the short call and the short put expire worthless and Floyd keeps the $450 option premium minus commissions. On the downside, the risk is owning 600 shares and having the stock price fall dramatically. On the upside, there is an "opportunity risk" if the stock price rises above $64.50. In this case, selling the straddle would not perform as well as simply holding the 300-share position and not selling the straddle.

Whether or not writing the straddle performs better than waiting depends on the price action of Fluctuation and Floyd's trading decisions. The short straddle establishes buying and selling prices that meet Floyd's initial objectives, but it is impossible to know in advance whether this strategy will perform better than his other alternatives.

USING LEVERAGE

Floyd's use of leverage changes the percentage risk of the covered straddle strategy. By selling three straddles when 300 shares are owned and cash is not available to purchase stock if the short puts are assigned, Floyd risks losing $2 for each $1 stock price decline below the breakeven point. Figure 16–2 graphically depicts Floyd's position, and Table 16–3 contains supporting profit-and-loss calculations.

The differences between Figure 16–1 and Figure 16–2 are the profit potentials and the slopes of the lines. This is the trade-off of leverage: higher profit potential and higher risk.

EXPIRATION MECHANICS EXPLAINED

At any stock price above $60 at expiration, the short puts expire, the short calls are assigned, and Floyd's owned 300 shares are sold. The resulting position is a cash balance of $19,350, $18,000 from selling 300 shares at $60 plus $750

FIGURE 16–2   Floyd's buy stock and write straddle

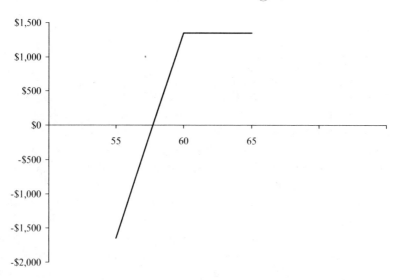

Capital:	$18,000
Own 300 Shares	@ $60.00
Sell 3 60 Calls	@ $2.50
Sell 3 60 Puts	@ $2.00

TABLE 16–3 Floyd's Buy Stock and Write Straddle—Profit-and-Loss Calculations

Stock Price at Expiration	Long 300 Shares @ $60 P/(L)	Short 3 60 Calls @ $2.50 P/(L)	Short 3 60 Puts @ $2 P/(L)	Total P/(L)
$64	+$1,200	($450)	+$600	+$1,350
$63	+$900	($150)	+$600	+$1,350
$62	+$600	+$150	+$600	+$1,350
$61	+$300	+$450	+$600	+$1,350
$60	-0-	+$750	+$600	+$1,350
$59	($300)	+$750	+$300	+$750
$58	($600)	+$750	-0-	+$150
$57	($900)	+$750	($300)	($450)
$56	($1,200)	+$750	($600)	($1,050)
$55	($1,500)	+$750	($900)	($1,650)
$54	($1,800)	+$750	($1,200)	($2,250)

from selling three calls at $2.50 each plus $600 from selling three puts at $2 each. For simplicity, transaction costs have not been included in these calculations.

If the stock price is below $60 at expiration, the short calls expire, the short puts are assigned, and 300 shares are purchased at $60. Since Floyd has no additional cash, the purchase of these 300 shares will be financed by margin loans. For example, if the stock price were $55 at expiration, the account equity would be $15,350. This is calculated by taking the initial investment in stock of $18,000, adding the option premium received of $1,350, and subtracting the stock loss of $3,000 (600 shares purchased at $60 that are now trading at $55).

The breakeven stock price at expiration is $57.75, not including commissions; because 300 shares are purchased at $60 and 300 are purchased at an effective price of $55.50.

If the stock price is below $60 at expiration, the short puts are assigned and the ending position is long 600 shares with margin debt of $16,650, the $18,000 purchase price of 300 shares at $60 less the option premium of $1,350. The maximum theoretical risk is $34,650, 600 shares purchased at

$60 minus $1,350 of option premium. The short puts contribute the increased profit potential and the increased loss potential. This is the double-edged sword of leverage.

ASSESSING RISK

Some observations can be made about Floyd's risk. First, the leverage is equal to buying stock on margin: Two units of stock are purchased for each unit of capital. The breakeven price, however, is $57.75, which is lower than the breakeven price of buying stock on margin at $60. Second, the breakeven price of $57.75 is higher slightly than the breakeven price for covered writing on margin of $56.50 per share (buy stock at $60 and sell 60 call at $3.50). Therefore, the risk of this strategy is somewhere between covered writing and buying stock on margin.

USING THE LEVERAGED VERSION OF BUY STOCK AND WRITE STRADDLE

The existence of leverage makes any strategy an aggressive strategy, suited only for those with experience in trading on margin. Also, because buy stock and sell a combination (or straddle) has limited profit potential, it is an income-oriented strategy. Finally, if the stock price is above the strike price of the call or below the strike price of the put at expiration, assignment of a short call or short put will occur. This strategy, therefore, is likely to involve several transactions and related costs.

A typical scenario is buying stock and selling options, then selling or buying stock through assigned options, then selling stock and/or selling more options. Consequently, the leveraged version of this strategy is suited only for those traders who are actively involved in watching the market and managing their positions and who trade in sufficient numbers of shares and options to get volume discounts on commissions.

An additional point to consider: One characteristic of aggressive traders with experience buying stock on margin and trading short term is decisiveness in cutting losses. The presence of leverage can make losses mount fast, and the only remedy is to take action, i.e., sell the stock, or at least buy protective puts to limit the loss.

TRADING A NEUTRAL-TO-BEARISH FORECAST

Meet Laura, an aggressive trader with $30,000 in trading capital, who trades both the long and short sides of the market. She also trades on margin to leverage her trading capital. Right now Laura is forecasting sideways price action for most of the market, but she believes that Dropco, which is currently at $75, is more likely to trade down than up. Consequently, Laura uses a neutral-to-bearish variation of the covered combo strategy described earlier.

The first part of Laura's strategy is to *sell short* 400 shares of Dropco stock at its current price of $75. The second part is to sell the 70–80 combination, which involves the simultaneous sale of four 70 puts for $2.50 each and four 80 calls at $3 each. Figure 16–3 graphically depicts Laura's position, and Table 16–4 contains the supporting profit-and-loss calculations.

Possible Outcomes

If the stock price rises, contrary to Laura's forecast, the breakeven stock price at expiration is $80.25, not including commissions, as shown in the third row of Table 16–4. This is the average price of an 800-share short position if 400 shares are sold short at $75 and 400 shares are sold short at $85.50, the effective price if the calls are assigned. At any stock price above $80 at expiration,

FIGURE 16–3   Laura's short stock and short combination

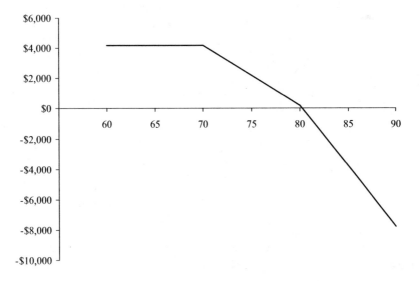

Capital:	$30,000
Short 400 Shares	@ $75.00
Sell 4 80 Calls	@ $3.00
Sell 4 70 Puts	@ $2.50

TABLE 16–4 Laura's Short Stock and Short Combination—Profit-and-Loss Calculations

Stock Price at Expiration	Short 400 Shares @ $75 P/(L)	Short 4 80 Calls @ $3 P/(L)	Short 4 70 Puts @ $2.50 P/(L)	Total P/(L)
$90	($6,000)	($2,800)	+$1,000	($7,800)
$85	($4,000)	($800)	+$1,000	($3,800)
$80.25	($2,100)	+$1,100	+$1,000	-0-
$80	($2,000)	+$1,200	+$1,000	+$200
$75	-0-	+$1,200	+$1,000	+$2,200
$70	+$2,000	+$1,200	+$1,000	+$4,200
$65	+$4,000	+$1,200	($1,000)	+$4,200
$60	+$6,000	+$1,200	($3,000)	+$4,200

the short puts expire and the short calls are assigned. As a result of the call assignment, 400 shares are *sold short*. Laura would then be short a total of 800 shares.

Laura Risks a Margin Call

Laura faces the risk of unlimited losses on a position of short 800 shares if the price of Dropco rises above $80. In fact, if the stock price were to rise above $80, it is a certainty that she would get a margin call from her broker, because her account equity of $30,000 is not sufficient to support an 800-share position in an $80 stock. Typically, the margin requirement for stock is 50 percent of market value, although some brokers have a higher requirement. Laura's 800 shares at $80 per share have a market value of $64,000, 50 percent of which is $32,000. If Laura receives a margin call, then she must either deposit additional cash or close some or all of the position. Closing the position at a stock price above $80 is likely to result in a loss, a possibility that Laura must consider before engaging in this strategy. She must also decide that she is prepared to assume this risk.

If the stock price is below $70 at expiration, the short calls expire, the short puts are assigned, and 400 shares are purchased at $70. The purchased shares will cover Laura's short stock position, leaving her with no position except cash, which includes a nice profit. For example, if the stock price were

$66 at expiration, the account equity would be $34,200. This is calculated by adding the beginning account equity of $30,000, the $2,000 profit on the stock (a $5-per-share profit on 400 shares), and the option premium received of $2,200.

Laura's View of Risk

The existence of both short stock and leverage makes the short stock and short combo strategy suitable only for aggressive traders who receive specific approval from their brokerage firm. Also, this strategy involves several transactions and related costs and therefore is suited only for traders who actively watch and manage their positions and who trade in sufficient numbers of shares and options to get discounts on commissions.

SUMMARY

In their basic form, covered combinations and covered straddles involve the purchase of stock with half of the available cash and the simultaneous sale of a call and a put. The remaining cash is left on deposit earning interest and is used to purchase stock if the short put is assigned. This is an income-oriented strategy that is appropriate for investors and traders with a neutral market forecast who want to buy at the low end of the predicted range and sell at the high end. The effective buying and selling prices established by the sold options provide reference points that can be used as part of the subjective decision-making process. If there is not sufficient cash on hand to purchase the shares, then the obligation of the short put is not truly covered.

The covered combination and covered straddle strategies have variations involving leverage and short stock. The variations involve using all available cash to purchase (or short) stock and, simultaneously, writing combos or straddles. If options are assigned, the stock position created will require the use of margin or margin loans. Using leverage changes the breakeven price and increases the risk in percentage terms. It also increases the chances that a margin call will force a liquidation of the position. The variation involving leverage, therefore, is suitable only for experienced traders who have received the specific approval of their broker.

C H A P T E R 17

CASH-SETTLED INDEX OPTIONS AND ETF OPTIONS

INTRODUCTION

A BIG INFLUENCE ON THE DEVELOPMENT OF NEW FINANCIAL PRODUCTS IN THE 1990S WAS THE MOVE TO INDEXING. By creating investment vehicles that were linked to various market indexes, some financial managers were changing the stated goal from "beating the market" to "matching the market." Although the first index-targeted products, such as Vanguard's S&P 500 Stock Index Fund, the Kansas City Board of Trade's futures contract based on the Value Line Index, the Chicago Mercantile Exchange's futures contract based on the S&P 500 stock index, and the Chicago Board Options Exchange's cash-settled options on the OEX Index, were created in the 1980s and earlier, it was in the 1990s that new index-linked products multiplied. Exchange-traded funds, or ETFs, began trading in the mid- to late 1990s and have grown dramatically in trading volume.

This chapter is not meant to be a definitive treatise on cash-settled index options and ETF options. Rather, given the background that has been presented on stock options, this chapter will explain some of the unique aspects of these options and offer pointers for short-term traders. Cash-settled index options will be explained first, and a discussion of ETF options will follow. In each section, the discussion will first explain the important differences in contract specifications between regular stock options and options on index-linked products. Second, some theoretical pricing differences from regular stock options will be presented. Finally, some practical complications that short-term traders of options on index-linked products may encounter will be explained.

THE BASICS OF CASH-SETTLED INDEX OPTIONS

The theory of index options is simple: Investors and traders can focus on the overall market rather than on specific stocks. In theory, index options work the same way as regular stock options, and, in theory, index options can be traded in exactly the same way as regular stock options. The reality, of course, is somewhat different from the theory.

> **INDEX OPTIONS**
> *The price in dollars equals $100 times the quoted price. (Just like regular stock options!)*

Cash-settled index options have been designed to be easy to understand and easy to trade. Prices are quoted just like those of regular stock options: in whole dollars and 10-cent increments above $3, and in whole dollars and 5-cent increments below $3. The price of an index option in actual dollars is $100 times the quoted price, just like the price of a stock option. Consequently, the price of an OEX 600 call trading at "4.50" is $450, not including commissions. Strike price intervals vary from contract to contract, because the underlying index level can range from 40 to 2,000. Popular OEX index options, for example, have strikes every five index points (600, 605, 610, and so on). Other index options, however, have strike prices every 10 or 25 index points.

The underlying asset of a cash-settled index option is a dollar value equal to the index level multiplied by $100. If Debbie owns an option on QRS stock that is trading at $63 per share, for example, then the underlying dollar value of an option on 100 shares is $6,300. Similarly, if Debbie owns an option on the OEX index that is trading at 621.50, the underlying dollar value for this option is $62,150, which is $100 times 621.50. As the index rises and falls, then, the underlying dollar value also rises and falls.

OPTIONS ON BROAD-BASED AND SECTOR INDEXES ARE AVAILABLE

The popularity of index options has led to the introduction of options on more and more indexes. There are options on broad-based indexes and on sector indexes. Broad-based indexes are designed to enable investment decision making concerning the market as a whole, and sector indexes, or narrow-based indexes, focus on a specific industry. As explained later, broad-based index options have unique tax treatment.

Examples of broad-based index options are DJX options, which are linked to the Dow Jones Industrial Average; SPX, or S&P 500 index options; and RUT, or Russell 2000 index options. Some sector index options are OIX, or CBOE Oil Index options, and MVB, or Morgan Stanley Biotech Index options.

CASH-SETTLED INDEX OPTIONS VERSUS OPTIONS ON STOCK INDEX FUTURES

The cash-settled index option contracts that are the subject of this discussion should not be confused with futures contracts or with the options on those futures contracts that are traded on the Chicago Mercantile Exchange, the Chicago Board of Trade, or the Kansas City Board of Trade. Cash-settled index options can be traded only through brokers licensed by the Securities and Exchange Commission (SEC), the same brokers who handle stock transactions. Futures contracts and futures options can be traded only

> *Cash-settled index options are traded on options exchanges regulated by the SEC.*

> *Options on stock index futures are traded on commodities futures exchanges regulated by the CFTC.*

through futures brokers who are licensed by the Commodities Futures Trading Commission (CFTC).

CASH SETTLEMENT

A significant difference between cash-settled index options and regular stock options is what is delivered and received when an option is exercised. For equity options, of course, the underlying instrument is the stock itself. For index options, however, the underlying instrument is a cash value that is based on the level of an index. The index consists of var-

> *Stock options are deliverable.*
>
> *Index options are cash-settled.*

ious numbers of shares of different stocks. Delivery of the individual shares that make up the index would be a cumbersome and expensive process. For this reason, the concept of cash settlement was developed.

Cash settlement means that, upon exercise, the option writer pays the in-the-money amount to the option buyer. The *in-the-money amount*, in real dollar terms, is $100 times the intrinsic value of the exercised option. In the case of an index call, this is calculated by subtracting the option strike price from the index settlement value and multiplying the result by the index multiplier. In the case of a put, the in-the-money amount is calculated by subtracting the index settlement value from the strike price and multiplying the result by the index multiplier.

The settlement value of an index may be determined after an afternoon market close, as it is for OEX options (known as "p.m. settlement"), or after an expiration Friday morning opening, as it is for SPX options (known as "a.m. settlement").

Consider an example in which Lee, an index option trader with a bullish opinion, purchases an OEX March 640 call for $6.50, or $650. If the settlement at expiration is 654.00, Lee's call will be 14 index points in-the-money, and it will be exercised. Lee will receive $1,400, the in-the-money amount of 14 times $100. Lee's profit, in this case, is $750 ($1,400 − $650). Alternatively, if the index settles at 643.00 at expiration, Lee receives $300 (3 × $100) when the call is exercised. This produces a loss of $350 ($650 − $300). A third possible outcome is the index settling below 640 at expiration. In this case, Lee's call expires worthless, resulting in a total loss of the $650 Lee paid.

When Lee exercises, who is assigned? Just as with regular stock options, writers of index options receive assignment notices, and they must fulfill the terms of the option contract. In the case of index options, a randomly assigned option writer pays the in-the-money amount in cash.

THE HIGH LEVERAGE OF INDEX OPTIONS

Leverage means that two related securities experience different percentage price changes. Consider a stock trading at $50 and a 50 call on that stock trading at $3. If the stock price rises 10 percent to $55 at expiration, the 50 call, at $5, will have risen approximately 67 percent. Similarly, a 10 percent decline in the stock price, to $45, at expiration would result in the 50 call expiring worthless, for a 100 percent loss. The call, therefore, is "leveraged" relative to the underlying stock, because its price tends to change more in percentage terms.

Understanding the concept of leverage is important, because price comparisons are frequently made between index options and regular stock options. The absolute price of cash-settled index options is often greater than the absolute price of stock options. Such a comparison, however, does not take into consideration the percentage of underlying value and the potential leverage.

90-day 500 index call: $10
90-day 50 stock call: $3

Which one is "cheaper"?

The difficulty of comparing cash-settled index options and stock options will be illustrated by considering an index call with a strike price of 500 that is trading at $10, or $1,000, when the index is at 500.00 and a stock call with a strike price of 50 that is trading at $3, or $300, when the stock price is $50. The index call may initially appear more expensive than the stock call. However, when the option prices are considered in terms of a percentage of the underlying instrument and the potential leverage, the index option appears cheaper, relatively, than the stock option.

First, the 50-strike stock call, at $3, is 6 percent of the underlying stock's price. The price of the 500-strike index call, however, is only 2 percent of the underlying index. Second, if the index level rises 10 percent, to 550, at expiration, the 500 call will be worth $50, or $5,000, a 400 percent increase from $10. If the stock price rises 10 percent to $55 at expiration, the 50 call will be worth $5, approximately a 67 percent increase from $3.

Despite its higher absolute dollar cost, the price of the 500-strike index call is a lower percentage of the underlying index value than is the price of the 50-strike stock call. Also, the index call is more highly leveraged than the stock call. Why this situation exists will be explained next.

THE LOWER VOLATILITY OF INDEX OPTIONS

Consider this question: Is it more likely, less likely, or equally likely for a typical stock to rise or fall 10 percent or for a typical index to rise or fall 10 percent?

Specific events affect individual companies, and general events affect the whole market. The price of an individual company may rise or fall 10 percent in response to a specific event or a general event; but general events do not affect all companies in the same way. Therefore, in order for an index to change by 10 percent, some stocks in the index must move by more than 10 percent. Consequently, the likelihood of an individual stock price moving 10 percent is greater than the likelihood of a group of stock prices, or an index, moving 10 percent.

Since options are similar to insurance policies, as explained in Chapter 2, and since indexes are less likely than individual stocks to have a "big move," as just explained, index options are "cheaper" than stock options—not in absolute dollar terms, but in percentage terms. The 500-strike index call described above was 2 percent of the underlying index value, while the 50-strike stock call was 6 percent of the underlying stock value. The result of this is that index options have a higher potential leverage than stock options. Percentage terms are only one way of describing relative value. Another, more mathematically sophisticated, comparison takes into account potential price movement, or volatility.

"CHEAPNESS" VERSUS LEVERAGE

While the higher leverage of index options may appeal to short-term traders who buy options, there is a corresponding higher risk for writers of index options. The speculative writing of index options, therefore, is an activity that should not be undertaken lightly. The risks of writing index options, as well as the risks of selling any uncovered options, should be thoroughly examined and understood prior to engaging in this strategy.

EXERCISE STYLE—AMERICAN VERSUS EUROPEAN

The popular OEX Index options are American-style, which means that early exercise is permitted. Other index options, such as the SPX and RUT options, are European-style, meaning that early exercise is not permitted. Since exercise style varies by index option contract, it is crucial for index options traders to fully understand the risks involved in strategies involving short index options.

"Covered" and "Uncovered" Index Options

The cash settlement feature has significant implications for writing American-style index options. Written, or short, American-style index options may not be covered, even though, in similar strategies with stock options, those options would be covered.

Traditionally, a covered call is a short call position that exists in conjunction with at least one of three other positions: long stock, long another call with a lower strike, or long another call with an equal strike. If the short call is assigned, delivery can be fulfilled either by delivering the owned stock or by delivering stock purchased through exercising a call (although even this may not be possible in rare circumstances, such as a tender offer that is expiring). With equity options, price fluctuations do not pose a risk for the covered call writer, because shares can be delivered regardless of intervening price fluctuations.

Consider, for example, a stock option spreader named Adam who purchased an XYZ 50 call for $3 and sold an XYZ 55 call for $2, the total spread cost being $1, or $100. Assume that on a morning two weeks prior to expiration, when XYZ had closed at $70 the day before, Adam receives an assignment notice on the short 55 call. If the 50 call had closed at $20 and the 55 call closed at $15, Adam would have a paper profit of $4, or $400, on the 50–55 call spread. If on that morning XYZ opens at $62, down $8 from the previous close, the 50 call is likely to open around $12, a decline of $8 from the previous close. Such an event is of no concern to Adam, because his assignment requires him to deliver stock at a price of $55, and the 50 call gives him the right to buy stock at $50. In this situation, Adam buys stock at $50 via exercise and delivers it to meet the assignment at $55. Consequently, Adam realizes the profit of $4 per share, even though the stock price dropped sharply overnight.

> *Index Option Spreads*
>
> *The short option is not necessarily "covered."*

If a similar situation were to occur with cash-settled American-style index options, however, the result would be very different. A short American-style index option is not considered to be covered by an owned index option with a lower strike price, because day-to-day price fluctuations in the underlying index affect the amount of cash received or delivered. An assigned index option writer cannot exercise an owned index option until the next day, when, in all likelihood, the index level will have changed.

As an example, assume that Adam, instead of spreading XYZ stock options, had purchased a 650 American-style index call for $3, sold the 655 call for $2, and thus created the 650–655 index call spread for $1, or $100.

If the index closed at 670 on that fateful day and the 650 and 655 calls closed at $20 and $15, respectively, and if the short 655 call were assigned, then Adam would be required to pay $15, or $1,500, in cash to the owner of the 655 call. Because Adam did not receive notice of the assignment until the next morning, however, he could not exercise his long 650 call and be guaranteed of receiving the $20, or $2,000, based on yesterday's index settlement price of 670. The cash amount received from Adam's exercise today will be determined by today's index settling price. If the index settles today unchanged at 670 (or higher), then exercise of the 650 call results in the receipt of $2,000 (or more), a sufficient amount to meet the assignment from the previous day. If, however, the index declines sharply on day 2 and settles at 662, for example, exercise of the 650 call results in the receipt of only $12, or $1,200, an insufficient amount to cover the assignment of $1,500.

If this outcome occurred (i.e., the index settled at 662), the index call spread purchased for $1, or $100, would result in a loss of $400! The 650 call was purchased for $3 and closed at $12 (by exercise), resulting in a profit of $900. The 655 call, however, was sold for $2 and closed at $15 (by assignment), resulting in a $1,300 loss. The net loss, therefore, was $400—$100 paid to initiate the spread and a net $300 paid when assignment of the short 655 call and subsequent exercise of the 650 call occurred.

Vertical Spreads with European-Style Index Options

The possibility that the loss from a vertical spread could exceed its cost is one of the reasons that European-style index options were developed. Since early exercise is prohibited by the option contract, the problem just described and other problems caused by early exercise do not exist with European-style index options of the same expiration month. Consequently, traders who are exploring the strategy of spreading index options, either buying or selling spreads, might be well advised to start with European-style index options. There are, however, a few additional considerations to keep in mind.

First, because the early exercise feature has value, American-style index options frequently trade at a higher price than corresponding European-style options. Index option spread traders may discover, therefore, that spread prices for European-style index options are slightly lower than those for American-style index options. Buyers of index spreads will undoubtedly find this an advantage; but spread sellers will find it a disadvantage.

European-Style Options—Unique Pricing Characteristics

The lack of early exercise has implications for deep in-the-money European-style options. They may trade at a discount to parity even when there is considerable time to expiration. An option trading at parity, it will be recalled, is an in-the-money option with no time value, or an option trading exactly at its intrinsic value. For European-style options, it is possible to trade *below* intrinsic

> *Deep in-the-money European-style index put options can trade below parity.*

value because arbitrageurs, being unable to exercise early, will bid and offer for options at prices that are tied to the cost of carry.

It is beyond the scope of this book to explain cost of carry and arbitrage, but deep in-the-money European-style index options can trade below parity. This can be observed by using Op-Eval4. Using the single option calculator, make sure that "Index" and "European" appear in the boxes at the top. Then input the following settings: "Stock Price," 25; "Strike Price," 50; "Volatility %," 30; "Interest Rate," 1.5; "Dividend," 0; and "Days to Expiry," 90. The resulting value for the 50 call and the 50 put are 0.000 and 24.8154, respectively. The 50 put is approximately 0.20 below intrinsic value. Thus, an arbitrageur, in theory, could buy the 50 put for $24.80, and buy the stock for $25, and earn a riskless profit of $0.20 plus dividends at expiration in 90 days. However, since $0.20 is approximately equal to the 90-day interest cost of financing the purchase of the stock plus dividends, an arbitrageur would actually bid a lower price than $24.80 for the 50 put. The important conclusion for index option traders to grasp is that the theoretical value of European-style options can be less than their intrinsic value.

It is important for nonprofessional options traders to be aware of these concepts, because the difference in pricing of European-style options relative to American-style options in the marketplace should be taken into consideration when choosing a strategy and anticipating results.

TAX TREATMENT OF BROAD-BASED INDEX OPTIONS

According to the 2003 issue of "Taxes and Investing," a brochure published by the Options Industry Council,

> "Mark-to-market" and "60/40" treatment applies to "broad-based" U.S. stock index options .... [A]ssets which require mark-to-market treatment generally must be treated as [closed] at their fair market value on the last business day of the taxable year, even if they have not been [closed] .... The combined gains and losses are netted, and the net gain or loss is then treated as 60% long-term capital gain or loss and 40% short-term capital gain or loss.

This brochure is available from the Web site of the Chicago Board Options Exchange at www.cboe.com.

USING OP-EVAL4 TO PRICE INDEX OPTIONS

In theory, using Op-Eval4 to price index options is simple. There are, however, a few practical complications.

STRIKE PRICE AND DAYS TO EXPIRATION
The easiest inputs to determine are strike price and time to expiration, because index options are identified by their expiration month and strike price. Op-Eval4 users need only count the days to expiration.

INTEREST RATE
Although dividends and interest rates are complicated to determine in theory, users of Op-Eval4 can easily find satisfactory approximations. In theory, the correct interest rate is the cost of funds, or borrowing rate, used by index arbitrageurs who buy or sell the underlying stocks in the index and sell or buy

index options in the hope of profiting from price discrepancies. A close approximation to this rate is the 90-day Treasury bill rate, which is widely published in business journals. Users of Op-Eval4 should know how to find the 90-day Treasury bill rate and be sure to use a current rate.

DIVIDENDS

Calculation of the dividend yield of an index is complicated in theory, because individual stocks pay dividends on different schedules. Op-Eval4 uses formulas that assume that dividends are paid continuously and evenly throughout the year. While this difference may sound significant, fortunately it generally is not. Dividends are spread out sufficiently so that users of Op-Eval4 do not have to be overly concerned with this issue. Use the index dividend yield numbers presented on Mondays in the *Wall Street Journal, Investor's Business Daily*, or *Barron's*.

INDEX LEVEL OR "STOCK PRICE"

Much care should be taken when selecting the appropriate value for the index level, or "Stock Price," when valuing index options with Op-Eval4. For regular stock options, the price of the underlying stock is readily observable. With index options, however, the situation is more complicated. Although the current level of the underlying

> *Stock index futures prices can affect stock index options prices.*

index is readily observable and can be used most of the time, there are times when this is not the appropriate number. A detailed explanation of pricing index options is beyond the scope of this book. However, a brief discussion of the complicating factors is warranted.

The concept of put-call parity, discussed in Chapter 8, is that the prices of calls, puts, and the underlying stock must have a certain relationship with one another or there will be arbitrage opportunities. Whenever prices are "out of line," professional traders will adjust their bids and offers and force prices back into line. Although it is beyond the scope of this book to explain them in detail, there are also arbitrage relationships between stock index options and stock index futures contracts. Consequently, price fluctuations of stock index futures contracts above and below their theoretical value can affect stock index options prices.

As long as stock index futures contracts are trading at prices that approximate their theoretical value, stock index options can be priced using the current index level as the "Stock Price." However, if supply-and-demand conditions in the stock index futures markets cause these contracts to trade sufficiently above or below their theoretical value, then professional options market makers may make bids and offers for stock index options based on arbitrage relationships with the futures contract. Consequently, the index options prices will appear to be out of line if the current index level is used as the "Stock Price" in option-pricing models. When this occurs, index options traders must adjust the "Stock Price" and be very careful how they interpret the information from Op-Eval4.

In order to understand how to make the necessary adjustment to "Stock Price," the following brief explanation of stock index futures pricing is necessary.

Calculating a "Fair" Stock Index Futures Price

In a simplified form, the "fair value" of a futures contract is

$$\text{Spot Price} + \text{Cost of Carry} = \text{Futures Price}$$

If a futures contract is "overvalued," arbitrageurs will borrow money, buy the underlying instrument, and sell the futures contract. On the futures delivery date, they will deliver the underlying cash commodity, receive cash equal to the sold futures price, and pay off the loan with interest. The difference is their profit.

If a futures contract is "undervalued," purchasers of the underlying instrument will profit by buying futures and earning interest rather than paying cash for the underlying commodity and storing it.

For stock index futures contracts, the existence of dividends requires an adjustment to the formula given here. Dividends received by arbitrageurs are income, and they, effectively, reduce the cost of carry. Consequently, the formula for stock index futures is

$$\text{Spot Price} + \text{Cost of Carry} - \text{Dividends} = \text{Futures Price}$$

Cost of carry and dividends are generally presented in annual rates and must be adjusted to fit the specific time period in question. For a specific time period, the formula for stock index futures is

$$\text{Spot Price} + \left[\text{Spot Price} \times (\text{Cost of Carry} - \text{Dividends}) \times \frac{\text{Days to Expiration}}{\text{Days per Year}} \right]$$
$$= \text{Futures Price}$$

A Specific Example

For example, to use the formula to get a rough estimate of the fair value of an index futures contract, make the following assumptions:

Days to expiration: 47
Treasury bill rate: 5.2%
Dividend yield on the index: 2.8%
Cash value of index: 440.00

A *rough estimate* of the fair value of the index futures contract is

$$440.00 + \left[440.00 \times (0.052 - 0.028) \times \frac{47}{365} \right] = 441.36$$

Interpreting the Information

If the futures contract is trading at approximately 441.36, as calculated here, then the current index level of 440.00 can be used in Op-Eval4 as "Stock Price." The 440 call with 47 days to expiration should be approximately 1.36 greater in value than the 440 put with 47 days to expiration. Also, if the actual market prices of the index options are typed in, Op-Eval4 will calculate accurate implied volatility numbers.

However, if the index futures contract is not trading near 441.36, then the price of the underlying instrument must be adjusted accordingly. If, for example, the index futures contract is trading at 443.36, two points above fair value, then, in theory, the "Price of Underlying" typed into Op-Eval4 should be raised to 442.00. In theory, the options prices will now be consistent with put-call parity.

Practical Problems in the Real World

While all this is good in theory, there are some real-world practical problems. When futures contracts are trading at a significant premium or discount to fair value, market conditions are probably very hectic. "Very hectic" means that there are erratic price fluctuations and possible delays in order processing as a result of a heavy volume of orders. Consequently, it may be difficult to tell exactly where the index futures are trading or where the underlying cash index level is, because both are changing so rapidly and erratically. Such a situation is theoretically impossible, but it does occur in practice.

Although the market action in October of 1987 was extreme, there are occasions when hectic trading activity causes stock index futures and stock index options to trade at prices that are significantly different from those implied by the theory of futures and options pricing. Index options traders must be aware of the risks of such market action and prepare themselves accordingly.

Inability to Profit from "Price Discrepancies"

Even if the price discrepancies just described are detected, it is virtually impossible for nonprofessional traders to take advantage of such a situation.

The only "riskless" method of profiting from a price discrepancy is to create an arbitrage. But this is impossible for nonprofessional traders, for at least two reasons. First, commissions and other transaction costs for a nonprofessional trader would almost certainly be greater than any profit potential from an observed price discrepancy. Second, entering orders and getting executions at the observed prices is highly unlikely because of the hectic market conditions.

The Fallacy of Buying "Undervalued Options"

The belief that one can take advantage of price discrepancies by purchasing "undervalued options" is based on a misunderstanding of option price theory. An option (either a stock option or an index option) will appear undervalued at one particular moment only because a pricing model, at that moment, yields a higher "value." A trader who purchases this option will profit only if the option returns to its "theoretical value" *and all other things remain constant.* But all other things never remain constant, especially in the hectic market environments just described.

"Undervalued," in the context used here, refers to an option with an implied volatility below its expected volatility. "Returning to theoretical value," in such a case, means that the implied volatility of the option rises to the expected level. This is known as the *vega effect,* vega being the change in option price attributable to a change in volatility. It is possible, however, that the price of the underlying index could change adversely even though the implied volatility may be changing to the expected level. The change in option price attributable to a change in price of the underlying instrument is called the *delta effect.* The buyer of the "undervalued option" could lose money if the delta effect is greater than the vega effect.

INDEX OPTIONS AND CHANGING VOLATILITY

An additional complicating factor in trading index options is the changing levels of volatility. Implied volatility, it will be recalled, is the volatility percentage that justifies an option's current market price. Implied volatility, is, in some sense, the "market's opinion" of possible movement. Consequently, as the market's opinion changes, the implied volatility level changes. Constantly changing implied volatility levels is a characteristic of index options.

CBOE's Volatility Index—The VIX

One measure of the level of implied volatility in index options is the CBOE's Volatility Index (VIX). This index is calculated by weighting the implied volatilities of all SPX options. Some traders use VIX as a general indication of index option implied volatility. Two years, 2002–2003, of the VIX, calculated daily, are presented in Figure 17–1. This information from the VIX reveals that implied volatility levels for index options change frequently and substantially.

THREE-PART FORECASTING

Keeping in mind the complications of trading index options discussed earlier, the three components of an option's value that are most subject to change are index level, time to expiration, and implied volatility. Options traders should attempt to forecast all three, not just the price of the underlying index. For long-term options, changes in interest rates also have a substantial impact, and traders of these options should add this fourth element to their forecast.

A three-step process to follow when contemplating an index option trade is as follows: First, use the current option price and time to expiration to determine the implied volatility. This can be done with Op-Eval4, assuming normal market conditions, with stock index futures contracts trading approximately at fair value. Second, forecast the change in index level, the expected time period over which the change will occur, and the implied volatility level at the end of the change. Third, use Op-Eval4 to estimate the option price after the predicted change. If this process indicates a loss or insufficient profit, then the trade should not be made.

The three-step process just described involves gathering information, making a specific forecast, and estimating results. This is a careful, thoughtful process rather than a haphazard, impulsive one.

EXCHANGE-TRADED FUNDS

Exchange-traded funds, or ETFs, are shares of trusts that hold portfolios of stocks designed to closely follow the price performance and yield of specific indexes.

ETFs are not mutual funds. Although practices vary slightly from mutual fund to mutual fund, dollars invested in a mutual fund are given directly to the mutual fund, and the manager of the mutual fund purchases stocks, bonds, liquid investments, or other investments, depending on the stated purpose of the mutual fund. The unit value of a mutual fund, known as the net asset value, or NAV, is determined at predetermined intervals, such as daily based on the closing prices. An investor in a mutual fund is said to "purchase units" in the mutual fund. To withdraw money from a mutual fund, an investor notifies the mutual fund of how many units are to be "sold," and the mutual fund remits

FIGURE 17–1 VIX, 2002–2003

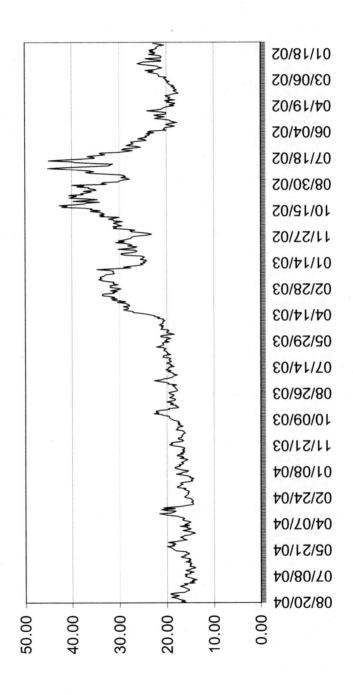

cash based on the next NAV calculation. Investors in mutual funds are assured of getting in and getting out of a mutual fund at the current NAV.

ETFs operate differently from mutual funds. ETF shares represent a portion of ownership of a trust that holds a portfolio of securities designed to follow an index. The ETF shares are traded on an exchange, just like individual stocks. As a result of this trading, the price of the ETF shares can fluctuate above and below the net asset value of the underlying shares owned by the trust. It is possible, in theory, to deal with the trust directly and get the net asset value, but the minimum transaction is very large—typically 50,000 shares or more. In practice, only wealthy individuals and institutions can deal directly.

ETFs have four advantages and four disadvantages relative to mutual funds. The advantages are that they can be purchased and sold during trading hours, they can be sold short, they have very low fees, and, according to some tax experts, they are more tax-efficient than mutual funds. Be sure to check with your tax advisor to assess your situation regarding taxes.

The disadvantages of ETFs are, first, that purchases and sales involve brokerage commissions. Direct investments in no-load mutual funds do not involve commissions. Second, as stated earlier, ETFs do not always trade at their net asset value. This may be an advantage or a disadvantage, depending on the specific transaction price relative to the current index level. The third disadvantage is that, practically speaking, individual investors must buy and sell shares in the market; dealing directly with the trust requires large sums of money. Finally, there is "slippage" in trading ETFs. Slippage is the spread between the bid price and the ask price and is an added cost.

ETFs are available from a number of issuers, who have registered trade names. For example, iShares, or "Investment Shares," is a registered trademark of Barclay's Global Investors, N.A. There are over 50 iShares available. HOLDRS, or holding company depository receipts, is a registered service mark of Merrill Lynch & Co., Inc. VIPERs, or Vanguard Index Participation Receipts, is a registered trademark of Vanguard, Inc.

OPTIONS ON ETFs

ETFs trade like shares of stock, and options on ETFs are operationally similar to options on stock. They are physically settled, which means that exercise and assignment create buy and sell transactions in the underlying instrument. Early exercise is possible, because they are also subject to American-style exercise. Long-term options, or LEAPS, are also available on some ETFs.

Strategies

Strategies applicable to ETFs options include the full range of strategies applicable to stock options. There are, of course, trade-offs. Options on individual stocks tend to trade at a higher level of implied volatility than ETF options. As a consequence, covered writers and other option writers may tend to favor options on individual stocks. However, the higher implied volatility is an indication of the higher risk of owning individual stocks relative to owning a diversified portfolio. The hoped-for higher profits are also a compensation for assuming higher risks.

Investors must decide what they feel comfortable with: options on individual stocks or on some market index. This is a personal decision that individual investors and traders must make personally. Some people are more comfortable trading "the market." Of course, those people have to decide what "the market" is. Is it the large-capitalization companies represented by the Dow Jones Industrial Average and DJX index options or the S&P 500 stock index and SPX index options? Or is "the market" some other broad-based or sector index? Some people think they know enough about a particular company, its fundamentals, and its trading patterns to feel confident about focusing their trading efforts on that company. The decision between index options, ETF options, and stock options is not a right or wrong issue. It is a personal choice.

SUMMARY

Options can be traded on many market indexes and exchange-traded funds (ETFs). These options enable investors and traders to focus on the overall market rather than on specific stocks. In theory, index options are exactly the same as regular stock options. However, the cash settlement feature of index options and the existence of stock index futures contracts mean that there are real-world, practical differences between index options and stock options. ETF options, however, are just like stock options. They are deliverable options subject to American-style exercise.

Op-Eval4 can be used to value index options, but traders must know the "fair value" of the relevant futures contract and the current market price of that contract. If the two are approximately equal, then the current index level can be used as the "Stock Price" in Op-Eval4. Otherwise, an adjustment must be made.

The volatility component of index options prices fluctuates and is an important factor to be considered. The CBOE's Volatility Index (VIX) can be used as a measure of the current level of implied volatility. When trading short-term index options, traders should forecast the index level, the time period, and the level of implied volatility. Traders of long-term index options should also include a forecast of interest rates.

5

Investing and Trading Psychology

18

THE DIFFERENCE BETWEEN INVESTING AND TRADING WITH OPTIONS

FINANCIAL MARKETS ARE MADE UP OF THREE DISTINCT TYPES OF PARTICIPANTS: INVESTORS, SPECULATORS, AND MARKET MAKERS. Although each of these types of participants seeks to make profits, each uses the markets in different ways, with different strategies, different time horizons, different degrees of leverage, and different ways of measuring results. A common misconception is that options can be used only to speculate. Nothing could be further from the truth! In fact, the primary theme of this book is that options have an important role in a long-term investing program. It is therefore important to distinguish the risk characteristics and objectives of investment strategies, those of speculative strategies, and those employed by market makers.

OPTIONS GIVE INVESTORS MORE ALTERNATIVES

Although whole chapters could be written on what distinguishes the three types of market participants, only a few significant differences need to be identified here. Investors generally have a longer time horizon, they measure their results against market averages, they do not leverage their investment capital, and they buy at the offered price and sell at the bid price.

> *Options give investors more alternatives.*

Investors use option strategies that reduce their risk or enhance the income from their stock portfolios, and they do not use margin loans to increase their leverage. The message to be taken from Chapter 2 (profit-and-loss diagrams) is this: Options provide investors with more alternatives—more risk profiles from which to choose. Without options, stock market investors have only three alternatives: buy stock, buy Treasury bills, or buy a combination of the two. The challenge of investing with options is to understand the investment objectives achieved by each strategy and to match the appropriate strategy with the market forecast. Unfortunately, the value of options as risk management and investment tools is as yet undiscovered by many investors.

Unlike investors, speculators are oriented toward shorter-term market risk, they believe in "high risk, high return," and they frequently trade on margin. Also, speculators treat options as an independent trading activity that is not related to stock trading. The only similarity to investors is that speculators also buy at the offered price and sell at the bid price.

Market makers operate in a third way that is not easily understood by newcomers to options. Market makers attempt to earn the spread differential between the bid price and ask price. Primarily, they seek arbitrage opportunities, and by managing their positions, they attempt not to assume the risk of market direction. Market makers hope to make only a small amount on each trade, but they hope to do a high volume of trades. The subject of market making is not discussed in this book. Interested readers should refer to the work of Sheldon Natenberg.

INVESTORS' AND TRADERS' MOTIVATIONS CONTRASTED

An example that contrasts the motivations of the investor and the speculator is the strategy of selling put options. A speculator who sells a put is predicting a market rally. If the prediction is correct, either the put will be repurchased at a lower price or it will expire worthless and achieve the maximum profit potential. The speculator has no interest

> *Is assignment on a short put always "bad"?*

in buying the underlying stock and just wants to benefit from the expected short-term change in the option's price. The receipt of an assignment notice is viewed as a bad event by the speculator.

An investor's goal, in contrast, is to buy "good stocks" at "good prices." Therefore, when an investor sells a put, the investor hopes that the put will be assigned and the stock will be pur-

> *Must your*
> *thinking*
> *be changed?*

chased. That's right—investors actually hope for assignment. This is a big difference. Exercise and assignment are viewed as good, or at least acceptable, events by investors.

If it is difficult for you to accept the notion that being assigned on a short put is a positive event, it may be that speculative thinking is very deeply ingrained. To understand thoroughly how options can be used to achieve investment objectives, it is necessary to get out of the "speculative mentality" when thinking about options.

Investors use options to protect or enhance a position in an underlying stock. An example of using options for protection is buying a put on stock that is owned; this strategy limits risk and allows participation in a price rise at the same time (less the cost of the put). An example of enhancement is selling a call when the underlying stock is owned and hoping for assignment. If the stock is assigned, a more favorable selling price than the current stock price may be achieved. If the call expires worthless, income may be increased. Each of these strategies, of course, has a trade-off. Buying a put for protection has a cost; selling a call when the underlying stock is owned limits profit potential.

INVESTORS DO NOT USE LEVERAGE

Leveraging investment capital is the sphere of the speculator. When purchasing stock, leverage is typically accomplished through the use of margin debt: borrowed money that enables $1 of capital to buy up to $2 of stock. The result is greater profit or greater loss from any price change. Investors, in comparison, pay cash in full when purchasing stocks and do not expose their holdings to the risks of leverage.

WHEN OPTION POSITIONS ARE *NOT* LEVERAGED

At expiration, if in-the-money option positions are exercised, stock transactions are created. If an option position exists on a share-for-share basis with the underlying stock, or if the investor has sufficient cash to pay for the stock position created, then that option strategy does not involve leverage.

Consider the case of John, an investor with $7,000 in a money market account (or Treasury bills) who also owns a 70 call on Power Industries, for which he paid $500, or $5 per share. John has sufficient cash to pay for the stock if the call is exercised. Furthermore, John fully intends to exercise the call if it is in-the-money at expiration, because he wants to add Power stock to his long-term investment portfolio. This strategy, buy call plus T-bill, as explained in Chapter 5, offers John the trade-off of limited risk in exchange for a higher effective purchase price if the call is exercised. To see that John's total position is not leveraged, consider what his position is if Power stock is at $60 at option expiration. John will not exercise his option and will lose only the $500 he paid for the call, which is less than 10 percent of his investment capital. It is also less than the $1,000 loss he would have had if he had paid $7,000 for 100 shares.

Now consider the case of Sharon, who writes a call against 100 shares of Egan Enterprises that she owns in a cash account. Sharon's use of the call is known as covered writing. As discussed in Chapters 6 and 7, covered writing offers the trade-off of establishing a potentially higher selling price or potentially increasing income in return for limiting profit potential. If the stock is above the call's strike price at expiration, assignment of the call will result in Sharon's selling her Egan stock and receiving cash. This strategy does not involve leverage. In fact, there is less risk for Sharon with the covered call strategy than with owning Egan stock outright, because the call premium she received reduced her net investment.

As a third case, consider Debra, an owner of 1,000 shares of Peters Consulting that is currently trading at $30 per share. If Debra employs the protective put strategy discussed in Chapter 8, she will buy ten 30 puts and thus limit the risk of her investment in Peters. Should the price of Peters decline, Debra will be able to exercise the puts and sell her stock at $30. This position is not leveraged, because the puts are purchased on a share-for-share basis with the owned stock.

INVESTMENT STRATEGIES VERSUS SPECULATION

The strategies described in Part 2 are investment strategies for at least three reasons. First, they are *stock-oriented*. They involve the underlying stock or have the goal of purchasing or selling the under-lying stock at a "good price." A "good price" is a subjective determination that every investor must make independently. Second, the strate-gies in Part 2 do not involve leverage. The underlying stock is owned or there is sufficient cash (or liquid assets) available to pay for the stock. Third, all the strategies discussed in Chapters 5 through 10 can be established in a cash

> *Basic option strategies can be established in cash accounts.*

account at many brokerage firms. Perhaps this is most significant, because cash account transactions meet the lowest-level risk parameters used by brokerage firms and can be employed by the largest number of investors who are new to options.

The speculative strategies discussed in Part 3 differ in several ways from those in Part 2. First, the nature of the forecast is unique to speculation. Short-term traders need a three-part forecast that includes a specific stock price forecast, a specific time frame, and a view on how implied volatility will change. Second, the presentation of every strategy in Part 3 involves a discussion of short-term option price behavior. Short-term traders must understand the concepts of delta and time decay discussed in Chapter 4, and they must have realistic expectations about how different options with different strike prices and different expiration dates behave so that they can choose among them. Third, speculators manage their trading capital very differently from the way in which investors manage their capital. Speculators must be diligent in deciding how much trading capital will be committed to one trade. They must also maintain a sharp eye on when to take profits or to cut losses.

SUMMARY

Financial markets involve the interaction of investors, speculators, and market makers, who buy and sell options for different reasons. Investors seek strategies that protect or increase the income of their stock holdings. Speculators, in contrast, seek only short-term trading profits. Market makers set bid and offer prices based on arbitrage opportunities and try to avoid the assumption of market risk.

> *Investors use options to accomplish investment objectives.*

The use of leverage is the most basic difference between investors and speculators. Speculators like leverage; investors do not. Option strategies with an investment orientation meet one of two criteria: either (1) option positions exist on a share-for-share basis with the underlying stock, or (2) the investor has sufficient cash to fully pay for the stock position created by option exercise or assignment.

Options can play a role for both investors and speculators. Perhaps because speculative thinking is deeply ingrained, many option users gravitate to speculation. The challenge, therefore, is for investors to alter their thinking so that they can use options effectively to target long-term investment goals.

19

GETTING STARTED

EVERYONE SHOULD HAVE A COMPREHENSIVE PERSONAL FINANCIAL PLAN. Included in this financial plan should be goals for portfolio growth and allocation of investments, from conservative to speculative. Criteria for selecting investments should be written down and adhered to. Only with consistency and discipline can any financial plan succeed over many years.

Planning and discipline are especially important in the use of options. The range of possible uses for options is so wide that an investor who plunges into options trading blindly, without analyzing how a strategy fits into a comprehensive plan, is courting disaster. Of course, creating such a plan is so personal and so individual that there are no right or wrong ways to make a plan. There are, however, some guidelines that all investors, regardless of experience, should know. This chapter will present some advice for newcomers to options and/or investing, review the traditional approach to investing, discuss strategies that four different types of investors might find most appropriate, and, finally, describe an organized method for strategy selection.

THOUGHTS FOR BEGINNERS

Options are not a first step in investing. The first step should be learning about the financial markets in general and the stock market specifically. Basic experience with investing in stocks is an absolute requirement. Prior to the first option trade, an individual should have, to some extent, "suffered the slings and arrows" and the various "outrageous fortunes" (both good and bad) that are an inevitable part of investing in the stock market.

Acquiring sufficient knowledge to get to the point of buying individual stocks is not the overwhelming, time-consuming task that many newcomers fear. The first thing to do is to learn about some companies—the history of their stock prices, their past earnings performance, their products and markets, and their prospects. Reading the newspaper business section once or twice per week, calling for—and reading—annual reports, and raising the subject of investing in conversation are excellent ways of starting to learn. Many people have good ideas and enjoy talking about investing, but are reluctant to raise the topic because there seems to be a perception that "few people invest" or "nobody wants to talk about the market." Frequently, it takes only someone to break the ice, and a new, interesting area of conversation is opened.

Learning about investing is a gradual process, but beginning investors must learn an important lesson: patience. As the cliché goes: "Rome wasn't built in a day." Neither can "learning about the market" be accomplished in a short time.

The second step is developing a good method of picking stocks. Whether it is a fundamental approach, a technical approach, or a combination of the two, a stock selection method coupled with experience in market prediction will increase an investor's confidence in his or her decision-making abilities. Without these basics, anyone new to options is doomed to fail, but with some practice and patience, most people can develop good investing skills. As an added plus, the decision-making and stock-selection skills that are developed will be a valuable personal asset throughout life—and not only in investing.

THE SPECTRUM OF INVESTMENTS

The risk/reward spectrum covers a range of investments, from low-risk–low-reward (such as certificates of deposit and Treasury bills) to high-risk–high-reward (such as high-risk stocks, speculative option strategies, and "junk" bonds). A related, but different, concept is that of investment goals, i.e., "income-oriented" or "growth-oriented."

Traditionally, financial advisors suggest that investments be spread across the risk/reward spectrum and diversified among investment goals in accordance with the investor's individual situation. They also suggest that limits be set, both for risk and for the percentage of assets invested in one particular investment and in one type of investment. Some of the goals and related types of investments are the following:

Goal of Investment	Examples
"Aggressive" capital growth	New issues, speculative investments
"High-quality" capital growth	Growth-oriented blue chip stocks
Balanced capital growth and income	Stocks with increasing dividends
"High" income	Utility stocks, corporate bonds
Conservation of capital and income	T-bills, CDs

THE HIERARCHY OF RISK

Typically, financial planners suggest that a larger portion of investments be oriented toward less risk and a smaller portion be oriented toward greater risk, as illustrated in Figure 19–1. Although the exact percentage in each category varies, the concept is that investments should be spread across a "hierarchy of risk" in accordance with individual goals and risk tolerance. For example, a

FIGURE 19–1   The hierarchy of investment risk

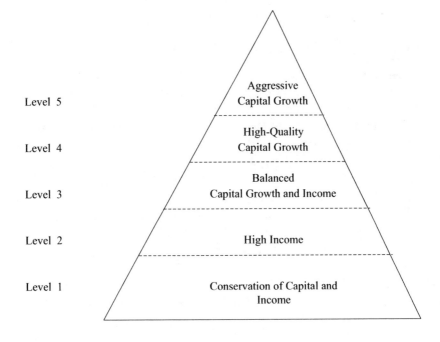

young person who is saving for retirement in 30 years may have a larger percentage of her investments in growth-oriented investments, and an older individual who is approaching or in retirement may have a larger portion in income-oriented and conservation-of-capital investments.

OPTIONS AND THE HIERARCHY OF RISK
Some people might think that options fit only the top tier, Level 5, of the hierarchy of risk. Not so!

The cash account option strategies discussed in Chapters 5 through 10 can be used to pursue the objectives of *all levels of risk*. Covered writing (Chapter 6), the strategy in which stock is purchased and calls are sold on a share-for-share basis, for example, is an income-oriented strategy involving stock ownership. Depending on the "riskiness" of the underlying stock, covered writing might be either a Level 2 or Level 3 risk.

Buy calls plus Treasury bills (Chapter 5) and married puts (Chapter 8) are short-term risk-management techniques for acquiring stock. Remember, the investment or speculative orientation of the use of options depends on an investor's willingness and ability to purchase the underlying stock. These strategies, therefore, could be used for investments in Levels 2, 3, or 4.

The option strategies that fit into the highest level of risk are the margin account and trading strategies in Chapters 11 through 16.

FOUR BROAD CATEGORIES OF INVESTORS

Since there are a wide variety of investment goals, risk preferences, and financial conditions, it is not possible for one set of guidelines to apply to all investors. Therefore, four distinct types of investors will be defined, and appropriate strategies will be suggested for each. The four types of investors are *the beginning investor, the income-oriented investor, the growth-oriented investor*, and *the well-capitalized investor*.

THE BEGINNING INVESTOR
Definitely lacking in experience and potentially lacking in investment funds, the beginning investor must first establish goals. The exact amount of investment capital required before a beginning investor should select a strategy involving options is difficult to determine. Many financial advisors recommend, however, that beginners first have some liquid savings—for the proverbial rainy day. After that, advice typically runs along the lines of "choose your

investments carefully with an eye to long-term growth." An individual retirement account (IRA) is frequently recommended to young investors because of the favorable tax treatment.

Covered writing is an appropriate strategy for beginning investors for at least two reasons. First, it is stock-oriented. Being stock-oriented means that success with this strategy is most likely if the underlying stock is chosen wisely. Covered writing, therefore, capitalizes on the skill in stock selection developed while learning about the market. Second, if the static and if-called returns are known (and deemed acceptable), a covered write will have a definite goal and an easily measured result. These are important attributes for beginners at anything. Also, covered writing is a good beginning strategy because the time element of two to four months or longer teaches beginning investors to be patient. Also, covered writing is allowed in tax-deferred IRA accounts, where many young people have long-term savings.

Covered writing also helps beginning investors gain decision-making experience, because a decision must be made at every expiration. If the stock price is below the strike price at expiration and the call expires, a decision must be made between simply holding the stock, selling another covered call, and selling the stock and making another investment. If the stock price is above the strike price as expiration approaches, a decision must be made about whether or not to roll the call, as explained in Chapter 7. If early assignment occurs, a decision must be made whether to repurchase the stock or to move into something else. During the first year of covered writing, a beginning investor's experience will increase dramatically. This investor will have made three or four investment decisions, while a buy-and-hold investor will have made only one.

When does a beginning investor buy calls? One situation is when the necessary funds to buy a stock are anticipated, but are not currently available. In this case, as explained in Chapter 5, an at- or in-the-money call is purchased. The expiration month is chosen so that the required funds to pay for the stock in full will be available on or before the expiration date. After acquiring stock via this method, it is not necessary that options be used again on this particular holding, because the goal of "adding a good long-term stock to the portfolio" has been achieved.

Please note that no trading or speculative strategies have been suggested for beginning investors, as they should spend their time studying the market in search of good-quality investments. Options can play a role in this long-term plan, when appropriate, by helping investors pursue their risk-management or income-enhancement objectives.

THE INCOME-ORIENTED INVESTOR

Income-oriented investors may be in retirement or experiencing high short-term expenses, such as a child in college. Whatever the reason, the need for income-oriented investments points to strategies beyond covered writing. Writing puts on a nonleveraged basis (Chapter 9) is a second income-oriented strategy, and covered straddles and covered combinations, without leverage (Chapter 16), are a third. Return calculations must include all transaction costs, and investors must remember that these strategies involve the risk of owning the underlying stock. Stock selection and managing one's investments, therefore, play as important a role as ever.

THE GROWTH-ORIENTED INVESTOR

Growth-oriented investors have many opportunities to use options to pursue their investment objectives. When entering higher-risk Level 4 or Level 5 stocks, these investors can use the buy calls plus Treasury bills to pursue the goal of short-term risk management. As explained in Chapter 5, the call is used as a limited-risk way of participating in a forecasted stock price rise. If the forecast is correct, the stock can be purchased via exercise of the call and paid for with the funds that have been invested in Treasury bills. During the life of the call, the investor can rest easier knowing that the risk is limited to the premium paid for the call.

If an investor is indecisive about selling a stock, regardless of its risk level, the insurance strategies discussed in Chapter 8 also pursue the goal of short-term risk management.

When the forecast calls for a neutral market, growth-oriented investors might write puts and buy Treasury bills (Chapter 9) as an alternative to placing limit buy orders below the current market price.

Buying stock with a ratio call spread (Chapter 15) pursues the goal of increasing profits over a limited stock price rise without increasing risk. Growth-oriented investors who understand this strategy may find times when it is possible to add a ratio call spread to a stock position that, given their market forecast, offers an opportunity to increase profits. The strategy need not be implemented on an entire position. If, for example, 200 shares are owned, options might be used as follows: Buy one at-the-money call and sell two out-of-the-money calls. This ratio call spread involves only 100 shares, or half of the holdings. If the stock price rises as predicted, then profits can be increased over a limited price range on those 100 shares. If the stock price rises more than expected, then the second 100 shares can rise to the full extent of the move. Transaction costs must be considered, and if the stock price is above the strike price of the short calls at expiration, then 100 shares will be sold when exercise of the long call and assignment of the two short calls occurs. This possibility must be anticipated and planned for.

THE WELL-CAPITALIZED INVESTOR

This investor is assumed to have a variety of investments with varying objectives and risk levels. Unfortunately, many people in this situation start by asking the wrong question. They frequently want to know, "How much of my money should be in options?" This is the wrong question, because the focus should be on investment objectives, market forecasts, and opinions on specific investment opportunities. Rather than thinking of options as a separate investment vehicle, these investors should view options in the context of how they might accomplish their investment objectives.

The well-capitalized investor can use the full range of option strategies discussed in this book where appropriate. For the income-oriented portion of the investor's assets, covered writing, writing puts and buying Treasury bills, and buying stock and writing straddles—all on a nonleveraged basis—pursue the goal of income.

When a market forecast calls for short-term risk management, buying calls and Treasury bills or buying married or protective puts are the appropriate strategies to consider. Adding a ratio call spread to growth-oriented holdings can add leverage over a limited price rise.

For Level 4 and Level 5 risk investments, the well-capitalized investor can use the trading strategies discussed in Chapters 11 through 16.

STRATEGY SELECTION FRAMEWORK

All four types of investors should know their priorities and think carefully about the selection of any strategy. The following discussion presents a simple, four-step approach for selecting strategies. The goal is to help all investors and traders think clearly and develop realistic expectations so that an appropriate strategy can be chosen, given a specific forecast.

The four steps are (1) know your situation, (2) state your market forecast clearly, (3) identify your specific objective, and, finally, (4) choose a strategy that will meet your goals if your forecast is accurate.

KNOW YOUR SITUATION

Many investors take it for granted that they know their situation. Since the use of options requires specific thinking, however, it is worth reviewing some examples. "I'm bullish" is not a situation; it is a forecast. "I would like to increase income" is not a situation; it is a goal. A situation is "I have cash to invest," or "I own stock with a profit that I am willing to sell," or "I own stock with a loss." These different situations, given the same forecast, may lead to the selection of different strategies.

STATE YOUR MARKET FORECAST CLEARLY

The idea of stating a market forecast clearly has been discussed before. Being "bullish" is not specific enough for the purposes of investing or trading with options. "The stock price will rise from $51 to $54 in the next three to five weeks," and "the stock price will trade at or below $40 between now and expiration" are clear market forecasts.

IDENTIFY YOUR SPECIFIC OBJECTIVE

This is quite different from what is required of a typical buy-and-hold investor. Examples of specific objectives are, "I want to sell my stock at $51.50," or "I would like to leverage my investment without increasing risk if the stock price rises as I predict," or "I am willing to buy stock at an effective price of $28.75." In contrast, just wanting to "make money" is not specific enough to lead to the selection of a particular option strategy.

CHOOSE A STRATEGY THAT WILL MEET YOUR GOALS

The previous three steps may or may not lead to the selection of an option strategy. Figure 19–2 illustrates how situations, market forecasts, and goals can lead to the selection of a strategy. This is presented in a conceptual manner; it can be used in real situations only after actual prices and commissions have been considered.

Line 1 in Figure 19–2 illustrates that for an investor who owns stock and has a neutral market forecast, selling a covered call pursues the goals of increasing income or selling at a higher price. Notice that Line 1 can start from either owning stock with a profit or owning stock with a loss.

Line 2 starts at "have cash to invest." For an investor in this situation with a neutral market forecast, writing puts and buying Treasury bills pursues the objectives of increasing income and buying stock below the current market price. Line 3 starts in the same place as Line 2, but the neutral-to-bullish forecast and the different objective of adding leverage without more risk leads to the strategy "buy stock with ratio call spread."

Line 4 illustrates that this process does not always lead to the selection of an option strategy. For a very bearish investor who owns stock, either with a profit or with a loss (Line 4 has two starting points), and who has the objective of eliminating risk, selling the stock is the logical strategy. A protective

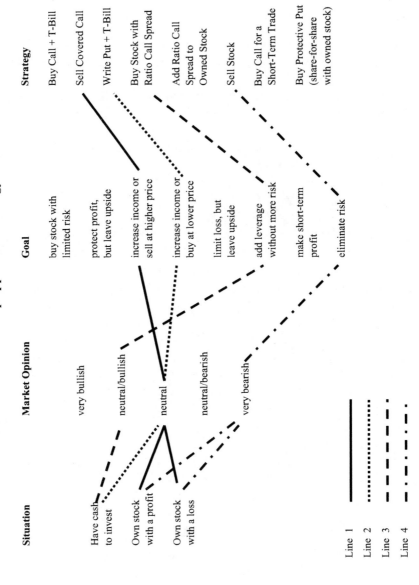

FIGURE 19–2   A 4-step approach to strategy selection

287

put, remember, if exercised, would result in a lower effective selling price for the stock than the current market price and therefore would not eliminate risk.

SUMMARY

Options are not a first step in investing. Investors must have an understanding of the financial markets in general and the stock market specifically before considering options.

Options can be used to pursue the investment objectives of all levels of the hierarchy of risk. Covered writing is income-oriented and may be appropriate for Levels 2 and 3. Buy calls and Treasury bills and married puts are short-term risk management strategies designed to acquire stock, and they can be used to acquire investments in Levels 2, 3, and 4. The trading strategies in Chapters 11 through 16 are potentially Level 5 strategies, but some are also suited for Levels 2, 3, and 4.

Beginning investors should consider starting with covered writing, because it is conservative and stock-oriented. Covered writing and writing puts and buying Treasury bills pursue the goals of income-oriented investors. Buying stock with a ratio call spread might help growth-oriented investors leverage their investments on part of a position, and buying calls plus Treasury bills can be considered when entering new positions. The entire range of option strategies is available to well-capitalized investors, because their investments are diversified across the hierarchy of risk and involve many different goals.

A simple, four-step strategy selection process promotes organized thinking and realistic expectations. The four steps are (1) know your situation, (2) state your market forecast clearly, (3) identify your goal, and (4) select a strategy that will meet your goals if your forecast is accurate.

20

LEARNING TO TRADE

INTRODUCTION

TRADING HAS AN ALLURE FOR MANY PEOPLE. There are no customers, no suppliers, no employees, and no bosses. Traders can even set their own work schedule. As experienced traders will say, however, "trading is a hard way to make an easy living." Trading involves a unique combination of hard work, patience, and discipline. A trader has to be sufficiently disciplined so that trading decisions can be made objectively, rather than emotionally. Yet intuition plays an important role, and what is intuition if not emotion?

This chapter will offer some thoughts on how one might learn to trade. It is impossible to say that all questions will be answered, or even that all issues will be raised. Yet it is reasonable to suggest guidelines for the beginner. Portions of this chapter are adapted from another book by the author, *Trading Index Options*.

SELECTING TRADES IS PERSONAL

Although a specific discussion of market forecasting is beyond the scope of this book, some comments about developing a technique are warranted.

Anyone can be right once, but was he lucky or smart? Most successful traders work hard. They constantly study the market. They read books, and they are open to new ideas. They have their own methods of gauging market direction and market sentiment, and they make trades based on indicators, not on impulse. Even with hard work and discipline, there will still be some losing trades, but hard work and discipline should improve the chances of success over a period of time and a group of trades. Traders must, therefore, develop logical and repeatable methods of trade selection and market prediction.

There are many market forecasting techniques. Some of the common ones are technical analysis, trend following, range trading, moving-average crossovers, and indicator-based methods such as stochastics and relative strength. Which method works best? In the opinion of the author, all of these methods work, *if* the trader can work the method! No method of market forecasting or trade selection works all the time or in every market. Consistency, discipline in following an approach, and having an intuition as to when and when not to act on a "signal" is what makes trading an art, not a science.

Every business has both subjective elements and objective elements, and trading is no exception. The subjective elements are sometimes referred to as the "art" of a business. The objective elements are dubbed the "science." Designing a dress or a coffeemaker or any other consumer product is an art, but making it economically in mass quantities is a science. The art for a trader is developing a forecasting technique for stocks, and this is usually an evolving process. The science for an options trader is understanding option price behavior and having realistic expectations for the profit potential of a strategy. Both are essential elements of a systematic approach, albeit with subjective elements.

TRADING IS A BUSINESS

Trading, or speculating, is a business activity that involves buying and selling, or selling and buying, the goal of which is to make money. Some people object to trading being called a business, but success at any activity requires a thoughtful approach. Can you imagine a large company building a new plant without thinking through the desired benefits and the potential problems in advance? Can you imagine a successful salesperson who does not plan her sales calls and her follow-up contacts? Trading is no different. Whether you plan to trade occasionally, more than occasionally, or full-time, you need a plan that includes certain essential elements.

The first element of a plan for part-time trading is allocating sufficient time to trade. How much time per day or per week will be devoted to trading?

Some traders spend as little as two or three hours per week and have successful results. The key is consistency.

So-called hobbyists at trading might spend a few minutes every day checking their positions and then devote one hour every Tuesday night and two hours every Saturday morning to do in-depth study to generate new ideas. That could add up to 16 hours or more per month.

The second element is fun. If it is fun to check the market, and if it is fun to work on Tuesday nights and Saturday mornings, then the time will not seem like a burden. However, if two or three weeks go by, and you have not checked your positions or generated new trading ideas, then maybe your actions are speaking louder than your words. Maybe you don't really want to be a trader.

A third element is sufficient capital. There is no specific rule about the amount of capital required to start trading. However, your capital must be sufficient to withstand losses during the learning phase. Keep in mind that capital devoted to trading is *risk capital*; it does not include other types of capital, such as emergency savings, long-term investments for retirement, or targeted savings such as savings for a home.

Getting consistent information is an important fourth part of a trading plan. Will you get trading ideas from newsletters or from the Internet? How will you check on your current positions, and, for entering trades, how will you know when a stock or option reaches the target buy or sell price? How much will this information cost you? Regarding new trading ideas, there is so much information available that it can easily be overwhelming. In one afternoon of listening to stock market radio and television shows and reading one market-oriented magazine, a trader can easily get 20 trading ideas. This leads to the next important part of a trading plan.

It is essential that you develop an objective method of trade selection. How will you sift through the many, many trading ideas that you get from one source or another? Developing an individual trading style, as described earlier, will absorb the most time initially, but then implementing your trading plan is a repetitive process. First you hear about an idea, then you get a chart, then you apply your method, and, finally, you accept or reject the idea. Perhaps you decide to wait for a target price to be reached, but then how do you follow up to see if your target price is reached?

A final element of a trading plan is having a realistic profit target. A trader with $10,000 of trading capital should not expect to make $1,000,000 in a year, and a trader with $1,000,000 should expect to make more than $10,000. It is reasonable for new traders to set more modest goals than experienced traders, but a goal is important. A profit target is something to shoot for. It can be the basis for measuring whether a trader did "well" or "poorly." A goal also gives a sense of satisfaction if it is achieved.

Although every trade should be initiated with the conviction that a profit will be made, the profit target just described should be a goal for a series of trades or for a period of time. For example, a trader might target "an average profit of 10 percent on 10 trades," or "a profit of $15,000 for the next six months or a year."

"Profit as a percent of invested capital" is a typical measure of investment success, but it is inappropriate for trading. Trading requires time, so the target profit should take into consideration the value of the trader's time and the desired rate of return. Arguably, there should also be a risk premium, because trading success is not guaranteed.

Consider a trader with $50,000 of trading capital who earns $10,000 net profits before taxes during one year. On the one hand, this profit is 20 percent of invested capital. On the other hand, if this trader spends 10 hours per week studying the market, or 520 hours per year, then $10,000 amounts to less than $20 per hour "wages." Seen in this light, the profit is not so impressive. Nevertheless, having a profit goal is an important part of planning. Setting a profit target is subjective. Every trader should think hard about how much, realistically, he hopes to make, and his plan should be consistent with that target.

ATTRIBUTES OF GOOD TRADERS

In the author's experience, good traders have three key attributes: an entrepreneurial desire to succeed, a love for the markets they trade, and a dispassionate attitude toward money.

An entrepreneurial spirit is needed, because traders must have a willingness to risk their own assets. Entrepreneurs are also reputed to love what they do. Love for the market can come only from within, because no outside force such as a boss can mandate that the job of trading be done well. There is only an individual's internal drive to look for trading opportunities. It must also be fun to develop a trading system, to watch prices fluctuate, and to initiate and close positions. If the individual loves the process itself, then profitable trades will offer encouragement and losing trades will be seen as learning experiences. The desire to "figure out the market" will provide sufficient motivation to get better at what many people find to be a frustrating challenge.

DISPASSIONATE ATTITUDE TOWARD MONEY

Since trading is about making money, some might wonder why traders must develop a dispassionate attitude toward it. Think about some people who have achieved great financial success. Henry Ford was an engineer who was interested in making cars; Michael Jordan loves basketball; Bill Gates is obsessed with computers. Only their passion could fuel the creativity and drive necessary to overcome the obstacles that are inherent in the entrepreneur's path. Money was a by-product of that passion, not the focus of it. It should also be noted that if financial success is not achieved, the person who loves the activity itself will still have had fun and a sense of personal satisfaction. In either case, the entrepreneur wins!

This means that those who are contemplating trading must ask themselves, "Do I like trading enough? Do I like following the market enough? Am I willing to suffer the humiliations I undoubtedly will experience? Am I willing to stick it out? Is trading that much fun?" These are personal questions that can only be answered by each individual. So look within yourself; think about how much you really enjoy trading. Go through the process of developing a market forecast, evaluating some alternatives, selecting a strategy, opening a position, living with its fluctuations, and closing it. Pay attention to yourself, your behavior, and your feelings. Are you excited? Are you concentrating? Is it fun? Or is it a chore?

We do what we love, and we do what we love because of the process, not because of the money. Of course, if we do not make money, we will not last long. Hence the importance of skill.

LEARNING THE SKILLS TO TRADE

The idea of being a "born trader" is a misconception. Trading skills can be learned. Three key skills that traders can acquire are the ability to act on an instinct, the ability to look forward without being unduly influenced by the past, and the ability to follow a strict trading discipline.

ABILITY TO ACT ON INSTINCT

Trading decisions cannot be brooded over for days, or even hours. Regardless of how specific a trading system is, conditions are never perfect. A trader must, therefore, develop the ability to "pull the trigger"—to have the instinct to initiate a trade and the ability to act on that instinct despite imperfect conditions.

ABILITY TO LOOK FORWARD WITHOUT BEING
UNDULY INFLUENCED BY THE PAST

Looking forward is essential because continued success is not possible if a trader is psychologically paralyzed by the results of the last trade. Some trades will result in losses. Others will be closed at a fraction of their potential profit. These are frustrating experiences, but they are inevitable. A trader must look forward to the next trading opportunity objectively, regardless of the outcome of the last trade.

ABILITY TO FOLLOW A STRICT TRADING DISCIPLINE

Trading discipline means the willingness to be guided by objectivity rather than emotion. In order for a trading technique to succeed, trades must be initiated in accordance with the tenets of an individual's trading system. Positions must be closed without regard to profit or loss when a signal to close a profitable trade is received or when it is clear that a market forecast is wrong. Otherwise emotion will rule the day, yanking the hapless trader back and forth with every hiccup of market action.

Assuming that an individual has the entrepreneurial desire to trade, these three skills—acting on instinct, looking forward, and trading with discipline—can be learned by engaging in the process. Make some trades! In the beginning, trade small, one or two options at a time. Concentrate on initiating trades and closing trades; do not be overly concerned with profit. Every new venture requires an investment. In the business of trading, this means making a series of losing trades.

By initiating a trade when you think conditions are right, you are practicing the skill of acting on instinct. By closing a position when one of the parameters is met, you are practicing the skill of trading with discipline. And by focusing on the next trading opportunity, you are practicing the skill of looking forward without being unduly influenced by the past.

If your trading technique is a good one, and if you are implementing it properly, you have a good chance of realizing net profits after a series of trades. But there are no guarantees in the business of trading. Profits will not occur on every trade; nor will they occur fast enough to satisfy impatient beginners. Yet, with continued work, results are likely to improve.

TRADING PSYCHOLOGY

To be sure, trading is difficult to learn and even more difficult to implement. That's because it involves a style and pace of thinking that is different from that required by almost any other activity. As a result, traders must consciously work at developing a healthy trading psychology; this involves unlearning old, unproductive mental habits and replacing them with new ones. For example, the maxim, "If it ain't broke, don't fix it," does not apply to trading. Short-term trends do not last forever, and a profitable trade that is not monitored and closed at a profit can rapidly become a losing trade. Thus, a profitable trade should keep a trader just as occupied as a losing trade, because in either case the time will come to close that trade and be done with it. "If a position ain't broke, watch it, and be prepared to close it" more aptly applies to trading.

Another distinction between trading and other activities is the role of hindsight. In most businesses it is impossible for anyone to look back and see the results of an alternative course of action. A trader, however, can know with 100 percent certainty what "should" have been done. Checking current prices is all that is required to see how a different strategy would have performed. The bane of trading is that there will always be a strategy with more profitable results, and rarely, if ever, will a trader buy at the lowest possible price or sell at the highest. Perfect hindsight is a reality of trading. Adapting to this reality is both difficult and essential. Otherwise, a trader will waste valuable mental energy brooding over "would have ... should have ... could have" regrets.

PERCENTAGE THINKING

Traders must accept the idea that they will have a percentage of profitable trades and a percentage of losing trades. While seemingly obvious, this concept of *percentage thinking* and its implications are often overlooked by novice traders.

Accepting this notion psychologically means that losses can be taken in stride, and that losing positions can be closed objectively when the forecast changes or when a stop-loss point is reached. Even though every trade is entered with the same confidence, experienced traders base their trading decisions on current market conditions and their forecasts—not on the results of the last trade.

Traders who have not fully adapted to the psychology of percentage thinking exhibit different behavior. They tend to initiate new positions too soon after profitable results, and they tend to wait too long after losing trades. They also tend to keep a losing position open in the hopes that "it will come back" and become profitable. It is as if they are saying, "I wasn't wrong, I was just early." Certainly the market does return at times. But at other times, losses continue to grow, with results that can be devastating.

Over time, the results that count are the net results of all trades. Traders must therefore learn to accept small losses and look forward to the next trading opportunity. For beginners this means two things. First, set a stop-loss point when a trade is initiated. Second, objectively close the position and realize a loss if that point is reached.

BUILDING CONFIDENCE

It is much easier to talk bravely about "win some, lose some" than it is to actually handle one's emotions after making a series of trades in which some are winners and some are losers. It is reasonable, therefore, for beginners to ask how they can build the confidence necessary to continue trading after experiencing losses. Confidence in trading frequently depends on three things: knowledge of past market behavior, trading small, and a reasoned approach to selecting trades.

Knowledge of the history of market movements builds a trader's confidence because, in financial markets, history tends to repeat itself. If one has some perspective on past patterns of price action—and if one has an idea of how bad things can get when a forecasting technique gives an incorrect signal—then it is easier to ride out tough times. It is possible to get such a perspective by studying the market, learning its past, and remembering the price behavior that has been observed. Over time, much will be learned about "typical events" and "rare events."

Tensions can run high during volatile markets. Most traders with large positions will naturally experience a higher degree of anxiety than those who are trading small. A trader who closes a position and realizes a small loss from such market behavior will learn that the experience is not as disastrous as she might have imagined. Moreover, that trader will remain relatively relaxed, a mental condition that supports objective thinking. Beginning traders especially should take this point to heart, because realizing too big a loss is very discouraging.

A systematic approach to trading is the third key element that builds confidence. Such an approach means that there are specific reasons for making trades rather than just hunches. A system reinforces a trader's belief that decisions will be right (i.e., profitable) more often than wrong (i.e., losing). Consequently, developing a logical technique for forecasting the market is essential.

BALANCE AND FOCUS

The topics discussed here take a great deal of study and reflection. For those who love the process, it is more fun than work. Yet focusing on one's trading activity should not become an obsession. Trading should be only one part of a well-balanced life that includes other important interests. Focusing on trading means knowing current market conditions; it does not mean trading all the time. Devoting two to four hours per week, divided into 15 to 30 minutes per day, might be enough. Trades do not have to be made every day, or even every week. There are times to be sitting on the sidelines with no open positions. Moreover, a break from the intense concentration required by active trading will do the trader's mind some good. It will then be possible for him to return to the market refreshed and ready to make a new trade.

SUMMARY

Trading is difficult to learn and even more difficult to implement, because it involves a style and pace of thinking that is different from that required by many other activities. Emotions experienced when trading can also interfere with the learning process. This means that traders must strive for a healthy, objective trading psychology. Traders must also develop a market forecasting technique that they have confidence will make more correct forecasts than incorrect ones. Although trades based on objective criteria and implemented with discipline can result in losses, a series of such trades should have a better chance of showing a net profit than a series of lucky trades. Despite the amount of effort that trading requires, focusing on one's trading activity should not be an obsession. Trading should be only one part of a well-balanced life that includes other important interests.

There are no guarantees of success, but anyone who attempts to make trading a business by starting with sufficient capital, working at a measured pace, and striving to trade with discipline has a chance of succeeding.

This book has followed a proven outline for learning to use options. First, draw profit-and-loss diagrams and master the mechanics of exercise and assignment, and second, understand the difference between investing and speculative uses. Third, commit yourself to adapting to the psychological differences between investing and trading with stocks and investing and trading with options. Fourth, define a specific goal up front, and choose a strategy that will achieve the goal if your market forecast is correct. Finally, traders must develop realistic expectations about how option prices change prior to expiration.

By keeping these guidelines in mind, by gaining experience and nurturing patience, and by selecting stocks and strategies with a reasoned approach, any investor can succeed in the world of options.

Index

About the Author

James B. Bittman is the senior staff instructor at The Options Institute, the educational arm of the Chicago Board Options Exchange. He has been a successful options trader for more than two decades and is the author of *Trading Index Options,* and *Trading and Hedging with Agricultural Futures and Options* and coauthor of *Options: Essential Concepts.*

CD-ROM WARRANTY

This software is protected by both United States copyright law and international copyright treaty provision. You must treat this software just like a book. By saying "just like a book," McGraw-Hill means, for example, that this software may be used by any number of people and may be freely moved from one computer location to another, so long as there is no possibility of its being used at one location or on one computer while it also is being used at another. Just as a book cannot be read by two different people in two different places at the same time, neither can the software be used by two different people in two different places at the same time (unless, of course, McGraw-Hill's copyright is being violated).

LIMITED WARRANTY

Customers who have problems installing or running a McGraw-Hill CD should consult our online technical support site at http://books.mcgraw-hill.com/techsupport. McGraw-Hill takes great care to provide you with top-quality software, thoroughly checked to prevent virus infections. McGraw-Hill warrants the physical CD-ROM contained herein to be free of defects in materials and workmanship for a period of sixty days from the purchase date. If McGraw-Hill receives written notification within the warranty period of defects in materials or workmanship, and such notification is determined by McGraw-Hill to be correct, McGraw-Hill will replace the defective CD-ROM. Send requests to:

> McGraw-Hill
> Customer Services
> P.O. Box 545
> Blacklick, OH 43004-0545

The entire and exclusive liability and remedy for breach of this Limited Warranty shall be limited to replacement of a defective CD-ROM and shall not include or extend to any claim for or right to cover any other damages, including, but not limited to, loss of profit, data, or use of the software, or special, incidental, or consequential damages or other similar claims, even if McGraw-Hill has been specifically advised of the possibility of such damages. In no event will McGraw-Hill's liability for any damages to you or any other person ever exceed the lower of suggested list price or actual price paid for the license to use the software, regardless of any form of the claim.

McGRAW-HILL SPECIFICALLY DISCLAIMS ALL OTHER WARRANTIES, EXPRESS OR IMPLIED, INCLUDING, BUT NOT LIMITED TO, ANY IMPLIED WARRANTY OF MERCHANTABILITY OR FITNESS FOR A PARTICULAR PURPOSE.

Specifically, McGraw-Hill makes no representation or warranty that the software is fit for any particular purpose and any implied warranty of merchantability is limited to the sixty-day duration of the Limited Warranty covering the physical CD-ROM only (and not the software) and is otherwise expressly and specifically disclaimed.

This limited warranty gives you specific legal rights; you may have others which may vary from state to state. Some states do not allow the exclusion of incidental or consequential damages, or the limitation on how long an implied warranty lasts, so some of the above may not apply to you.